UNLOCKING THE
MEANING OF *LOST*
AN UNAUTHORIZED GUIDE

LYNNETTE PORTER 1957-
DAVID LAVERY

SOURCEBOOKS, INC.®
NAPERVILLE, ILLINOIS

Published by Sourcebooks, Inc.
P.O. Box 4410, Naperville, Illinois 60567-4410
(630) 961-3900
Fax: (630) 961-2168
www.sourcebooks.com

Library of Congress Cataloging-in-Publication Data

Porter, Lynnette R.
  Unlocking the meaning of Lost : an unauthorized guide / Lynnette Porter, David Lavery.
    p. cm.
  Includes bibliographical references and index.
  ISBN-13: 978-1-4022-0726-6
  ISBN-10: 1-4022-0726-3
  1. Lost (Television program) I. Lavery, David II. Title.

PN1992.77.L67P67 2006
791.45'72--dc22

2006006321

Printed and bound in the United States of America

VP 10 9 8 7 6

UNLOCKING THE MEANING OF *LOST*

CONTENTS

ACKNOWLEDGMENTS

The original idea for doing a book on *Lost* was Lynnette Porter's, and it is to her that I owe my greatest debt in making this project work. Thanks for being such a knowledgeable and wonderful collaborator.

Thanks to Uwe Stender for hooking us up with Sourcebooks. Thanks to Peter Lynch for your interest in our project.

Thanks, as always, to my wife Joyce, with whom I have gotten *Lost* since the first episode. After over a quarter century she is still the woman I would most want to crash on a desert island with.

I also want to thank Hillary Robson-Reeder. In many respects this book's third author, she wrote the first draft of the fandom chapter, as well as drafts of several entries in the "*Lost* Ancestors" chapter. As I learned in many conversations even before this book began, her knowledge of *Lost*, especially the *Lost* fandom and conspiracy theories, is second to none. Lynnette and I are in your debt; it's hard to imagine this book coming together without your help. Thanks, too, for your excellent website at www.unlockinglost.com.

—David Lavery

Having an insightful collaborator is always a gift, but having fun while working with a knowledgeable colleague is even better. Thank you, David, for your valuable ideas and good humor throughout this project.

Hillary Robson-Reeder also deserves my thanks for her hard work and for sparking my interest in even more areas of fandom.

Peter Lynch and Whitney Lehman at Sourcebooks, thank you for your enthusiasm for *Lost* and this project.

Thanks, too, to my family—Jimmie, Bart, Nancy, and Heather.

I couldn't get *Lost* with better people.

—Lynnette Porter

INTRODUCTION

GETTING *LOST*

"At the pit of exhaustion from directing Mission Impossible, all I could think about—all I wanted to do— was write or direct another episode of Lost. Put it this way: If I hadn't helped create it, I would be a fan—and I'd be absolutely furious with myself for not thinking of it first."
—J. J. ABRAMS

In September 2004, the ABC network series *Lost* debuted on U.S. television. Within a year, the series had gone international, running in such countries as Canada, Australia, Brazil, Colombia, France, Germany, Greece, Iceland, Israel, Italy, Malaysia, New Zealand, the Netherlands, Norway, Spain, and the U.K.; North America, South America, Europe, Asia, Africa, and the Middle East were all watching *Lost*. Everywhere the series is broadcast, *Lost* brings in high ratings and frequently is the top or one of the top three programs.

A godsend for ABC, a network that had not had a hit show in years, its popularity makes it more than just another series from the U.S. sold around the world. During the second season in the U.S., the series again has topped ratings charts, not only winning its time slot on Wednesday nights, but frequently the entire night's programming. Its Season Two ratings have actually increased (current episodes are averaging 17.8 million viewers, up from Season

One's 15.9 average). As the series begins its second season in its jaunt around the globe, the trend in high ratings continues worldwide. Beyond the wildest expectations of ABC executives, the cast and crew, and even series creators, *Lost* has taken on a life of its own. Everyone, it seems, wants to get *Lost* these days.

THE PHENOMENON

In the U.S., the series has consistently been in the Nielsen Top 20 and almost always won its timeslot in the tricky Wednesday 8:00 p.m. (7:00 p.m. Central) time period, becoming the second highest rated new show during the 2004–2005 U.S. broadcast season. With the order for a full season of shows in October 2004, the number of episodes was upped a few times until a three-hour finale in May 2005 ended *Lost*'s first season with twenty-four episodes, an unusual number in modern television practice. Long before ABC announced the rest of its schedule for fall 2005, *Lost* had won renewal for a second season. A second-season move to the 9:00 p.m. timeslot (8:00 Central) allowed writers to introduce more adult themes, including the island's first (albeit brief) sex scene. Even with the introduction of new characters and the demise of favorites, *Lost* has continued to attract new viewers and maintain its ardent fan base.

In addition to its prime-time hit status, *Lost* became noted for several innovative firsts in broadcast media:

- By late 2005, *Lost* had become the most frequently downloaded series for iPod.
- It is one of the first U.S. series to be simultaneously broadcast in Spanish as well as English.
- It will soon be available for viewing on mobile phones. *Lost* is trendsetting not only as a television series with intriguing plots and characters, but as a successful product available via many types of media outlets.

The marketing for the series branches into many directions and reaches fans and prospective viewers in sometimes unexpected ways. During August 2005, the pilot episode was popular among passengers on Virgin Airline's Britain-to-U.S. flights. How unusual for a graphic depiction of a plane crash to be viewed (repeatedly) by passengers crossing the Atlantic! The DVD set, complete with extras such as actors' auditions and episode commentaries, sold well; its release in September 2005, just prior to the beginning of the second season in the U.S., encouraged more people to catch up so that they would understand new episodes. Fans who like to read as well as watch *Lost* storylines could buy a series of novelizations, beginning in late 2005; a mystery written by a doomed author on Oceanic 815 is scheduled to be published in 2006. Fans' imaginations (and purchasing power) were inspired by *Lost* conventions at which actors and the creative team behind the series answered questions, posed for photo ops, and shared inside secrets. (Creation Entertainment presented the first official convention in June 2005 in California, with the promise of more conventions to come.) Either individually or collectively, *Lost* people appeared at such fan venues as San Diego's Comic-Con and at other science fiction, comic book, collectible, and television conventions. The actors, writers, directors, and producers seem as eager to talk with fans as fans are to attend these events.

Lost has been popular with critics as well as fans. During its first season alone, this difficult-to-classify, multi-genre series was nominated for or received awards for such diverse criteria as visual effects, family programming, scriptwriting, directing, acting, and themes involving the accurate portrayal of drug use. *Lost* won the 2005 Emmy for Outstanding Drama Series, the 2005 and 2006 Golden Globe for Best Television Series—Drama, and, in December 2005, *Entertainment Weekly* named the cast of *Lost* its Entertainer of the Year. (A list of *Lost*'s many nominations and awards can be found in appendix B, "Awards and Nominations.")

LOST POPULARITY

What makes the series so successful? It takes more than a beautiful cast or a tropical island to attract viewers. The diversity of awards and nominations and the fervid enthusiasm of its fans demonstrate that many people discover multiple strengths in *Lost*. Successfully blending genres and combining the best aspects of storytelling from classic television and movies, *Lost* provides intriguing action and plot twists to keep audiences hooked from week to week. Perhaps most importantly, however, it pulls viewers into the personal stories of a group of human beings with a broad range of experiences and different worldviews representing at least a half dozen cultures and countries. Audiences watch *Lost* because they care about the castaways.

The basic premise of *Lost* seems simple: forty-eight people initially survive a plane crash on a supposedly deserted tropical island. When no one comes to rescue them (at least during the forty days of the first season), the individuals learn that they must pull together in order to survive. What happens to them individually and collectively during that time makes riveting television as they wrestle with private demons and struggle to survive on an island full of human and inhuman dangers.

Their lives are further complicated, and the drama thickened, by the introduction of the "Tailies," a small group of survivors from Oceanic 815's tail section. The newly enlarged society attempts to understand the information revealed in the Dharma Initiative's research projects in the Hatch and other abandoned stations on the island. The Others, who many viewers might label terrorists, continue to bedevil the castaways.

ABOUT THIS BOOK

What makes *Lost* more than popular, but actually cultlike in its fandom? Why do so many millions of viewers worldwide tune in each week, or grouse about a hiatus between new episodes? Most importantly, why is *Lost* significant to Western culture? What does the success of *Lost* say about viewers and the world at large?

These are some of the many questions we explore in *Unlocking the Meaning of* Lost: *The Unauthorized Guide*. It has been written for anyone seriously interested in the show:

- Those who study television programs and their cultural impact
- Fans of the series who want a closer look at the many influences on *Lost*'s storylines and characterizations, as well as the way that *Lost*, in turn, is influencing popular culture

Completed at the end of 2005, nine episodes into *Lost*'s second season, the book's five chapters cover the immediate and potentially long-term significance of this immensely popular series. The first season's fourteen major characters and twenty-four episodes (twenty-five including a summary episode shown in the U.S.) are discussed in the most detail, but Season Two's new characters and first nine episodes also are included.

The book consists of several parts, beginning with the series' creation. The many meanings of "lost" are revealed and discussed in part 2, and spirituality and philosophy take center stage in part 3. Part 4 offers a variety of "keys" to understanding *Lost*, including a look at its many ancestor texts and the importance of its fandom and a plethora of supplementary materials: a glossary, character sketches and connections, a list of similar names. An epilogue, in which we briefly consider the future of *Lost*, two appendices—an episode guide and a list of awards and nominations the series has received—bibliographies, and an index of people, places, and key themes in *Unlocking the Meaning of* Lost complete the book.

As new developments about the series are revealed, please check our website at www.unlockinglost.com for updates.

As we discovered, being *Lost* can be an exhilarating ride in participative television viewing. We hope that you also will find yourself as you enjoy getting *Lost*.

PART ONE:

CREATING *LOST*

"If [Lost] works at all, it's because the audience and the characters want to know the answers to the same questions. The mysteries that we're grappling with while watching the show are the same ones they're grappling with, and that's part of the fun."

—J. J. ABRAMS

LOST AND **ABC**

Though originally described by ABC Entertainment president Stephen McPherson as part of a new fall 2004 line-up that would be "not spectacular, but good," *Lost* has turned out to be by any measure a spectacular success, a key ingredient in the resurgence of a network "that recently seems to have set the world record for airing stinkers."

In 2003–2004, ABC lost viewership for the third straight year in the prized eighteen to forty-nine age demographic. But shows like *Lost* and its fellow (even bigger) hit *Desperate Housewives* reversed that trend. In its first week (September 22, 2004) *Lost* had the best opening for a drama in nine years. Throughout the season, it would average eighteen million viewers a week and consistently rank among the top ten programs, while proving to be a major international hit as well.

McPherson gets much of the credit for ABC's 2004–2005 ratings comeback. But it was his fired predecessors Susan Lyne—

who discovered and supported *Housewives*—and Lloyd Braun—
Lost's biggest backer and the benefactor who provided the $12
million dollars for making the pilot—who identified and greenlit
the properties that would make it possible. In January 2004,
Braun brought the basic concept—what Damon Lindelof suc-
cinctly calls "Plane Crashes on Island"—to J. J. Abrams, who was
already helming *Alias* for the network. (An earlier script by *Tuck
Everlasting* coauthor Jeffrey Lieber had been rejected.)

Already heavily committed to the development of other projects,
Abrams was initially unimpressed:

> I was like, "Why? What the hell's that show? How
> would that work?" I just didn't get it. Then I started
> thinking about ways [of doing it] that, for me at least,
> would be thrilling. If the island wasn't just an island
> and if you started to look at where they were as part
> of the ongoing story, it started to become increasingly
> clear that this was a big idea.

One of those creative individuals who thrive on multi-tasking,
Abrams would sign on and ask for help. And at that moment, *Lost*
truly began.

CHAPTER ONE

THE MAKING OF *LOST*

J. J. ABRAMS

"I lucked into this incredible medium. The hours are brutal, the pressure's tremendous, and the need for material is insatiable. But it's so exciting to work with the same group of people on a long-term basis, and you're writing something you know is going to get shot. That just doesn't exist in features."

—J. J. ABRAMS

Abrams is sometimes spoken of as *Lost*'s sole creator. As simplistic and incorrect as that notion may be in the collaborative medium of television, it is understandable. In an era in which it has become more customary to equate prime mover and show—Joss Whedon's *Buffy the Vampire Slayer*, David Chase's *The Sopranos*, David Kelley's *Ally McBeal*, Aaron Sorkin's *West Wing*, Winnie Holzman's *My So-Called Life*—the temptation to speak of J. J. Abrams's *Lost* was perhaps irresistible.

The son of producer Gerald Abrams, Abrams has wanted to make films since he was a teenager. A screenplay he wrote while a student at Sarah Lawrence College eventually became *Taking Care of Business* in 1990. Other scripts likewise found their way to the screen: *Regarding Henry* (1991), *Forever Young* (1992), *Gone Fishin'* (1997), and *Armageddon* (1998), none of which made their author a big name in the business. "[A]s someone who was an accredited writer on *Armageddon*," Abrams admits, "my one real question is, is that something you really want to publicize?"

They did lead, however, to development (with Matt Reeves) of a television series for the WB: *Felicity*, which ran from 1998 to 2002. Like his contemporary Whedon, Abrams imagined his future would be in film, not the small screen. But he found himself fascinated by television's possibilities.

Fantasies about expanding the parameters of *Felicity*'s narrative universe by making its college co-ed heroine a spy led to the creation of *Alias* (2001–2006). Because *Alias*' creator, in the words of Mark Cotta Vaz, "has memory circuits wired to the mythic mainframe of pop culture," his new series was a generic amalgam, a mixture (in Stafford and Burnett's taxonomy) of spy drama, comedy, romance, family drama, science fiction, Hong Kong martial arts, *Twilight Zone*, *thirtysomething*, *Mission Impossible*, and *Avengers*. "I loved all sorts of movies and television," Abrams would tell Kevin Dilmore. "I loved Irwin Allen disaster movies, James Bond movies. I was a fan of cheesy ABC shows of the 1970s like *The Six Million Dollar Man* and *The Bionic Woman*. When I was a kid, I loved all that stuff." *American Werewolf in London* is likewise mentioned as a major influence, as are the films of David Cronenberg.

Hybridizing genres was not the only pleasure Abrams found in *Alias*. While making *Felicity* he had been reminded of what "he always enjoyed about writing: capturing small, private moments that resonate with viewers, then weaving them into a narrative that's compelling to watch." He sought to fill *Alias* with such moments. His acknowledged displeasure with the series' third season (during which his hands-on involvement diminished due to other commitments) stemmed in large part from its neglect of them.

Abrams's experiences with *Felicity* and *Alias* taught him important lessons about the kind of imaginative universe he might want to live in: "When you write a pilot, you're building a dream space…You want to populate that area with as many fun props as you can, so that when you're living in it for hopefully years, you're not bored." Abrams built into the *Alias*verse the sci-fi indeterminacy of Rambaldi, the Renaissance scientist and inventor whose discoveries were five hundred years before their time, which has enabled fantastic expansion of its storytelling capability as needed in order to prevent his boredom—and ours.

So it should not surprise us that, when given the opportunity to colonize the dream space of a South Pacific island, he would need it to be something more than *Gilligan's Island*, or *Cast Away*, or *Lord of the Flies*, or *Survivor*. To Edward Gross' question about why his new creation *Lost* needed a monster and all the other mysteries of the island—why it couldn't just be a drama about survival—he replied:

> It wouldn't work for me. Personally, [the monster is] what interests me. Someone else I'm sure could do the show with that absent from it entirely, but it wasn't the version I was interested in. For me, it was like looking at the show in a long term. What is the series beyond survival? What is the series beyond relationships such as trust and betrayal? What would give the show story tent poles that were compelling and mysterious and bigger than the obvious stuff that you see play out? Increasingly it became clear that it was about adding an element that was, for me, hyper-real....It's just my tendency. Whether it's smart or successful storytelling or not, it's just what interests me.

In episode commentaries and in mini-documentaries on the *Alias* and *Lost* DVDs, Abrams shows himself to be wonderfully knowledgeable about all aspects of filmmaking, from special effects to scoring. But he has clearly thought long and hard about his own creative path and explains it with eloquence:

I'm not sure how the process works in me...but I know that when I'm writing, there'll be moments that will occur to me inspired by a premise, and then the premise changes inspired by moments. Then moments change and new ones appear because of what the premise is telling you. Then another idea occurs to you, but that means the premise will change. It's sort of *writing as nanotechnology,* creating something from nothing. There is no tried-and-true method. It just sort of happens in the weird way it happens, and you hope at the end of the day that the piece works as a whole and you can't quite tell which idea inspired which. *(authors' emphasis)*

One of the many keys to the mystery offered by *Lost*'s inquisitive and imaginative fans is that the island is overrun by nanotechnology (the now in-development use of molecule-sized machinery to control the structure of matter even at atomic levels). Like much Internet speculation (discussed in part 4), the idea seems ingenious but unlikely. *Lost*'s nanotechnology is behind the camera, not in front of it, released by Abrams's imagination but alive now and endlessly evolving in the series' narrative drive.

THE REST OF THE TEAM

In various media interviews during *Lost*'s first season, both cast and creators made the analogy between the survivors of Oceanic 815 and the group of actors and actresses who came together in Hawaii to perform as a synergistic ensemble. Each major character's complex and often unexpected pre-island backstory has been revealed in *Lost*'s richly textured flashback sequences; the actors' pasts have been investigated not in flashbacks but in places like *Entertainment Weekly* or *People.*

But the creators of *Lost* have rich stories too. How did they end up on the island?

"The deal on *Lost*," Abrams told Edward Gross, "was always that I was going to help mount the show, but not run it day to day." That assignment would fall to two relative unknowns.

DAMON LINDELOF

"You'll have to ask J. J. why he needs me (hell—I'm still asking myself that), but as to why I need him? Come on."

—DAMON LINDELOF

Television creativity, with its recombining of widely different sensibilities on divergent projects, can often energize new potential in writers, directors, and producers. The TV past of Damon Lindelof—as a writer on *Nash Bridges* (1996) and writer-producer on *Crossing Jordan* (2001–2003)—would not seem to foreshadow the achievement of *Lost*.

But Lindelof, a graduate of NYU's film school, had a personal list of influential TV series that Abrams would certainly find likeminded: *"Twilight Zone, Incredible Hulk, Six Million Dollar Man, Hill Street Blues, Police Squad* (six glorious episodes!), *Twin Peaks, Misfits of Science, X-Files, Profit, Quantum Leap, Buffy, South Park, The Tick* (cartoon version), *Mr. Show, Dexter's Lab*, and the greatest show ever—*The Simpsons."*

Even while working on *Crossing Jordan*, Lindelof aspired to do more. He confessed to *Ain't It Cool News*: "I'd been an *Alias* addict for almost three years…and had been pushing my agents (and anyone who'd listen) just to get a meeting with J. J. [Abrams]. Ultimately, it was Heather Kadin (an incredibly bright woman who defies the term 'network executive') who pitched *me* as the person to sit down with J. J. on this concept."

Hence Lindelof found himself, in spring 2004, perfectly positioned to become the chief collaborator with Abrams on *Lost*. Immediately recognizing their simpatico imaginations, Lindelof and Abrams, with some assistance from Jesse Alexander and Jeff Pinkner, *Alias* staff writers, hammered out a full outline of the pilot that would eventually be filmed. Four days after the idea had first been proposed, at the end of development season for the network, the series was greenlit by ABC. Eleven weeks later the pilot was in the can.

The benefits of his collaboration with Lindelof were not lost on Abrams either. In August 2004 he told *Television Week*: "Damon showed up and I couldn't stand that we had never worked together.... He was incredibly smart. He had a point of view and seemed to have a take on what this show could be. He pitched, in the room, this idea for how he had to open the show, which is literally shot for shot what's there."

In addition to his central role in transforming *Lost* from dream into reality, Lindelof penned, with Abrams, the two-part pilot. On his own, Lindelof wrote:

- "Tabula Rasa" (1.3), in which we learn that Kate is a fugitive, captured in Australia by a U.S. marshal who was retuning her for trial in the U.S. when 815 went down
- "Confidence Man" (1.8), exploring Sawyer's criminal past
- "Homecoming" (1.15), a Charlie-centric episode concerning his post-DriveShaft struggles with heroin addiction

Collaborating with Jennifer Johnson, Lindelof also scripted "Whatever the Case May Be" (1.12), in which Kate acquires, in a bank robbery, that toy airplane that means so much to her. With Cuse, he coauthored:

- "Deus Ex Machina" (1.19), with its Locke flashbacks in which the island's mystery man is flimflammed out of a kidney by his biological father and Boone is seriously injured doing Locke's bidding
- The three-hour finale, "Exodus" (1.23 and 1.24), in which (among other things), the *Black Rock* is revealed, the black smoke rises, Rousseau steals a child, the Hatch is opened, the raft is launched, and Walt is taken captive.

When members of the cast and crew of *Lost* came to the stage to accept their 2006 Golden Globe award in January 2006, it was Lindelof, fittingly, who held the statuette and who delivered the acceptance speech. J. J. Abrams remained in the background, silent.

CARLTON CUSE

"We're on a first name basis with all our viewers."
—CARLTON CUSE ON *The Adventures of Brisco County, Jr.*

Carlton Cuse was no stranger to a mixed-genre television series when, long after the series had built a full head of steam, he joined *Lost* as Lindelof's co-showrunner in October 2004. (Cuse and Lindelof had collaborated before on *Nash Bridges*.)

One of his early (1993–1994) ventures in television as an executive producer was with *The Adventures of Brisco County, Jr.*, a Fox series scheduled in the Friday night slot preceding *The X-Files* and later relegated by TNT to Saturday morning reruns. However, *Brisco* was far from a typical Western or a children's show. Part comedy, part science fiction, part drama, and part buddy series, its snappy dialogue defied the "Thank you, ma'am" and "This town ain't big enough for the both of us" school of Western dialogue. Double entendres and comments on nineties' culture (that's 1990s,' not 1890s') permeated the episodes. For example, an Elvis impersonator becomes a recurring character, and a slab of beef placed on a bun is eternally saved from being known as a "cow patty" by Lord Bowler's timely comment.

Cuse, who created *Brisco* with Jeffrey Boam, also wrote the teleplay or story for seven episodes spanning different genres and playing with popular culture icons. "The Orb Scholar," the second episode in the series, begins the mythology of the mysterious orbs. Episode 20, also written by Cuse, completes the orbs' story with a time-traveler denouement.

A few *Brisco* plot elements foreshadow ideas later found in *Lost*. In the series' final two episodes, Brisco and Lord Bowler fake their deaths before a firing squad. In *Lost*'s first season, Shannon and Charlie seem to die, only to be spared that fate. The concept of killing off main characters—or teasing viewers with that idea—is nothing new to *Lost*.

Plays on words also grace both series. *Brisco* features a lawyer named Socrates; *Lost*'s characters include John Locke and

Rousseau. *Brisco's* "chapter" or segment titles include "The Blast Supper" and "Spur of the Moment" (from the pilot); an episode about Dixie Cousins is entitled "Deep in the Heart of Dixie." *Lost's* episode titles often refer to song titles or lyrics, such as "Born to Run" (1.22) or play with the theme of the episode, such as "Whatever the Case May Be" (1.12), about the marshal's briefcase.

Brisco County, Jr. isn't a prototype for Jack Shephard (Matthew Fox), but the two share common traits. Brisco fails to gain his father's approval and support while his father is alive. Commitment shy around Mae West-esque good "bad girl" Dixie, he is genuinely fond of her and looks after her.

Similarly, *Lost's* Jack is a good man who sometimes keeps secrets or strays from the moral high ground. Like Brisco's father, Jack's dad dies before father and son work out their differences. Jack, too, sees his father's ghost (or hallucinates the visions) and gains insights from seeing the apparition. He shies away from greater involvement with bad girl Kate, but his attraction to her is obvious.

Cuse demonstrates an attraction for a "buddy" theme in *Brisco* later echoed in *Nash Bridges*. (On that series, Cuse worked with Daniel Roebuck, who was brought into *Lost* as short-lived science teacher Leslie Arzt.) As in all series in which Cuse is involved, a wide variety of often quirky characters come together to pool their disparate knowledge and skills for the greater good in plots occasionally otherworldly. Although Cuse doesn't blatantly steal from his previous work, the themes of friendship, father/son relationships, and supernatural or mystical elements operating in an otherwise logical world frequently turn up in a Cuse series. A latecomer to the island, Carlton Cuse has become one of its most influential inhabitants.

In *Entertainment Weekly's* "Best of 2005" issue we learn that the "Jewish and empirically minded" Lindelof and the "Catholic and willing to leap beyond logic" Cuse are a kind of Scully and Mulder, whose very different conceptions of reality are in many ways reflected in *Lost*'s ongoing clash between "man of science" Jack and "man of faith" Locke.

The clash has proved effective, despite others' doubts. In fact, the Powers That Be at the FBI originally felt that Scully's medically trained skepticism and Mulder's open-to-conspiracy-thinking faith that the "truth is out there" on *The X-Files* did not seem a promising collaboration. *X-Files* creator Chris Carter knew better: the collaboration of opposites may produce a generative, expansive, ongoing creative friction. When Lindelof invited Cuse to become one of the "*Lost* boys," he demonstrated the same wisdom. The collaboration of Abrams and Lindelof resulted in a strong foundation for the series; the partnership of Lindelof and Cuse, in turn, has energized its ongoing evolution as a serial narrative.

Lost's strong creative team has nevertheless faced, and will continue to face, a myriad of challenges.

Lost in a Good Story: The Problem of Serial Creativity

"[C]ontinuous serials must of necessity build and sustain a cult status to stay on the air…viewers supposedly cannot bear to miss an episode. To stimulate and maintain that level of interest, you need to draw viewers into watching the show and then keep them hooked."

—Marc Dolan, "The Peaks and Valleys of Serial
Creativity: What Happened to/on *Twin Peaks*"

In a column in *Entertainment Weekly* entitled "*Lost*'s Soul," Stephen King offers some fascinating speculations on what lies ahead for a series he has touted as the best on the small screen. "There's never been anything like it on TV for capturing the imagination," he insists, "except *The Twilight Zone* and *The X-Files*." And yet he fears *Lost* might succumb to the same serial narrative fate as the latter, a great series that ended badly because it violated the Nietzschean dictum to "die at the right time," remaining faithful instead to what King deems "the Prime Network Directive: Thou Shalt Not Kill the Cash Cow." "I could have throttled the executives at Fox for doing that, and Chris Carter for letting it happen," King rants, and he has no desire to experience déjà vu all over again.

As *Lost* became both a mainstream top ten show *and* an international cult phenomenon, the extraordinary tests faced by the *Lost* castaways have turned out to pale by comparison to those Abrams, Lindelof, Cuse, and company face. Not since *Twin Peaks*, another rule-breaking, genre-defying ABC series that started strong but flamed out in its mystifying second season, and *The X-Files*, a *Lost* ancestor with a complex and perplexing mythology that perpetually promised but seldom delivered solutions to the myriad puzzles it raised (alienating its fans in the end), has an episodic television story faced greater narrative challenges.

How can *Lost* sustain its suspense while retaining the good faith and credibility of a deeply inquisitive viewership determined to puzzle out its mysteries? Can it become a "long-haul show" (Sarah Vowell's term) while maintaining immediate watercooler buzz? How can *Lost*'s creative team out-imagine its obsessed, ingenious fan base? ("People who post online—they're infinitely smarter than anyone working on the show," Abrams effused on *Jimmy Kimmel Live*.) Must *Lost*, of necessity, eventually disappoint?

Challenges to *Lost*'s ongoing development came from above as well as below, from network doubts as well as fan demands. Both before and during *Lost*'s first season, ABC made its concerns about the show's course well known. *Daily Variety* reported in July 2004 that the network had expressed alarm over the series' fear factor, evidently worried too much of the scary might drive away viewers, especially in *Lost*'s early evening time slot. In mid-season, David Fury, who had been a major contributor as both writer and director for both *Buffy the Vampire Slayer* and *Angel*, reported in an interview in *Dreamwatch* that network interference had intensified.

Fury had written or cowritten several pivotal *Lost* episodes, including "Walkabout" (1.4), in which we learn that survivalist Locke had been confined to a wheelchair when he boarded

Oceanic 815; "Special" (1.14), which focuses on Michael, his mysterious, possibly telepathic son Walt, and the reappearance of a geographically anomalous polar bear; and the marvelous (and very funny) "Numbers" (1.18), which reveals that Hurley is a multi-millionaire after winning the lottery with numbers to be found on the mysterious Hatch Locke and Boone discovered in "All the Best Cowboys Have Daddy Issues" (1.11).

Because each of these episodes introduces elements of the fan tastic, it shouldn't surprise us that *Lost's* deviations from standard television realism, a given in Fury's tenure on *Buffy* and *Angel*, were on the mind of both interviewer and writer when he sat down to talk with Tara DiLullo: "We didn't run into any network interference," Fury admits, "until roughly around episodes 9 ["Solitary," written by Fury] and 10 ["Raised by Another," written by Lynne E. Litt]." The network, he suggests, became "terrified" at the creative team's decision to "goose things and take it a bit further" and asked that the "hard to explain things" be avoided.

Why would a network that once had the audacity to air *Twin Peaks*, one of the most bizarre series ever to air on the small screen, be terrified by the plans of Abrams, Lindelof, Cuse, and Fury? Had not the central mystery of *Twin Peaks*, "Who killed Laura Palmer?"—certainly the greatest puzzle TV had seen since the question of "Who shot J. R.?" in 1980—been satisfactorily answered? Laura, it was clear, had been killed by her father while under the control of BOB, a psychopathic supernatural parasite emanating from the ghostly Black Lodge which manifested periodically in Glastonbury Grove outside of the town of Twin Peaks! As *Twin Peaks* finally began to disclose its "answers" in its second season, such as the identity of BOB, the ratings had, of course, plummeted.

But that was so last century. Surely ABC couldn't be worried that its new Goose That Laid the Golden Nielsens could be destroyed by the "goosing" Lindelof wanted to undertake? Weren't the fans anxious to be goosed? Fury, who has since left the show, admitted to "a frustration for me as a viewer, in that I'd like some clearer answers [to *Lost*'s mysteries], but those answers were resting in the area of sci-fi and that's where we had to draw the line."

At this point, Fury's efforts to say what he isn't allowed to say become completely enigmatic—as enigmatic as *Lost* itself:

> We were holding back, but it's not like we want to burst forth and admit we are a sci-fi show in the closet coming out....It's more about trying to find the elements of the island that become the metaphors for character stories that we are trying to tell. It's about trying to find those mystical elements and yet give them an element of being possibly mystical, or not, by perception.

Using a metaphor drawn from one of *Lost*'s genetic ancestors, he even manages to find a way to make this triangulation sound like a good thing:

> We are respecting the network's desire to not make the show too "out there" too fast....We were trying to approach the show from the Scully perspective and always try to have a reasonable explanation for everything, despite anything that seems out of the ordinary. That was our self-imposed mandate because the networks are scared of genre television. But it wasn't a constraining element. It was more of a way of looking at the show in a way that helped keep things more subtle and grounded and that's a good thing.

While the Powers That Be at the network, Fury observes with disarming cogency, "are content with the mysteries, they are not content with the answers."

Hyperconscious of the classic "surprise/acceptability problem" Marc Dolan identified (see the epigraph), Fury knows very well such a situation has inherent risks: "There is the challenge of how long an audience will be invested in the show and in these characters without getting enough concrete answers." If "we answer some of these questions, and if we do it in the most reality based way, I think people will feel cheated." On the other hand, supplying answers to *Lost*'s enigmas "in the most interesting sci-fi way" could well result in "alienat[ing]"—a telling word choice—"the core audience of the series." Did we mention that Fury is no longer with the show?

LOST IN SEASON TWO

Now, nine episodes into Season Two, *Lost* is perhaps the most-imitated show on television. All the networks, seemingly no longer concerned that SF/fantastic story lines might drive viewers away, have prolifically experimented with science fiction and the fantastic in their fall schedules. *Threshold* on CBS, *Night Stalker* on ABC, *Supernatural* on the WB, *Surface* on NBC (most now cancelled), and *Invasion*—*Lost*'s partnered follow-up show on ABC, have come and gone (mostly gone). *Lost* nevertheless remains firmly perched on the horns of its indigenous creative dilemma, though at least we have now gone down the Hatch.

Lindelof and Cuse's Season One finale last spring gave with one hand and took away with the other. We were left wanting to know more about the crash itself, but only saw the survivors boarding the plane and learned nothing new about the flight itself or the crash. We longed for insight into the mysterious numbers, and though the proliferating 4, 8, 15, 16, 23, 42 had repeated cameos, they remained inscrutable. We saw (and heard) more of the Monster than ever before, and yet it still dwells in the mystery. We met the Others (we think) but still have no idea who/what they are and why they were wearing winter clothes. The Hatch was opened, but we still had no idea where or to what it led. And, by all indications, the fan base was not entirely pleased by the lack of answers. *Entertainment Weekly* reports that throughout summer 2005 the cast had to bear "the brunt of fan angst."

With new individuals added to the creative team—Elizabeth Sarnoff (*Deadwood*) and Craig Wright (*Six Feet Under*) joined the show from HBO; independent film auteur Darren Aronofsky signed on to direct an episode—*Lost* seemed ready to face the challenges of a sophomore season. Not surprisingly, however, Season Two developments have not met with complete approval. Although "Man of Science, Man of Faith" (2.1) began in the Hatch, introduced its sole inhabitant—Desmond and his forced mission—we could only surmise why the numbers with which Hurley had won the lottery had to be input into a computer or what might happen if they were not. We watched the Dharma Initiative orientation video (shown earlier in the season than originally planned due to fan displeasure about the too slow pace of narrative revelation) but still found ourselves disoriented. Subsequent episodes offered new insights into the pre-island lives of Jack, Kate, Shannon, Hurley, Locke, and new characters like the Tailies Ana Lucia and Mr. Eko, but earlier *Lost* mysteries (the cause of the plane crash, for example) remained, and new ones proliferated.

Lost's perhaps too-open-ended mysteries—so essential to maintaining the lift necessary so the story doesn't crash on a narrative desert island—are not the only fan irritants. Message boards and other websites reveal unhappiness with other series developments. The Tailies, some fear, are already unduly distracting from, and competing for screen time with, the original survivors. And for the first time the series has its own disliked-by-many character in Ana Lucia. Some, it seems, have begun to fear that the shark (perhaps the one with the Dharma logo that menaces Sawyer in "Adrift" [2.2]) might be ready for jumping.

The dangers *Lost*'s creative team faces are very real and have proved fatal, either in the short or long term, to all previous episodic television. But then the *Lost* boys are not governed by a traditional paradigm. As both creative consultant Jeff Pinkner (in an interview on the Season One DVD set) and Lindelof have acknowledged, *Lost*'s ongoing narrative drive is modeled, in what may be a television first, on the storyworld of video games. As in a video game, in which players acquire new weapons and capabilities within its digital geography and learn more about how to play from the collective knowledge of gamers online, both *Lost's* characters and its audience are acquiring sequentially the "tools" they need to play. In an interview for *The Lost Chronicles*, Lindelof recalls a moment very near the show's inception when Abrams had insisted "that whatever we wanted to do in *Lost* we had to build all that stuff into the pilot, we had to stock this world with all the elements and hints and clues." *Lost* is clearly well-stocked, both by the creative team and the fans.

"With most shows, the 'watercooler' moments are what you see on screen," Lindelof would tell *Entertainment Weekly*. "With *Lost*, what gets people talking is what they think they saw. A Dharma Initiative logo on a shark. Sayid on a TV in Kate's flashback....The greatest thing about *Lost* is that people can own it. They can plug in, engage, interact, and imagine."

"The mantra at [ABC] these days," *Newsweek* reported at the time of *Lost's* inception, "handed down by [former Disney CEO Michael] Eisner, is 'It's a marathon, not a sprint.'" From the outset, Abrams and company have insisted that the story they want to tell is complex enough to take years to tell. We may be *Lost*—playing *Lost*—for a very long time.

PART TWO:

THE MANY MEANINGS OF *LOST*

Done well, a title can encapsulate not only a work's basic theme but its vision, purpose, and scope. Consider "*Lost.*" It captures the basic premise of the show: the survivors of Oceanic flight 815 are at least one thousand miles off course when their plane crashes, and no one, in the roughly forty days that make up the first season's events, has come to save them. To the outside world, it seems that the group is, indeed, lost, and as time passes, much less likely ever to be found. But the title does more than indicate the show's high concept.

"Lost" takes on many meanings in this series, just as in life. In this part, we look at life without technological necessities, much less luxuries. How do the castaways survive during the first forty days with very limited modern technology? How can they—or we—thrive in a culture without the latest gadgets? And how does their need for modern conveniences change as they begin to call the island "home"?

CHAPTER TWO

LOST WITHOUT MODERN TECHNOLOGY

LOST IN THE WORLD

We might not realize at first how unlikely it seems to be geographically lost. Tracking and communication devices abound in our world, and the modern concern is more about how to escape being found—at least for some downtime—than wanting others to track us down. After Oceanic 815 crashes, the survivors don't know where they are, and it seems obvious as the days wear on that their rescuers are looking in the wrong place, if indeed anyone is trying to find them. The survivors are "lost" in the geographical world; they don't know their location, although they try to signal they are alive to alert any aircraft or anyone listening electronically.

The island, itself a character, is part of the mystery of *Lost*. In fact, the pun can be made that this island truly is paradise *Lost*, much like a Garden of Eden in Christian mythology. It is beautiful, with everything humans need to survive: food, water, warmth, shelter, and even companionship. This beautiful, bountiful land is theirs to explore and cherish.

However, after their quite literal "fall," the far-from-innocent survivors discover the island is as full of secrets and perils as the technological world. A huge, menacing "monster" suddenly snatches survivors. Anomalous animals, such as polar bears, attack without warning. Cliffs from which to fall, rip currents in which to drown, and rising tides threatening their makeshift dwellings also imperil them. The survivors haven't yet been expelled from the Garden, but this particular "paradise" is often closer to hell than heaven.

LOST WITHOUT COMMUNICATION

We take communication for granted: speed dial a cell phone, text a friend, check email, leave voicemail. Part of being lost from the rest of the world is trying to find one's way without much technology. That a plane crashes and no one finds it seems odd in an age of global positioning satellites and international intelligence. A place so out of the way that no passing aircraft, whether search plane or commercial airliner, spots wreckage or locates a group of forty-eight people living on a small island seems incongruous with our concept of the world's "smallness." The sheer number of people in the world and the immediacy of global communication mean that someone somewhere knows what's going on at any time. It's difficult to be an anonymous citizen, much less to disappear without a trace.

In our society, a normal response to crisis involves counting on the global networks of satellites, the Internet, telephone and radio communications, and other broadcast technologies. Immediately after the crash, and continuing throughout the later episodes of the first season, technology and modern communication devices seem the best way for the survivors to be rescued. Technology is often perceived as a savior, especially in emergencies. The survivors of Oceanic 815 use several typical strategies to help others find them.

One of Boone's first acts after the crash is to open his cell phone and try to make a call. We hear a fast beep indicating a lack of signal. Boone tries again but still has no luck ("Pilot," 1.1). Where in the world could he be that a signal can't be generated if the phone is still working? After all, even during a flight, several thousand feet above the earth, passengers can make calls. How remote is this island if a signal can't be received? What does someone do if there's no way to call for help?

Shannon at first patiently waits for the rescue boat to arrive. When Boone offers her a candy bar, she sneers at his offer and then watches while he spitefully munches the snack. Shannon's reasoning? She will eat on the boat and not resort to candy bars when real food is headed her way. As she reminds Boone, the plane had a black box, and rescue is only a short time away. That possibly explains why Shannon gives herself a pedicure after finding her bag in the wreckage. She also tans on the beach once she changes into her bikini ("Pilot," 1.1). These pastimes are more important to her than salvaging goods from the plane or establishing a temporary home on the island; she assumes technology will find her and the other castaways soon.

Jack comes up with another idea, although he shares it with only a few people before he starts a trek into the jungle. Jack once took flying lessons, and so he knows that if he can locate the plane's cockpit, he might find a transponder and be able to use it to signal rescue planes. First, however, he has to find that section of the plane. Because Oceanic 815 split into three parts, the debris field must be wide, and Jack first tries to estimate where the cockpit might have fallen. Because Kate remained conscious as the plane descended and saw the plane break apart, she is able to point the way. She knows the direction of the cockpit, based on her knowledge of which direction the plane was heading when the fuselage broke apart.

Surprisingly, the pilot is found injured but alive in the wreckage of the cockpit and part of the first class section. He confides to Jack that the flight was far off course when turbulence eventually broke up the plane. The instruments, it seems, failed to work properly even earlier in the flight, and so the pilot turned toward Fiji for a possible landing. However, the airliner did not make it that far. With no accurate instrumentation and flying well off the flight plan, Oceanic 815, the pilot explains, will be difficult to find. A search grid most likely will not cover as wide an area as necessary to find the debris field. The one bright spot is that the still-functioning transponder is also in the cockpit.

Every moment of clarity on *Lost*, however, seems to be accompanied by a deepening of the mystery. The Monster suddenly rattles the cockpit and savagely pulls the pilot from the plane. In the frenzy to get out of the wreckage and run as far and as fast as possible, Jack has the presence of mind to grab the transponder ("Pilot," 1.1). Even in the face of danger, technology still seems the most likely way to get off the island.

During the first few days after the crash, Sayid manages to get the transponder working and to take it to higher ground where a signal can be sent. Because the battery power is limited, the window of opportunity for sending a distress is small. Sayid, accompanied by other castaways, tests the signal from an inland mountain.

Again, technology backfires on the survivors. Instead of being able to send a message, the transponder picks up a distress call on the frequency Sayid plans to use for his signal. The message further shocks the survivors: not only is the message in French from a woman stranded on the island, but the distress call has been on a loop being broadcast for sixteen years ("Pilot," 1.1).

Even if technology functions on the island, it seems to be ineffective. If a distress message broadcasting for sixteen years has not yet garnered a response, what is the likelihood this group of survivors will ever be found? (As Sawyer, one in the party accompanying Sayid on his mission, reminds the group, someone might have rescued the woman but not stopped the distress call. However, Sayid finds this unlikely, and, as it turns out, he is right. The Frenchwoman still lives on the island; technology has been unable to save her.)

Still, Sayid is determined to find a logical way to find where the Frenchwoman's distress call originated, go to that spot, and send a signal of his own. Among the communication devices salvaged from the plane (and retrieved from Sawyer's collection of gathered goods) are laptop computers and cell phones, from which Sayid cannibalizes parts to make three devices for triangulating a signal. Boone and Kate agree to help coordinate the transmission, but again things go horribly wrong.

This time the human element interferes: a cave-in traps Jack and Charlie at the same time that Boone, Kate, and Sayid try to coordinate their efforts. As a result, Boone delegates his tasks to Shannon, who almost forgets to turn on the device at the beach. Kate leaves Sawyer to take over for her inland while she runs to the caves to help save Jack. Sayid is even less fortunate; although Shannon and Sawyer come through, someone hits Sayid from behind just as he receives a strong signal and begins to figure out the location of the Frenchwoman's broadcast ("The Moth," 1.7).

Once the initial attempts to send a signal fail, Sayid's access to technology is severely limited, and he eventually gives up his plan to broadcast a distress signal or learn where the ongoing transmission originates. As long as the survivors can hope that they can send a distress call, they can keep up their morale and believe that soon they will return to their former lives—or at least a "safer" life away from monsters and Mother Nature. A communication device, like a cell phone or a transponder, only has value when it works. With no way to boost their limited technology's capability, and possibly with no one to hear a message anyway, the castaways gradually accept that they may be on the island much longer than they originally anticipated.

Late in the first season, however, communication technology once more seems a possible savior. Locke and Boone discover a drug runner's Beechcraft, its pilot long dead. The plane balances perilously over the edge of a cliff, hanging from the canopy of tall trees. Boone, manipulated by Locke into climbing up to the plane, finds that its radio still works, and he desperately sends a distress call. Miraculously, he receives an answer to his Mayday. But another mystery is revealed. The person on the other end of the transmission incredulously reports "We're the survivors of Oceanic 815!" The communication abruptly ends as the plane falls from the cliff, crushing Boone ("Do No Harm," 1.20).

In an interesting view of this broadcast from the recipients' perspective, the second season "catch up" episode about the Tailies' experiences reveals more about the broadcast. Bernard finds a radio in an abandoned bunker and tests the radio for a few minutes at a time to conserve its battery. During one check, he hears a Mayday and responds to it. However, group leader Ana Lucia squelches further use of the radio, believing the Others are trying to locate the castaways. Ironically, the message from Boone, if interpreted correctly by Ana Lucia, could have saved his sister's life. If one group of Oceanic 815 survivors had known about the other group, the merger likely would have been blood free ("The Other 48 Days," 2.7).

After Boone's death, Locke reluctantly leads Sayid to the plane, where the former communications officer scavenges the wreckage for equipment that might be used for another distress call ("The Other 48 Days," 2.7). However, at this point, technology only teases the survivors with the hope of communicating with the world beyond the island.

LOST WITHOUT MEDICAL TECHNOLOGY

Communication technology is immediately needed as the survivors attempt either to call for help or to leave the island. However, an even more pressing need, both immediately after the crash and in the following weeks, is the need for medical technology. We—and the castaways—have grown accustomed to having medicine "fix" anything. It is not surprising that Jack's (soon to be) ex-wife Sarah tells Jack that his need to fix people or situations is too great ("The Hunting Party," 2.11). As a doctor, and later as leader of the survivors, Jack medically fixes people physically and emotionally, but he also has the desire to control and fix dangerous situations. He seems to believe that every problem has a solution; he just needs to find it. Similarly, we often believe that medicine (and doctors) can perform miracles all the time; life-saving or life-prolonging treatments and medications are commonplace in the modern world. When the survivors, especially Jack, carry that attitude onto the island, they realize just how lost they are without modern medicine and the latest high-tech equipment.

Fortunately for the number of people saved or stitched by Jack in the first season, Jack survives the crash. He prescribes treatments for hives and rashes ("Solitary," 1.9), poor eyesight ("Deus Ex Machina," 1.19), and heroin withdrawal ("Hearts and Minds," 1.13). He stitches Sayid's leg ("Raised by Another," 1.10) and keeps Sawyer from bleeding to death ("Confidence Man," 1.8). He brings Rose ("Pilot," 1.1) and Charlie ("Whatever the Case May Be," 1.12) back to life through CPR. Jack is often a miracle worker, living up to his name as a good "shepherd" for his flock of survivors.

On ABC's *The View* in mid-May 2005 Matthew Fox, who plays the good doctor, noted that Jack has to "reinvent himself as a doctor." Because Jack is comfortable with medical technology, one of his first acts as a leader is to look for antibiotics in the salvaged luggage. Later, as supplies diminish, he rations aspirin and stronger medication as part of his treatments for Sawyer and Charlie and demands the last of Sawyer's alcohol as a disinfectant before Boone's surgery. Yet even though Jack is a talented surgeon with a compelling desire to save people, he is limited by his reliance on technology.

When Shannon suffers asthma attacks and no inhalers can be found, Jack expends his energy to coerce (and encourage Sayid to torture) Sawyer into giving up the inhalers. To Jack's chagrin, Sawyer does not have the medication; only Sawyer's belligerent pride, not protection of his salvaged goods, makes the former confidence man defy Jack ("Confidence Man," 1.8). In his quest for a technical/medical solution to the problem, Jack ignores the basic Hippocratic principle: first do no harm.

The medical technology problems are actually solved by Sun. Sun begins to plant an orchard and create a nursery when she realizes that her new little society may need to survive on their own ("Hearts and Minds," 1.13). Her knowledge helps in a variety of ways. In one of the first episodes, Sun shows Walt how to brush his teeth using a local plant ("Walkabout," 1.4). Later, Sun finds eucalyptus and makes a balm that helps Shannon breathe during an asthma attack ("Confidence Man," 1.8) and even finds sea urchin spines from which to make a fine enough needle for Boone's blood transfusion ("Do No Harm," 1.20). The young woman who was reared in prosperity and shown in flashbacks as more concerned with parties and romance than public service begins to find in herself the qualities of a healer. However, her approach to healing, and to life, differs from Jack's. Sun uses what is at hand and works with the natural world, a place where she frequently seems to find herself.

An episode late in the first season highlights not only Jack's and Sun's different approaches to healing, but their acceptance of technology, or the lack of it, in their treatments. In "Do No Harm" (1.20) Boone lies dying, his injuries too great for Jack's expertise, probably even without Locke's incorrect information about their cause. Jack diligently works to save the young man, to the point of transfusing his own blood into his patient. However, Boone's condition only gets worse, and Jack determines that the only possible way to save Boone's life is to amputate his crushed leg using part of the fuselage, with a heavy sliding door, to sever it.

This final effort seems horrific, not only for us, but for the castaways. Sun begs Jack to reconsider, and Boone becomes lucid long enough to persuade Jack just to let him go. Boone knows that he is too badly damaged to survive the amputation and that Jack has tried every method at his disposal to save him. Jack still contemplates the amputation for a moment, believing even yet that Boone might be saved. Sun's approach seems the more rational in this sad story; she agrees with Boone that sometimes people can't be saved and heroic measures do more harm than good. Boone dies, but part of his heroism, as Sayid later tells a grieving Shannon ("The Greater Good," 1.21), is that Boone wanted the few remaining antibiotics used not on a lost cause, but to help others in the future.

Even in the most modern hospitals, much less in the jungle, technology and gifted surgeons cannot save all patients. Jack's realization that he cannot always be a savior, with or without technology, is devastating. As one who relies on medical technology and the latest information to perform miracles, he has become accustomed to defeating death. However, as Sun and Boone understand, life is cyclical. Although it is sad to lose a friend—or one's own life—the grace and dignity of death should supersede the ability to simply prolong life. Sun's "natural" approach to healing seems to oppose Jack's "technological" approach. Whether the two come to balance each other in later episodes or if the distance between the two widens remains to be seen.

On the other side of the island, Ana Lucia's band of survivors faces a similar dilemma. Libby, who says that she completed a year of medical school before dropping out, sets a man's broken leg. When she later expresses concern that the man is near death because of an infection, Ana Lucia replies, "What do you want me to do about it?" ("The Other 48 Days," 2.7). She knows that they have no medical supplies or way to treat this, or any other, crash victim.

When Sawyer is forced to hike with the Tailies through the jungle, his infected shoulder wound also draws Libby's concern. However, with her limited medical skills and no technology to help, she can do little more than superficially treat the injury and try to provide emotional comfort ("Abandoned," 2.6). Although both groups of plane-crash survivors benefit from aid from trained medical personnel, technology is often the deciding factor in who lives or dies.

Jack's stash of medical supplies is replenished in the Hatch, but even that source is limited. What happens when Jack no longer has any antibiotics for treating cuts, much less knife or gunshot wounds, in the middle of a jungle? Claire fortunately gives birth to a healthy son; neither mother nor child apparently suffers from the very natural childbirth. Will future mothers be so lucky? If the castaways' permanent home becomes the island, how will they fare as they age? The castaways' need for medical technology only increases over time, no matter how many herbal remedies they develop or carefully they hoard the remaining pharmaceuticals. Will they be able to accept the greater likelihood of death as they rely more on a "natural" lifestyle than medical intervention to solve their health problems?

THE TEMPTATIONS OF TECHNOLOGY

Technology in the second season takes an ominous turn. The Hatch leads to an underground research base complete with a computer (however old), clothes dryer, stereo/turntable, film projector, and shower, among other "luxuries." However, being chained once more to technology is another way to lose one's way. Someone must enter a code (4, 8, 15, 16, 23, 42) and then push the Execute button every 108 minutes—or else the world will end. At least that is Desmond's theory, and no one yet seriously seems to want to challenge it. The Dharma Initiative's orientation film to the "volunteers" at Station 3: The Swan plays up the gravity of the situation as well ("Orientation," 2.3). A schedule is created so that one castaway always pushes the button at the appointed time.

Locke is eager to keep the system going and settles into the first shift. However, other castaways are reluctant. Hurley, after all, associates the code with the cursed numbers that seem to plague him since he won the lottery. Charlie only is lured into this mundane work with the promise of "good" or "fun" technology: Locke tells him that he can play records in the Hatch ("Everybody Hates Hugo," 2.4). Rose stays away from the Hatch and prefers doing laundry outdoors; the "creepy" factor is enough to turn her away from the Hatch's dryer ("Abandoned," 2.6). Some characters, like Claire, haven't yet been shown visiting the Hatch; perhaps baby Aaron is enough to keep Claire occupied on the beach.

The Tailies may not associate the Hatch with anything sinister because it has been opened by the time they arrive. Libby gladly hauls her laundry to the Hatch ("Fire + Water," 2.12). Her presence even lures love-smitten Hurley to accompany her. As time goes on, Hurley seems to overcome his initial reluctance to have anything to do with the Hatch. He and Charlie listen to music as they debate what women really want; their "guys' night in" keeps them happily in the Hatch ("The Hunting Party," 2.11). Over time, at least some survivors may choose to visit the Hatch more often rather than continue to live in more primitive conditions all the time.

Among the castaways we see the gamut of responses to technology, from love it to leave it. Many survivors still lack a comfort zone in dealing with the perils of technology to offset its convenience. Most castaways survive and even begin to think of the island as their new "home" during the first forty days before the Hatch is opened. If, like Rose, they can live without technology that long, they likely can continue to do just fine without it. Objects seem to matter to Rose less than relationships, especially with her husband Bernard. Hurley fears that the discovery of a well-stocked pantry—and Jack's decision to let Hurley decide what happens to it—will turn him into a social outcast; after all, winning the lottery and suddenly having more money than his friends once cost him his best friend and a relatively uneventful life ("Everybody Hates Hugo," 2.4). After Hurley makes his new friends happy with his distribution of the Hatch's food, he has a better feeling about the Hatch and is shown visiting more frequently. Charlie steers clear of the Hatch (and mundane office work) as long as he has somewhere else to go, usually with Claire and the baby. When Claire kicks him out of the "house," Charlie turns to music for solace, and the Hatch's stereo provides a welcome diversion ("The Hunting Party," 2.11). Technology, even on the island, can lead people to question what they value in life and how far they are willing to become slaves to technology in order to enjoy its benefits.

TECHNOLOGY AS A BARRIER BETWEEN PEOPLE

Technology often creates a barrier between people, instead of drawing them together. Email or voicemail, for example, are supposed to help friends and family keep in touch at any time and relatively inexpensively. However, the technology also can be used to avoid talking to people in person. Who hasn't sent a hasty email or preferred voicemail instead of having to deal with a person in real time?

In our world, technology often separates us. Although the Internet allows people to communicate with each other globally, a barrier separates those sending and receiving the communication. They aren't talking face to face. The technology may even be valued, in part, because it creates a comfort zone for the communication.

But what happens without technology, especially modern communication tools? The castaways have no such luxury of avoiding others with a technological barrier. If they want to communicate with each other, they must do it face to face. Just as they learn to fashion everything from traps to cradles from native resources, so they must also develop the inner resources to deal with the people around them. They often are lost in knowing how to deal with each other when they have to solve problems. They must relate to each other personally, without layers of technology to separate them.

When Hurley wants to confront the Frenchwoman about the numbers he feels are cursed, he cannot call her or send her a fax. He takes off into the jungle to locate her, a plan that seems to Sayid foolhardy at best and deadly at worst. After all, he has been tortured by the woman when he dared stumble into her booby-trapped neck of the woods ("Solitary," 1.9). Sayid is a savvy soldier and a veteran of covert operations, whereas Hurley apparently has no such experience.

Nevertheless, Hurley uses the right approach. He is brave (and lucky) enough to find Danielle and directly ask her what he needs to know. Probably surprised and impressed with his forth-right approach, Danielle tells him that, indeed, the numbers may be cursed. Hurley is relieved that his suspicions seem correct and spontaneously embraces the startled woman. "Thank you. Thank you so much!" Hurley exclaims, and then turns around to head home ("Numbers," 1.19). He has no ulterior motives, other than asking his question and getting an answer. Truly this is human communication at its finest—a scene that likely surprises us as well as makes us laugh.

Even in the second season, communication is not enhanced with the opening of the Hatch. The computer supposedly can be used only as an input device, not a communication tool ("Orientation," 2.3; "What Kate Did," 2.9). Even when Michael receives a message from Walt, or so he believes, the computer technology heartbreakingly separates them. Father and son only can "talk" a few characters at a time, and neither can be sure that the message is real. Michael wants to believe that Walt sends an instant message (although the old fashioned computer seems unlikely to perform that function), but he has no way of knowing exactly where his son is, or indeed, even if he is really communicating with Walt. Other technology fails to help, as well: the cable leading to the island (shown in "Solitary," 1.9) apparently supplies power to the Dharma Initiative's research stations, but it does not allow two-way communication.

Lack of communication spawns violence in the second season. The Tailies are unaware of Oceanic 815's other survivors until Jin, and later Michael and Sawyer, wash up on their side of the island. When the groups unexpectedly intersect, Jin, Michael, and Sawyer are beaten and held prisoner until their identities can be ascertained ("...And Found," 2.5). Because the Others know how to infiltrate the Tailies' camp ("The Other 48 Days," 2.7), Ana Lucia takes no chances when new people show up. Resorting to face-to-face communication and trusting other people not to attack when they are close enough to be seen face to face seem antithetical to safety. Trust is especially hard-won during the second season. Ana Lucia's shooting of Shannon ("Abandoned," 2.6) is one result. *Lost* shows the risk involved with face-to-face interaction but insinuates that it is still the best method of interpersonal communication.

THE LURE OF MODERN CONVENIENCES

Part of *Lost*'s appeal is our vicarious involvement with the survivors as they go back to basics. How people learn to survive in a different type of environment, reconcile with what they have lost, and find new benefits and priorities interest us. The survivors' dilemmas provide inspiration for many interesting plot lines and also make us wonder how we would live on the island.

After the initial trauma of the crash wears off, the castaways search for items that they can use from the wreckage. They sort clothing into practical and impractical jungle and beach wear. Kate reverently removes a pair of sturdier shoes from a crash victim before she hikes into the jungle to search for the cockpit. Hurley passes around the remainder of the flight meals, and the castaways share water bottles. Even luxuries, such as padded seats, make life a bit more comfortable ("Pilot," 1.1).

Other luxuries are shared or hoarded. On the day following the crash, Charlie asks if anyone has sunblock, and Shannon shares hers. Sawyer, however, gathers as much as he can from the aircraft and victims, becoming the source of all other luxuries, from books to laptop batteries to toiletries ("Pilot," 1.1). Later in the season, Hurley tries to coerce Michael into playing on the golf course by telling him the stakes are the last of the deodorant sticks ("Solitary," 1.9). What once was commonplace now takes on new importance.

Hurley initially builds a golf course to help others relieve stress. With the discovery of a set of clubs, including balls and tees, Hurley creates the perfect modern diversion. Common products of a commercial society—from lip balm to golf clubs—are comforting to the survivors as links to their past and to a world they understand. The need, for example, for sunblock may seem trivial to us, but this detail shows how people typically react on a tropical beach. How often have advertisements, as well as medical articles, warned of the dangers of sun damage and possible cancer? Especially when the survivors anticipate being saved within hours, or at most days, items like sunblock seem reasonable to value.

In the long run, though, they have to deal with bigger problems—such as the need for water, food, and shelter. Many are woefully (and humorously) unprepared to fend for themselves. Hurley and Charlie spend most of the day floundering in the surf before they spear a fish. Shannon flirts with Charlie so he will procure fish for her, not because she is interested in him but to prove to Boone she can find a way to get her own food ("Walkabout," 1.4).

Only Locke, who seems from the start to have "found" himself on the island, is initially more comfortable living a less technologically advanced lifestyle. Of course, he also is the only castaway with a suitcase full of knives ("Walkabout," 1.4). The self-proclaimed hunter successfully brings back boar and begins leading the others toward greater self-sufficiency. He seems to know how to do everything to survive, from tracking animals to building almost anything from native materials.

Jin, who, as we later learn, is the son of a fisherman ("...In Translation," 1.17), immediately provides food. He harvests sea urchins and prepares them for the others to eat. He seems especially solicitous of the heavily pregnant Claire, who feels her child move again once she eats his gift ("Pilot," 1.1). Jin also proves to be an effective fisherman, using his catch to barter for other goods for his wife and as a way to bridge the gap with fisherman-wannabe Hurley ("...In Translation," 1.17).

Kate soon uses her tree-climbing skills not to help send a distress call but to forage for fruit deeper in the jungle. Sun plants a garden and an orchard ("Hearts and Minds," 1.13). Charlie develops a knack for skewering coconuts ("Outlaws," 1.16). The communal need to find food takes precedence, and "necessities" like deodorant and coffee become luxuries prized as long as they last. However, the survivors' priorities shift rapidly in the days after the crash, and what was a necessity in their previous lives often becomes a luxury or an unimportant memory in their current situation.

Once again, *Lost* raises questions about what people really need in their lives. Is deodorant a worthwhile prize? Should alcohol be used for cocktails at sunset or medicinal disinfectant? How much is a fish worth? To put these issues in our terms—how valuable is this year's fashion? Is a new car worth trading hours of family time for a second job or overtime? Does the most recent flatscreen television necessarily trump a nine-inch model?

On an even larger scale, what do countries or cultures value? Should the global gap between "haves" and "have nots" be breached, and if so, how? Even something as simple as Locke's finding a coffee packet in the wreckage can (and probably does) instigate debates over what constitutes a necessity and what people can live without.

Early in the second season, the Hatch provides unexpected luxuries. After determining that the food supply might last one person about three months, Hurley receives Jack's blessing to distribute the processed food stored in the Hatch's pantry. Goodies like peanut butter, candy bars, and potato chips create a "normal" scene as the castaways laugh around their campfires and share the wealth ("Everybody Hates Hugo," 2.4). However, these unexpected pleasures provide only a welcome respite from island life and its typical fare of "natural" foods. After this treat, the castaways return to their routine. Of course, the food is gone but other luxuries, such as a shower and clothes dryer, appear to be used on a take-it-or-leave-it basis. After the first forty days, the castaways have learned about the necessities—water, food, shelter, even more clothing—and no longer "need" the technology provided in the Hatch.

The castaways' individual responses to the Hatch depend on the value they place on technology. Locke, for one, believes that the Numbers must be keyed and the Execute button pushed, or something very bad—like the end of their world—will take place. This response is the ultimate reliance on technology for life or death. At the opposite extreme is Rose, who seems content to stay far away from the Hatch unless she is given a specific job to do there, such as help Hurley take inventory of the pantry. The rest of the time we get the feeling that Rose would much rather stay on the beach, especially now that Bernard has returned from the back of the plane. Their responses mirror modern society, in which some people love the latest gadgets for status as well as convenience and others prefer a simpler life not revolving around technology that most likely will break down or otherwise fail them at some point.

THE TECHNOLOGY OF DESTRUCTION

One of the few types of technology that survives the crash is weaponry. Locke's suitcase of knives definitely comes in handy, used mostly to kill boar and serve as everyday tools (e.g., for cleaning the carcasses and cutting plants). Although they could be deadly weapons used against humans, they often have more benign purposes.

Firearms are another matter altogether. The suitcase of the marshal who held Kate in custody on the plane contains several handguns and lots of ammunition. Sawyer also takes a gun from the marshal's body, with which he shoots the first polar bear the survivors encounter ("Pilot," 1.1). At the time, of course, it seems like a good idea for Sawyer to confront the charging bear and shoot it point blank—one of the few times so far a gun only saves someone on the island.

Jack tries to regulate the use of firearms by locking the gun case and keeping the key on a string around his neck. When a situation warrants the possible use of guns, Jack issues them to those who know how to handle firearms, usually Sayid, Sawyer, Locke, and Kate ("Whatever the Case May Be," 1.12). Guns have a way of getting into other hands, however, usually with tragic results.

In "Homecoming," the hunting party of Jack, Sawyer, Kate, Locke, and Sayid surrounds pregnant Claire, who is being used as bait to capture the supposedly evil Ethan. The group only plans to snare him and learn why Claire was kidnapped and how he came to be on the island. (His name is not on the flight manifest for Oceanic 815, but clearly he lives on the island and seems very familiar with life there.) Information from Ethan will be valuable not only to solve the immediately interesting riddle of the kidnapping, but also to help the castaways learn more about the mysteries of the island.

Unfortunately, Charlie also gets his hands on one of the guns and figures out how to use the weapon. Without warning, he blasts several shots into Ethan ("Homecoming," 1.15). Charlie believes he is saving Claire from her kidnapper and most likely also wants to exact revenge because Ethan hanged him and left him for dead. Shooting Ethan haunts Charlie, however, even as he believes Ethan's death was justifiable in order for Claire and her baby to be safe. The easy availability of the technology for killing no doubt makes Charlie's emotional choice easier (would he confront his enemy as readily in a hand-to-hand battle?).

In a similar way, in "The Greater Good" Shannon feels betrayed that Sayid refuses to murder Locke, because she wants revenge for her brother's death. Both Shannon and Jack blame Locke for Boone's demise. Locke not only put Boone in danger, but lied about the way that he had been injured. Getting a gun from the locked case, she tracks Locke and angrily confronts him in front of Sayid, Kate, and Jack. As she fires the gun, Sayid knocks away her hand, so that the bullet only grazes Locke's head.

Shannon feels remorse only in that she hasn't achieved vengeance ("The Greater Good," 1.21).

When guns, or other destructive technologies, are available, they often wreak havoc. Rousseau, the Frenchwoman, also has a weapon and knows how to use it. She is cut off from the other survivors in part because she chooses to shoot first and ask questions later. She lives defensively and doesn't hesitate to use a gun. Whether her paranoia is the result of her island experiences or simply a manifestation of being isolated for so long, Rousseau trusts only herself.

Instead of finding other ways to solve their problems, Shannon and Charlie elect to pick up a gun and shoot another person. Other characters choose other paths. Even when dealing with an animal "enemy," such as the boar intent on destroying Sawyer's possessions, characters have other options. Sawyer decides not to kill the animal, although he points a gun at the boar that he had vowed to shoot on sight ("Outlaws," 1.16). He opts to confront the animal, but let it live.

The second season shows that life on the other side of the island often involves a near reverence for the gun that Ana Lucia takes from Sawyer ("Orientation," 2.3). The weapon gives her a sense of power over the Others, even as she realizes that having only a few bullets is not protection against a group of attackers. Unfortunately, Ana Lucia thinks she is defending her group against the Others when she shoots Shannon ("Abandoned," 2.6). Shannon's death at the hand of another Oceanic 815 survivor likely would not have occurred if a weapon other than a gun had been in Ana Lucia's hand ("The Other 48 Days," 2.7).

A lack of weaponry does not eliminate people's ability to kill others or exact vengeance, but the easy availability of weapons allowing longer range killing seems to determine the castaways' choice of whether to fight or flee, kill or confront their enemies in other ways. The castaways have to decide for themselves when and how to use weapons. They operate in a little society with no formal laws or ways to enforce them. They rely on their own judgment, and if they feel lost in their lives, they most often base their actions on momentary emotions, rather than rational deliberation. The one type of technology that, at one point or another during the first season, becomes easily available to many survivors is firearms. Choosing to use a gun to solve a problem may make characters feel more lost in their lives, more separated from who they want to be or even from other survivors.

As with other aspects of being lost, the use of technology for killing raises several questions. When is the use of deadly force reasonable, or even desirable? Is destructive technology necessary for survival? What strategies for mediating disputes or confronting enemies can be successful if destructive technologies aren't available? Does easy access to, say, firearms also make it easier for good people to lose their way when they search for solutions to problems? Does the use of deadly force make someone "bad" or "good"? As with other aspects of the meaning of "lost," many questions about the place of technology in everyday life parallel the survivors' experiences on the island with our experiences in our own culture.

Technology offers many benefits to a society, whether island bound or metropolitan. However, technology's virtues often come with a high price. The castaways, like us, must struggle with the issue of how much technology is necessary for a higher quality of life versus how much personal freedom and interpersonal "connectedness" is likely sacrificed in our reliance on technology. Although the castaways are often lost without the level of technology to which they've grown accustomed, they may find themselves to be equally lost with the Dharma Initiative's techno-scientific world.

CHAPTER THREE

LOST IN THEIR LIVES

"Lost" also captures the flagging spirit of the fourteen characters most prominent in the first season. At the time of the crash, each character is lost in his or her life. The survivors are disillusioned, addicted, imprisoned, and crippled in many ways. The irony of *Lost* is that as the survivors' probability of being rescued decreases each day, their likelihood of finding themselves and starting a new life increases. Jack explains to Kate in "Tabula Rasa" (1.3), "It doesn't matter…who we were—what we did before this…Three days ago we all died." What does matter is who these people become on the island.

Desmond, a world-class runner whose boat crashes on the reef, becomes a button pusher for a supposed doomsday computer. He is lost in this important but mindless task and the loneliness of his long-term mission. The Tailies, a dwindling number of survivors from Oceanic 815's tail section, face even more harrowing experiences than the survivors from the plane's center section. The "new" castaways are equally lost on the island and apparently in their lives, but they also are lost within the horror and shock of their terrorists' ferocity and cleverness. The Others attack them on their first night on the island and methodically drag nine people, including two children, into the jungle ("The Other 48 Days," 2.7.) Early second season episodes even reveal that the Others may have themselves lost their way from being researchers working on a peaceful scientific project to becoming scavengers, kidnappers, and murderers. Everyone on the island, it seems, for whatever reason, is lost in life.

"Lost" as a descriptor also can apply to the viewing audience. In a precarious post-millennium, post-9/11 world fraught with unexpected dangers, many of us find the old rules no longer applicable, global politics increasingly important, and the expectation to do more with fewer resources a new given. Dichotomies are deepening, dividing one religion against another, one political party against another, one country against another, one worldview against another. The illusion of an idyllic life on a tropical island may be as difficult for *Lost* characters to grasp as it is for *Lost* viewers.

And it's not just the extremes of terrorist dangers either. In regular life, we may feel equally as lost in our lives as the characters we watch. The dilemmas faced by the castaways—whom to trust, how much of oneself to reveal to others, and how to bridge seemingly insurmountable differences to coexist with others—are the predicaments of modern life, not just of this television fiction. During an ABC-TV segment of *20/20* in early May 2005, actor Dominic Monaghan explained that his character, Charlie Pace, has ongoing issues with "women and trust and intimacy" because of his previous choices and lifestyle. "For want of a better word, Charlie is lost." During a second season backstory, teenaged Shannon deals with her father's sudden death in a car accident and her stepmother's final rejection of her; a penniless Shannon must quickly learn to fend for herself ("Abandoned," 2.6). Jin faces extremely rough spots in his marriage and blames himself for being a workaholic husband who has become insensitive to his wife's needs. Many viewers likely deal with Charlie's, Shannon's, or Jin's issues, or other problems with family members and lovers that mirror problems encountered by *Lost* characters.

Being lost entails a separation from something—a person, a place, or even aspects of oneself. *Lost*'s survivors, in their ongoing search for what they think they need to become reunited, seek not to be lost. Because the characters are lost on the island, they provide viewers with dramatic and comedic possibilities for learning to live in a new environment. However, because this international group's carry-on baggage includes contemporary anxieties about relationships, world events, and personal traumas, their significance goes beyond the archetypes they represent. The characters reveal universally human fears and frailties as well as heroism and triumphs as they realize what they have lost and move toward finding what they need not only to survive, but to have a meaningful life.

In this chapter, we look at what it means to be "lost" in a variety of ways. We look at how the characters and audiences work together to find their way in a chaotic world, and find some meaning to their lives. Because the first season emphasizes fourteen characters from Oceanic 815 and the first few other characters (e.g., Rousseau, the Others on the boat) they encounter on the island, most discussion in this chapter is focused on these characters.

FIGURING OUT WHO THEY ARE

In a less technologically sophisticated environment, the survivors must deal with larger issues that force them to work together—finding food, water, and shelter and relying on each other for protection and companionship. They also have to deal with personal issues.

Even if no one else is looking for them, the castaways at least can begin to "find" themselves. They can search for the missing parts of their personalities, have the types of relationships they wanted in the past, and develop those qualities they admire and want to emulate. Even if they cannot achieve closure with people from their past who have wronged them or whom they have wronged, they can at least relate differently to those stranded with them. If they can indeed start a new life, they can, at least theoretically, become whoever they truly want to be.

So who are these people? At first, the group of fourteen castaways featured prominently in the first season's episodes seem to represent basic types. In fact, the opening narration to the April

27, 2005, "catch-up" or summary episode, appropriately entitled "The Journey," simplistically classifies several characters. For example, Jack, Kate, and Charlie are reduced to type: doctor, prisoner, addict. Initially the stereotypes are based on these limited first impressions of those who are *Lost:*

- Jack: an American surgeon/doctor, highly successful and professional, as evidenced by his dark suit and his friendly manner toward Rose as Jack attempts to alleviate her anxiety about the in-flight turbulence; a responsible leader who tries to save everyone, literally running from crisis to crisis to help others in the moments after the crash
- Kate: a woman who agrees to help Jack, despite her fears; a budding leader who later volunteers for more active treks into the jungle
- Sawyer: a redneck U.S. southerner who seems bent on starting fights and scavenging whatever he can from the wreckage; someone who is only out for himself
- Sun and Jin: a traditional Asian couple, who speak no English and prefer to remain separate from the others; Jin, a conservative, repressive husband; Sun, a subservient wife
- Shannon: a spoiled, blonde rich girl, more interested in how the crash affects her than anyone else, more interested in sun bathing and giving herself a pedicure instead of helping others
- Boone: also spoiled, with a penchant for nagging his sister; interested in helping others but often ineffective and needing guidance
- Claire: a worried pregnant Australian woman, fearful of going into labor immediately after the crash, and then concerned about the welfare of her unborn child
- Charlie: British, a heroin addict more concerned with his drugs than anything or anyone else
- Michael: a devoted American father whose first concern is to find his son, Walt, and then to provide him with shelter and water

- Locke: another American man willing and able to help when Jack first calls him to assist in moving an injured man from under the fuselage; someone at ease on the island and strangely separate from the others, as he sits in the sudden rainstorm, arms outstretched
- Sayid: a Middle Eastern man being stereotyped by Sawyer because of his ethnicity; a former member of the Iraqi Republican Guard
- Hurley: a helpful, rotund American man who pitches in but sometimes has trouble with what he's asked to do (e.g., he passes out when assisting Jack in makeshift surgery)
- Ana Lucia: a busy, direct American woman who is confident about who she is; on the island, a take-charge woman with a brutally pragmatic streak
- Mr. Eko: a religious man who also has special skills—such as tracking people in the jungle; a voice of reason who can occasionally overrule Ana Lucia's commands

The *Lost* world is definitely not "what you see is what you get." Characters who seem "nice" have shady pasts; authority figures, such as police officers, may become weapon happy. The Republican Guard soldier tenderly loves an upper-class American. The dedicated doctor decides to make war. The former junkie becomes a caring surrogate father. On the island, no one is who he or she originally seems to be or what we might have expected. As Hurley so aptly tells Jack about African American Rose's reunion with Caucasian Bernard, "Didn't see that coming" ("Collision," 2.8). Watching *Lost*, we probably think that line dozens of times.

Based on the castaways' words and actions immediately after the crash and limited knowledge of each person's past, we jump to conclusions about the characters; the survivors, too, determine someone's "worth" or "likeability factor" based on appearances.

- "Hurley" doesn't sound like a Hispanic name, but the young man is Hispanic.
- Beautiful women abound: Kate, Shannon, Sun. Claire is

pretty, too, but she is more likely categorized as "pregnant." As she tells Charlie a few days after the crash, the others often fail to look her in the eye, as if they think of her as a "time bomb of responsibility" ("White Rabbit," 1.5).

- Other characters may be defined by their skin color or racial traits: Sun, Jin, Walt, Michael, and Sayid may be defined by their culture, country, or race.
- Age may be yet another method of classifying castaways: Locke is noticeably older than many of the other men; Rose, although a secondary character in the first season, is an older married woman.
- Family relationships further characterize the group. Shannon and Boone are siblings—eventually amended to stepsister/stepbrother and one-time lovers ("Hearts and Minds," 1.13). Rose misses her husband, who she feels is still alive in another location, and later is proved right ("Collision," 2.8). Walt and Michael are son and father. Claire eventually gives birth to a son and takes on the role of mother ("Do No Harm," 1.20).

Occupation becomes a defining factor once the survivors begin to learn more about each other. Jack is identified immediately as a doctor and, largely because of his occupation, becomes the group's leader ("White Rabbit," 1.5). Charlie expects others to think him special because of his previous fame as the bassist in a one-hit rock band and is often disappointed when women fail to recognize him as a celebrity. Once Michael is defined as a construction expert, he gains status among the survivors, not only to lead rescue efforts when Jack and Charlie are trapped in a cave-in, but later to determine the caves are safe for habitation ("The Moth," 1.7). The expectation that Michael, if anyone, can build a raft seaworthy enough to escape from the island seems only logical.

Like the survivors, we can easily be misled into believing that stereotypes are true. As the story unfolds, however, the castaways' preconceptions about themselves and each other, as well as our preconceived notions about who is "good" or "bad" and why, are shown to be only partially true. The easy categorizations are shown to be only one small part of each complex character's makeup. The characters are all lost in their lives when the plane crashes, but for different reasons than we may initially suspect. This layering of characterizations not only makes the characters more human as they face universal problems, but it also plays with our concepts of good and evil, friend and foe.

Yunjin Kim, the actress portraying the Korean woman Sun, explained in a *Los Angeles Times* interview in May 2005 that, at first, the portrayals of the Korean couple as inscrutable Asians—with a dominant husband insisting on traditional values such as modesty—were criticized as being stereotypical. For example, Jin angrily motions for Sun to fasten the topmost button on her blouse when Michael talks with her; even in the heat, she must be modest and reveal as little skin as possible ("Pilot," 1.2). Sun initially is perceived as only an extension of her husband, submissive, obedient.

However, as with other characters who begin to "find" themselves on the island, Sun and Jin change. Sun reveals (at first to only a few people) that she understands English and develops a hesitant friendship with Michael and Kate, often as she explains the motivations for her husband's seemingly harsh or irrational acts. She explains to Michael, for example, that Jin attacked him not because Michael is African American and Jin a racist, as Michael believes, but because Michael wears a watch that belonged with her father's business goods. Through encounters like these, the characters become less stereotypes and more universally human.

Other major characters' multiple layers are revealed in their backstories, disclosed in a series of flashback scenes recalling significant moments in their pasts, revealing to audiences the reasons behind current reactions to situations or people. Although the survivors have the chance to start fresh on the island, their current actions often are based on past experiences and relationships.

By the end of the first season, we (but not necessarily the other survivors) know the a great deal about each character's past leading up to their departure on Oceanic 815 from Sydney, Australia:

- Happy-go-lucky Hurley seems neither happy nor lucky on his trip to the outback. Although he has won millions in a lottery, the money does not bring him happiness. His "luck" instead may be a curse.

- Although Claire is the only one of the fourteen main characters whose home is in Australia, she is leaving for her baby's new home in California. She leaves Sydney so her baby will be adopted by loving parents; the baby's father has abandoned them. To complicate issues further, Claire is hounded by a psychic who insists that only she must raise her baby.

- Jack's father is found dead in a Sydney alley, the result of a massive heart attack induced by alcohol. Estranged from his father, Jack feels guilty about his part in his downward slide. He argues with the airline representative and finally is allowed to take his father's body back to Los Angeles for burial.

- Kate is a prisoner of a federal marshal and is being brought back to the United States most likely to face sentencing for her crimes. Her capture is worth a $23,000 reward.

- In Australia, Sawyer murders a man who he thought once seduced his mother and stole from his father. Both acts apparently enraged Sawyer's father so much that he killed his wife and himself. However, the death that Sawyer anticipates for so many years fails to bring him either satisfaction or revenge, as he kills the wrong man after being set up by a former partner.

- Locke tries to go on a walkabout in Australia, a spiritual quest he had long planned. The only problem is that the excursion requires him to walk about and Locke is wheelchair bound.

- Charlie hopes for brother Liam's agreement to once again front their band DriveShaft so that the group can tour as an opening act. Since the band's demise two years earlier, Charlie survives by charming women and then stealing from them. His dreams of a return to fame are dashed when Liam refuses to return to the band. Charlie also disappoints Liam, who, himself a former addict, recognizes that his brother still uses heroin.

- Sayid stays in Sydney one day beyond his scheduled flight in order to claim the body of his college roommate, the man chosen to be a martyr for a terrorist cell. Coerced by American and Australian intelligence agents to infiltrate the cell (they promise he will be led to Nadia, an Iraqi insurgent and childhood friend he once helped to escape), Sayid succeeds and delivers the group's explosives. Although he tells his former roommate to flee when he learns that he is a double agent, the man takes his life in front of Sayid. To give his former friend a proper Muslim burial, Sayid refuses to leave Australia until he claims the body.
- Shannon and Boone sit together on the plane, but they are far from "together" in any other sense of the word. Boone flies to Sydney to rescue Shannon from an abusive boyfriend, only to discover that Shannon has set him up in order to get money. Once Boone pays off the boyfriend, Shannon and her friend plan to split the money. However, Shannon also is scammed this time and left with neither boyfriend nor cash. Inebriated and rejected, Shannon seduces her stepbrother and then tells him that they will never let anyone know.
- Sun and Jin are in Sydney because Jin needs to complete business for his employer, Sun's father. Although Jin hates his job and plans to start a new life in the U.S. after this business is completed, he has not, of course, revealed his plans to Sun, who dislikes the man her husband has become. Sun secretly speaks English and crafts a way to disappear. When the moment comes for her to leave her husband, however, she does not go through with her plan.
- Michael flies to Sydney to retrieve his son Walt. With the recent death of Walt's mother, and his stepfather's desire to

be rid of the boy, Michael finally gains the opportunity to be a real father to his son. However, Walt doesn't remember the father of his babyhood, and a belligerent ten-year-old boards the flight. Neither father nor son knows each other, and both must be anxious about their future relationship.

The second season continues the trend of troubling backstories ("Collision," 2.8). Ana Lucia Cortez is a police officer who, like Jack, goes into the "family business." Her mother is also an officer and her captain. While on patrol, Ana Lucia and her partner are called to a robbery. A young man runs out the front door that Ana Lucia is covering. He exclaims that he is a student, but when he reaches for his ID, he pulls out a gun instead. Ana Lucia is shot point blank, an act that not only injures her but kills her unborn child. Back on the job, Ana Lucia becomes a gun-happy officer who seems to mistrust most men. Although we don't learn why she was in Sydney, we get the feeling she may not have been on holiday.

These are not happy stories. Each character brings a great number of personal problems that must be resolved, and each seeks something to improve his or her life or to return to the "true path" from which he or she strayed. *Lost* is the one all-encompassing word to fit each of these characters.

All the characters go through metamorphoses during the first season, shattering the images we initially have of them and, just as in real life, making the line between good and bad characters ever fuzzier. *Lost* offers no simple answers or instant, permanent changes—just as in real life. The balance of relationships among characters, their moods and motivations, all change throughout the first season and sometimes within a single episode.

While remaining in character, the castaways also can surprise and shock. Anything but one-dimensional beings, they are complex, "real" people who are not completely good nor completely evil; who bravely set out to change aspects of their lives and then face setbacks; who are as biased, altruistic, annoying, lovable, strong, broken, mundane, and inspirational as anyone else we know. They go beyond lost souls to become just like us: people who are doing (sometimes) the best they can and otherwise muddling through a chaotic world that often seems intent on destroying them. Individually and collectively, the characters change during the first forty days since the crash.

ABC's *20/20* broadcast an extended interview with cast members in early May 2005 before the final three episodes aired. The actors commented on the reasons why their characters are so popular. Jorge Garcia (Hurley) knows that fans consider his character the "everyman"—the guy who often helps out and makes the castaways feel better with his friendly words or helping hands, but who also passes out or nearly faints every time he sees blood. He is not a traditional hero, and many viewers see themselves as a Hurley type of survivor.

Interviewer Elizabeth Vargas teased Daniel Dae Kim (Jin) about his new sex symbol status on the Internet. Although he laughed good naturedly at the comment, he also noted that Asian men were seldom seen on television "as heroes, as leading men." Commenting on the tender love scene between Jin and Sun, before Jin turned to the dark side as an employee of Sun's father, Kim added that he had "worked in this business for twelve years, and this show has given me my first on-screen kiss." In November 2005, *People* magazine included Kim as one of the sexiest men alive. The characters no longer seem like stereotypes. They are individuals who interest us because they are unique.

The cast as a whole represents what interviewer Vargas called "a mini U.N." Naveen Andrews (Sayid) explained that the characters' relationships and dealings with each other are a "microcosm...of society at the moment." Part of the appeal of *Lost* is that it mirrors what is going on in the world, and how viewers' and the characters' preconceptions of what an Iraqi, or a Korean, Aussie, Canadian, American, or Brit is likely to say or do. By the end of the season perhaps we can see more than the culturally loaded designation "Iraqi," instead finding Sayid interesting as a man who has had a certain set of experiences but has made individual choices and has personal preferences, strengths, and struggles.

In the second season, one character seems locked into the category of "bad girl," despite efforts to make her more sympathetic. Michelle Rodriguez expressed concern in November 2005 that her character is most hated by fans. Not only does she kill Shannon, but she emasculates female fan-favorite Sawyer. Still, "Rambina" also is made more sympathetic when cries in the arms of Mr. Eko ("The Other 48 Days," 2.7). Midseason she begins developing a closer relationship with Jack and shows a more playful side ("Fire + Water," 2.12).

At first, Ana Lucia may be pigeonholed as a bad girl for her frequent scowl and continuing crankiness, but other moody characters have done similar deeds. After all, both Charlie and Ana Lucia have shot and killed the unarmed men who once attacked them. Bad boy Sawyer mellows considerably after his ordeal on the raft and recovery from a gunshot wound; during the first season, we might not have anticipated that Sawyer would play a more-or-less friendly game of blackjack with Hurley and advise him about women ("Fire + Water," 2.12). Like real-life people, seldom is anyone completely good or bad; *Lost*'s many characters are well rounded and intrigue us with their strengths and faults.

As new characters are brought into the series and familiar characters continue to grow, the label-defying roles should continue to intrigue us even as these characters provide a mirror of international and interpersonal relationships in the larger world. The characters' growth shows not only how they are "lost," but how they may potentially change to find themselves. This, too, can help those of us who face similar types of trauma.

THE *LOST* GENERATION

Every viewer probably feels lost at some point in life. The world is changing rapidly, and for the current generation of young adults, "monsters" often lurk in unexpected places and defy easy solution. In many ways, we, but especially young people, are part of a lost generation.

The creators of *Lost* said at the end of the first season that new characters are to be introduced in subsequent seasons. Some characters die; others live but become less important over time; new characters gain prominence in the story. As in other aspects of real life, *Lost* mirrors the increasing uncertainties of modern life. Even though characters are loved by millions, they, too, can face untimely and unexpected ends.

As Season One drew to a close, the cast did not know which character would be eliminated. The anxiety leading to this revelation affected not only the cast but us as well. No one wants his or her favorite character (or the character he or she portrays) to die. A similar situation occurred when Maggie Grace's character Shannon died early in the second season.

However, as the creators reiterated in several interviews, that's life. Does that make deceased characters any less memorable or important? If we knew at the beginning of the series that Boone would die before the end of the season, would we still have loved him or cared about his backstory? Do we feel that we "wasted" our time learning about this character when he ended up being killed off? More importantly, would we feel that way about a friend or family member who fails to survive to a ripe old age, or who has a life-threatening condition?

Life is uncertain. Part of understanding what it means to be found is to know that loss occurs and how to handle this loss. Mr. Eko most likely knows that his brother is dead; Yemi is shot and roughly loaded on the Beechcraft just before it takes off. Yet Eko cries and asks forgiveness when he finds his brother's body on the island ("The 23rd Psalm," 2.10). Despite their disagreements and different lifestyles, the brothers loved each other, and the loss moves Eko to truly become a "priest" not only in name but in practice. At the opposite end of the scale is Charlie. Although

Claire and Aaron live, they are lost to Charlie because he lies to Claire about the Virgin Mary statue. Claire is angry not only that Charlie lies to her, but that he brings heroin into their home. When she kicks him out, Charlie obsessively tries to force his way back into her life. When Charlie almost burns down the camp and kidnaps baby Aaron to "save" him, the castaways shun him ("Fire + Water," 2.12). Charlie doesn't know how to deal with separation, or a temporary loss, of his newly created family; a long-term loss of Claire and Aaron in his life may be devastating.

Are we, or the survivors, ultimately going to be lost without a certain person? Is part of being found the ability to love others fully even though they might not be around tomorrow, either by choice or fate or some divine plan? These questions affect not only the characters on the island, who do not know their future or longevity, but we viewers (and *Lost*'s actors) who do not know which characters will live or die or disappear in the next few weeks. Dealing with loss is just another way of surviving being lost—for cast, characters, and audience alike.

Most people want their lives to have significance. They may want their fifteen minutes of fame, but they also want to leave an enduring (and preferably positive) legacy to future generations. They need to know that they counted or mattered. What is the legacy of a character (or a family member, friend, or colleague) who unexpectedly dies or is killed? In island terms, what mark did Boone and Shannon make on the world, or even the survivors who knew them for about a month? Living life on an isolated island brings up these questions, as viewers also may feel isolated in the little islands of their life—the small communities, mundane jobs, insular homes.

Lost brings up many issues about the meaning of life, of what it means to be lost and how to be found. These themes are important to audiences internationally. Many fans promised to "get *Lost*" even before the series debuted in September 2004 in the U.S. and Canada. They created websites for the series, attended events promoting the program, and passed around "get *Lost*" stickers. Since *Lost* debuted, more viewers worldwide have agreed to do the same.

Even our interaction with the series shows how much we tend to search for meaning and answers. Although some viewers are content to find meaning at the surface level of each episode, the fans who make *Lost* a cult series only begin at this level of deriving meaning. Hardcore fans not only watch an episode multiple times, but freeze images and post their findings on the Web. They work harder than most characters to decode the island's meaning (and the writers' cryptic messages). They play dialogue backwards; enlarge images; do research (e.g., Dharma sounds like DARPA, a U.S. governmental project in the 1960s that tried to manipulate the environment); and find layer upon layer of hidden meanings in their search for the answers.

This type of audience also demands answers. When not enough information was presented in "Exodus," fans protested at conventions, on discussion boards, and through email. Many viewers even like to know in advance what will happen, perhaps to have a head start on interacting with *Lost*'s subtext and decoding messages. In this way they make more meaning out of the series than can be gained through casual viewing. *Lost* offers hardcore fans the ability to make meaning for themselves, in a sense to find themselves not only as audience members but as equal castaways on the island.

In a world that demands vigilance, *Lost* is no exception; it is an exercise in paying attention to detail. Increasingly, interpreting meaning from body language, styles of clothing, and deviations from the "norm" is a fact of life. Unfortunately, as *Lost* illustrates, this type of interpretation often leads to an incomplete or inaccurate conclusion. Kate can convincingly take on a new persona, such as Annie on a ranch ("Tabula Rasa," 1.3). She believably tells a bank manager that she is a photographer and wins his support during a bank robbery ("Whatever the Case May Be," 1.12). Her body language, dress, and friendly manner belie the truth that she is a fugitive and a thief. We may have a tough time believing that the Kate we know and love from the island torched the house where her drunken father slept ("What Kate Did," 2.9). The signals Kate sends are often misinterpreted. Sawyer gives the other castaways a good clue about Kate's double life when he reveals that she has taken a dead woman's passport in order to mask her true identity ("Exodus," 1.23). Nevertheless, the castaways soon trust her again, and Kate remains a prominent member of the survivors' community. *Lost* not only encourages us to pay closer attention to everything that we see or hear, but to share information with each other so that we are more likely to interpret information correctly. How we respond to that information is then up to us.

The immediate interest in the series goes beyond its beautiful cast and location or its enticing mix of genres. It is based on the fundamental understanding that everyone faces personal monsters or loses his or her way at some point in life. Everyone at one time or another longs to make a fresh start. With *Lost*, the characters and audiences are all survivors of chaotic modern life who still seek answers to fundamental questions.

Lost and Found

All the characters are lost in many ways, but part of their journey is the important steps in finding themselves. Even though they may never be geographically found, they can better understand themselves and each other as they build a new society on the island. As the first season unfolded, it became apparent that although most of the castaways were strangers when they boarded Oceanic 815, connections between and among the passengers already existed. On *Lost*, truly no person is an island. Although the meaning of *lost* implies loneliness, the series shows that the castaways have connections that may pave the way to their being found—at least emotionally or spiritually, if not geographically.

"Exodus" (1.23–24) provides several clues to pre-crash connections among the characters:

- In a Sydney hotel a harried Hurley sees that the elevator to the lobby is full; he says he will take the stairs instead of crowding inside. Just as the door closes, an annoyed Charlie shouts a sarcastic "thanks" for stopping the elevator and then not getting on.
- On the phone at the Sydney airport, Michael tries unsuccessfully to convince his mother to take Walt; the new father already is fed up with his son's antics and uncertain of what to do. Locke rolls past the phone bank on his way to their mutual flight.
- Onboard the plane, Arzt helps heavily pregnant Claire lift her bag into the overhead storage bin, and as Hurley rushes to his seat so the plane can depart, he makes eye contact with Walt and gives him a thumbs up, receiving a grin in return.
- Just before the turbulence rocks the plane, Charlie bolts from his seat to avoid being stopped by approaching crew members. He clambers over Boone and an annoyed Shannon and pushes by Jack on the way to the washroom.

These minimal contacts on the day of the ill-fated flight show that even though we often are unaware of the people we encounter, we do make some connections with others in our everyday life. The nature of human existence is to make these contacts, even if they are fleeting and usually inconsequential.

On *Lost*, and perhaps in real life, nothing is inconsequential or random. As Locke notes in "White Rabbit" (1.5), "Everything happens for a reason." This line becomes increasingly important—and frequently repeated—not only in "Exodus" but in the second season. This tag line is a focal point for the second season's advertising in the U.S. and indicates that one theme for the continuing story is destiny or fate.

"Exodus" provides a multitude of connections between and among passengers, but the links between characters go beyond the day of the final flight:

- Sawyer meets Christian Shephard in a Sydney bar ("Outlaws," 1.16); later Sawyer tells Jack about the encounter, creating a friendlier bond between the two usually antagonistic characters ("Exodus," 1.23).
- When Boone pleads with a Sydney police officer to intervene in his sister's abusive relationship, Sawyer is paraded through the station in handcuffs ("Hearts and Minds," 1.13).
- Hurley's accountant assures the new millionaire of his financial worth even as he lists a litany of tragedies to befall the businesses in which Hurley has invested. Included in the list is the box company where Locke works ("Numbers," 1.18).
- Locke and Hurley share Randy as a boss, although at different companies at different times ("Everybody Hates Hugo," 2.4).
- Shannon's father dies in the emergency room where Jack meets and saves future wife Sarah, the other victim of their joint car crash ("Man of Science, Man of Faith," 2.1). Jack walks past Shannon as she learns of her father's death ("Abandoned," 2.6).

The strangest link between characters to date takes place as one of the mysteries in the second season. Jack's first backstory in Season Two includes a brief scene with a helpful runner. Desmond happens to be sprinting up stairs in the same stadium where Jack is literally trying to run away from his failure to perform a surgical miracle on Sarah. When Jack sprains his ankle, Desmond stops to help. He idly comments as he examines the ankle that he almost was a doctor but now is a runner training for a world run. When he asks Jack why he is running, Jack explains Sarah's desperate medical situation and his inability to fix her. Desmond asks Jack if he believes in miracles, but Jack indicates that Sarah's condition is impossible to fix. With a cryptic comment about seeing Jack in another life, Desmond jogs down the stairs and presumably out of Jack's life.

When Jack sees the miracle of Sarah's recovery for himself, he is overwhelmed with joy and surprise, but it is doubtful that he thinks of Desmond in connection with Sarah. However, when a man holding a gun to Locke's head begins to speak to him, telling Jack to drop his own weapon and threatening to kill Locke, Jack recognizes the voice. Desmond has a distinctive accent to American ears, and Jack's memory is further jogged when Desmond steps into view. Although older and now wild-eyed, Locke's captor clearly is the same man from the stadium a few years before ("Man of Science, Man of Faith," 2.1). Logically, the two men should never meet again, but in this other life on the island, logic seems to take second place to destiny or fate.

Even when we can't see the result of our everyday encounters, perhaps the everyday run-ins with others have a greater significance. Even in a moment's time, what we say or do may influence another and ultimately cause change in someone else's life. We may consider such transitory links between real people or characters coincidental, but what if they have more meaning than we may originally think? When we search for meaning in *Lost*, we should realize that perhaps a greater force than the castaways can accept or readily understand is at play. Only Locke seems unsurprised by whatever the island reveals, including strange connections between the castaways.

Links between characters also take place through dialogue, behavior patterns, or shared experiences. Structurally, the series' writers and creators enhance the links between characters by having one character repeat the dialogue spoken by another in a previous scene or episode or having one character's actions mirror another's:

- Rose tells Jack that she is letting him off the hook for his promise—to stay with her until her husband returns from the washroom ("Tabula Rasa," 1.3). Boone tells Jack that he is freeing Jack from his promise to save him ("Do No Harm," 1.20).
- Boone suggests that Jack perform a tracheotomy to save Rose, who is not breathing after the crash ("Pilot," 1.1).

Jack performs a tracheotomy to help Boone breathe after he is injured in a second plane crash—the Beechcraft's fall from a cliff ("Do No Harm").

- During a brief backstory scene in "Exodus" (1.24), Charlie struggles to hold onto his last baggie of heroin in a tussle with another addict. As the woman beats him, Charlie fends off blows as he protects the drugs instead of himself. "You're pathetic!" the defeated woman screeches in disgust. In current time on the island, Charlie lashes out at the distraught Danielle. Although the woman has returned baby Aaron, Charlie believes that she, not the Others, set the signal fire as a ruse. Charlie scornfully denounces Rousseau—"You're pathetic"—as he clutches the child and stalks off.

- Locke's heartfelt "Don't tell me what I can't do!" ("Walkabout," 1.4) is echoed by Jack at the end of the season ("Exodus," 1.24). Jack further says to Locke, "Don't tell me what to do," in the second season as he holds a gun on Desmond ("Man of Science, Man of Faith," 2.1).

Charlie's problems with Claire mirror brother Liam's early marital problems with wife Karen. Both brothers fall for blonde Australians with a baby (Liam's biological child and Charlie's surrogate child, respectively). Each woman believes that the man's behavior places her child in jeopardy and banishes the (surrogate) father from their lives. For Liam, the loss of wife and child prompts him to give up drugs and work a steady job. Charlie's resolution has yet to be determined ("Fire + Water," 2.12).

Characters who otherwise seem very different may share some common trait or experience, which then gives us a new perspective on a good or bad character. Although Rousseau is often described by other characters as crazy or dangerous, she is, as Sayid tells Charlie ("Exodus," 1.24), also a mother who lost her baby. Claire, who seems crazed by Rousseau's abduction of baby Aaron, also is a mother who loses her baby. Whether both mothers eventually lose or are able to be reunited with their children permanently remains to be seen.

Another resonating scene involves Locke. He insists on going into the newly opened Hatch despite Jack's recommendation that the castaways spend the night at the caves, where they can post guards and potentially keep the Others at bay. Kate follows Locke to keep an eye on him, but when she catches up, he tells her that he has been waiting for her. Locke then convinces a wary Kate to descend into the Hatch. After all, Kate is lighter and can fit into smaller spaces; she is the more logical choice to be lowered into the Hatch. Kate, however, sees the situation differently and suggests that Locke only wants to see if the Monster will eat her first ("Man of Science, Man of Faith," 2.1).

Perhaps Kate understands that Locke may not have had altruistic motives when he encouraged Boone to be careful but nonetheless to enter the Beechcraft. Kate must remember (as we do) that Locke may not be as trustworthy as he seems.

Desmond soon captures Kate and Locke, who stumble into his underground home. Obviously agitated, gun-wielding Desmond obsessively asks Locke, "Are you him?" ("Man of Science, Man of Faith"). The scene mirrors Rousseau's repeated "Where's Alex?" when she captures Sayid as he enters her territory ("Solitary," 1.9). Both Desmond and Rousseau are linked by their apparent longevity on the island, their knowledge of what may be a more sinister nature of the island, and a routine established to avoid "traps." They also are obsessive in their desire to find answers to the questions that plague them.

The story of the Tailies' first forty-eight days on the island parallels what the center section's survivors encounter during the same time. Both groups face monsters—everything from the Others to polar bears to natural dangers to the Monster. Both groups of survivors receive medical care by a trained professional who cannot save all victims of the crash. Some people drown, although they survive the plane's destruction; others survive only after receiving

CPR. Both groups find at least one gun. Both camps are infiltrated by one of the Others, who pretends to have been on the same flight and is at least indirectly responsible for the kidnapping of one or more castaways. Both groups find a research station from the Dharma Initiative. They locate a radio and attempt to send and receive signals. Both receive a message but fail to understand its ramifications. Although the two new societies differ (Ana Lucia's is more of a military dictatorship compared to Jack's benevolent socialism), they face similar dilemmas and accomplish similar goals during the first forty-eight days ("The Other 48 Days," 2.7).

Resonances in dialogue and situation indicate that the characters are not as isolated as they may feel. The good characters share background experiences or dialogue with not so good characters or those representing an opposing point of view. A seemingly throwaway line in one scene (such as Christian Shephard's "Don't cross that line" to a potentially philandering Jack) takes on new significance in a later scene (the Others' warning to Jack not to cross a line and, in effect, go to war against them) ("The Hunting Party," 2.11). These links again show the well-rounded nature of characters as well as the sense that they are all fallible humans who may need to hear repeated dialogue (i.e., advice, warnings) or repeat common experiences if they are to learn a lesson. If these characters are lost, perhaps ties to other people and situations can help them find themselves. ("Character Connections" and "Similar Names" list other similarities between characters and their experiences.)

Lost allows us to read personal meanings into the castaways' experiences. Like the characters, their dialogue or experiences may resonate with similar occurrences in our lives. One of *Lost*'s great strengths as a series is that it provides a mirror to the world and allows us to see commonalities among people and events.

PART THREE:

SPIRITUALITY

In *Lost*, a character's philosophy and spirituality (or lack of) are often closely linked, because the castaways face life-altering experiences almost daily. They need some foundation for their lives, some approach to making sense of what often seems to not make any sense at all.

A typical situation: During the first-season finale, "Exodus" (1.24), Hurley spies the *Black Rock*, which, in typical *Lost* fashion, is neither black nor a rock, but instead is a wooden sailing vessel grounded several miles inland. "How can something like that happen?" he questions aloud. Rousseau, guide for the expedition, merely quirks an eyebrow. "Do you live on the same island I do?" she replies as an explanation.

The inexplicable merges with the unpredictable throughout the series. Shortly after the survivors arrive at the *Black Rock*, science teacher Leslie Arzt suddenly is blown up during a lesson about handling dynamite safely. Hurley reels from the death of a man with whom he has just had a conversation. On the same trek, the group encounters the Monster once more, and Locke nearly lets himself be carried away.

On *Lost*, this is simply an afternoon on the island. Even more so than in the "real world," which has its own sudden, terrifying events, the island exploits every human fear. Natural disasters, humans bent on murder and destruction, and monsters that defy definition all prey upon the survivors' sanity. Even without these additional worries, the castaways continue to struggle to survive. Finding food, water, and shelter is traumatic enough most days;

on some days—and nights—they must evade the Others and the implied terror they bring.

The castaways naturally question the foundation of their previous lives and wonder if they need something more in order either to escape the island or survive the experience. Whether these people are religious or merely question what brought them to the island, they look for answers to life's larger questions: Why am I (are we) here? What is my purpose? Why does evil exist? Why are good people punished? Will I, or how will I, be held accountable for my actions? Do I control my future, or does someone/something determine what happens to me? What is the meaning of life in general (or life on the island)? As with most aspects of *Lost*, each character has a different answer to these questions or searches in different places for the answers. A *Time* article in January 2005 suggested that like "a religious text, *Lost* is open to endless interpretation."

Lost is a "non-religious" program, at least compared to other U.S. predecessors like *Joan of Arcadia*, *Seventh Heaven*, *Touched by an Angel*, or *Highway to Heaven*; spirituality as described in *Lost* does not rely only on a Christian belief system. Spiritual expression may be more personal than ritualized, more self-defined than ordained, more universal than unicultural.

Spirituality requires a belief in something beyond oneself— some higher power or supernatural being who does have the answers. Omniscience is an important role for whatever deity is revered. For some characters, God is that deity; for others, Allah; for at least one survivor, the island.

Spirituality also requires people to act based on their beliefs— to define what is right or wrong, to determine what is important or valuable. Within the range of the fourteen characters prominent during the first season, and with new characters added during the second, we see a wide range of belief systems at work, from those who frequently express their spiritual beliefs to those who seem to have none or who follow only their own counsel.

CHAPTER FOUR

LOST SPIRITUALITY

FORMAL RELIGION AS A WAY TO UNLOCK MEANING

Formal religion can be a powerful influence on one's life and worldview. Rose's Christianity (most likely Protestant); Charlie's, Hurley's, and Desmond's Catholicism; and Sayid's Islam affect the characters' actions and provide them with a framework for understanding the world. Although no characters thus far have identified themselves as pagan, elements of that spiritual expression also arise on *Lost*.

In addition, during Season Two, *dharma*, as in the Dharma Initiative ("Orientation," 2.3), becomes a key term, although it is far removed from Buddhist or Hindu concepts of dharma. Nevertheless, a spiritual understanding of life's meaning from a dharmic perspective is a focal point for the second season, especially when Oceanic 815's survivors begin to settle into life on the island. The Dharma Initiative's mission statement indicates that the funded experiments help to advance the human race. For many spiritually minded castaways or viewers, spirituality serves the same purpose, although people most likely do not want to be considered guinea pigs in an ongoing experiment.

Even if these characters do not consider themselves religious now, they still may react to the world based on earlier religious influences. Through the snippets of religions interspersed throughout several episodes, we can see the religion's influence on a character.

ROSE

Rose stands out as the most prominent religious character during the first season. Although she is not one of the major fourteen players, her smaller role is nonetheless influential, and L. Scott Caldwell portrays Rose as calmly confident. When Jack sits by her soon after the crash and tries to entice her to join the others down the beach, Rose merely watches the waves ("Walkabout," 1.4). She gradually talks about her husband and shows Jack her husband's wedding ring, which Rose wears when the couple flies. Rose knows, without a doubt, that husband Bernard lives and now wonders where she is. Jack may attribute Rose's certainty to post-traumatic stress or even denial, but Rose just knows, her faith unshakable. During the second season, Bernard is shown in a group of survivors from the tail section. Rose's faith is rewarded when she and Bernard reunite when the Tailies merge with the survivors from the plane's center section ("Collision," 2.8).

She is just as certain that God is good and each day is worth living. When a despondent Charlie mopes alone after Claire's abduction and his near-death experience at the hands of Ethan, Rose prods him into action and reminds him that other survivors have equally traumatic tales. However, she does more than just jar him from lethargy. She shares her religious beliefs as she and Charlie work. Whereas Charlie sees only an island of impending death, Rose finds beauty in her surroundings and has faith in the future. Rose tells Charlie that he needs to ask for help. "Who's going to help me?" he asks. As a new segment in the episode begins, the scene cuts to a close-up of the cross adorning the marshal's grave. The answer to Charlie's question is clear. For him, as for Rose, the answer lies in Christianity.

At the end of the episode, Charlie asks Rose how she can be so certain that she will see Bernard again; Charlie doubts whether he will be reunited with Claire. "It's a fine line between denial and faith. It's much better on my side," Rose assures him. A tearful Charlie asks Rose for help, because his troubles seem too great to bear. Rose prays with Charlie, beginning with a familiar Christian phrase, "Heavenly Father" ("Whatever the Case May Be," 1.12). Rose practices what no doubt she has often heard preached; her spirituality makes her who she is and gives her the confidence to live fully, even on an island of mystery and uncertainty.

During the first season, only Rose and Locke, whose island-based form of spirituality is strengthened over time, openly proclaim their spiritual beliefs and share their faith with others who seek answers or guidance. In the second season, Mr. Eko, whose backstory is entitled "The 23rd Psalm," has a similar spiritual bent. He also promises to pray for the survivors shortly after the crash. He imposes on himself a forty-day period of silence after, in self-defense, he kills two of the Others who attack him ("The Other 48 Days," 2.7).

CATHOLICISM

Other characters were once religious but strayed in their pre-crash lives. In one episode, Charlie explains to Jack that the cave in which they are trapped reminds him of the claustrophobic confessional booths of his youth ("The Moth," 1.7). In Charlie's first backstory, we learn that the young man tries to be a devout Catholic. On the day his band is offered a recording contract, Charlie visits the parish priest to confess sins from the night before. Charlie ruefully admits he had sexual relations with not one but two young women he just met, and he furthermore watched them have sex with each other. When the priest advises Charlie that he must choose one lifestyle over another, Charlie, surprising in his solemnity, declares he must give up DriveShaft. At least at one point in his life, Charlie values his God instead of wanting to be a rock god.

Also raised Catholic, Hurley harbors memories of frightening recent religious experiences. During Hurley's beloved grandfather's funeral, the family's priest dies suddenly—struck by lightning at the grave site ("Numbers," 1.18). Perhaps events like these turn Hurley from traditional spiritual beliefs toward a certainty that a curse plagues him for using the mysterious Numbers for personal gain. Being cursed and facing fate's retribution are not Church tenets, and Hurley seems to fall away from his religion and under the spell of superstition after a series of improbable "coincidences."

Down the Hatch, when Desmond desperately hopes that his repair job has fixed the computer needed to "save the world," he crosses himself before rebooting the system ("Orientation," 2.3). Although Desmond may never have strayed from his religion, his secular passion is channeled into running. Whether Desmond is truly good, as he seems in current time, or bad, as his cryptic messages to Jack during a backstory segment may lead us to believe ("Man of Science, Man of Faith," 2.1), he expresses a need for divine intervention when he faces a crisis.

Mr. Eko also is religious as a youth, until guerrillas raid his village. Eko murders a man at a guerrilla's command so that his younger brother won't be forced to shoot. Before he is taken with the gang, Eko gives his brother a crucifix. Yemi grows up to become a priest, and although Eko seriously strays from his religious past, on the island he accepts the role of priest after finding Yemi's body in the wreckage of the Beechcraft ("The 23rd Psalm," 2.10). Mr. Eko returns to his religion and even provides spiritual comfort to others.

CHARLIE

In other episodes the Catholic Church is merely a guise for illegal activity. Boone and Locke discover the body of a dead "priest"—a Nigerian drug smuggler in disguise ("Deus Ex Machina," 1.19). They do not know that unlike the drug runners, Yemi, Eko's brother, truly is a priest who accidentally becomes a passenger. Boone discovers that the broken Virgin Mary statues conceal bags of heroin. Days later, when Sayid and Charlie take a breather on their search for baby Aaron, they pause by the wreckage. Sayid shows Charlie where Boone died and explains the drug operation ("Exodus," 1.24).

Heroin introduces temptation once more into Charlie's life, and symbols within the storyline indicate the potential dangers if he takes this path. Perhaps the priest's body hanging from a tree mirrors Charlie's near-death by hanging; Charlie already has cheated death at least once and may not be so lucky again. The broken vessels themselves point to Charlie as a young man—a religious vessel himself—whose purpose is later defiled by drugs. Like the Madonnas, Charlie is broken spiritually; he undoubtedly will be tempted to return to heroin as a source of help.

One of Charlie's first acts early in Season Two is to take a Madonna away from Claire after she discovers it in his backpack. Charlie is playing with Aaron when Claire asks Charlie about the statue. When she comments that she did not know that he was so religious, he quickly replies that he is not, but nonetheless immediately trades the baby for the statue. Charlie keeps a careful eye on what he views as insurance in case something bad happens ("Adrift," 2.2). Karl Marx once insisted religion is an "opiate," but Charlie's opiate-filled Madonna statue fails to protect him and leads him to further emotional or physical crises.

Among the many subconscious or conscious reasons Charlie is attracted to Claire is because she is his real-life version of a Madonna. Although Aaron's conception is hardly immaculate, young mother-to-be and later mother Claire seems sweet and innocent in Charlie's eyes. She bears a child in difficult circumstances and places him in the rough-hewn cradle that Locke has built ("Numbers," 1.18). Charlie longs to protect Claire and her child, although the baby is not his. Charlie's protective streak becomes almost obsessive during Season Two, when he questions Claire's ability to care for the child and asserts what he feels is his rightful place with the baby. The Madonna and child image is further strengthened when Locke demonstrates how to swaddle Aaron; the newborn becomes a babe wrapped in swaddling cloths ("Abandoned," 2.6). For Charlie, this most Christian of images must resonate with his ideal of motherhood and parental love.

When Charlie has dreams of Aaron in danger, he envisions his mother and Claire as angels, urging him to save the baby. A white dove—and an early backstory flashback to a portrait in Charlie's childhood home of John the Baptist—symbolize baptism. After Charlie discusses his dream with Mr. Eko, the surrogate father becomes convinced that Aaron must be baptized. Convincing Claire to do so is difficult, because she recently has learned about the heroin-filled statue and sent Charlie away ("The 23rd Psalm," 2.10). Charlie's erratic behavior prompts her to want spiritual insurance herself, and Claire asks Eko to baptize her and her child.

The episode's title, "Fire + Water" (2.12), may offer several symbolic meanings, but baptism is an important one. Charlie faces baptism by fire, not only the blaze close to camp but an angry confrontation with the other castaways after he abducts the baby. Aaron's baptism is more traditional, with water blessed by a priest. Charlie is left outcast, in an emotional and possibly spiritual crisis now that his personal Madonna and child are unreachable, but he has fulfilled his mission to save Aaron, at least spiritually.

ISLAM

Other religions are mentioned in *Lost*, if not as frequently as Christianity. The modest attire worn by Muslim women, in particular Sayid's friend Nadia, indicates Islamic belief in modesty ("Solitary," 1.9). Sayid also stays in Sydney to claim the body of his former roommate and provide a proper burial, a choice that puts him on Oceanic 815 ("The Greater Good," 1.21). Islam makes one of Sayid's comments to Jack in an early episode more understandable. When Jack insists that the crash victims' bodies be burned, Sayid wants to wait to determine the religious backgrounds of those who died. Cremation in not acceptable to Islam. Sayid seems appalled at the wholesale cremation, which, as he emphasizes, may be against the victims' religious beliefs ("Walkabout," 1.4). We may not understand why at first, but once we hear Sayid's comment in "The Greater Good" (1.21) that cremation is wrong, we understand why Sayid responds so forcefully to Jack's pragmatic treatment of the dead.

Paganism, Nature, and New Age

Even pagan cultures receive a nod in *Lost*. As soon as Charlie dubs Claire's baby Turnip Head ("The Greater Good"), fans on the Internet speculated on the nickname's hidden meaning. The baby's head really does not look like a turnip to anyone but Charlie, so why would he choose that particular name? In Celtic cultures throughout what now is the U.K. (Charlie's homeland), people carved lanterns out of turnips for Samhain, more commonly known as Halloween among non-pagans. The frightening lanterns kept away evil spirits. Oceanic 815's flight date is listed on ABC-TV's Oceanicair website as September 22 (which is on or near a pagan equinox holiday). If that is the true crash date, and if the first season encompasses the castaways' first forty days (also a Christian biblical number), then Turnip Head's birth is on or close to Halloween.

What Internet fans may not consider is that Samhain is an autumnal or harvest holiday, and the castaways most likely are coming into spring if they are, indeed, still south of the equator. Little Turnip Head is not bound by the beliefs of a northern Celtic culture. Even if he is born on the night when spirits are closer to humans, the baby is not necessarily evil or even a talisman against it. Boone's spirit, for example, is not automatically transferred to the baby boy on the eve before the Day of the Dead, as some fans theorized. Nevertheless, the timing of the baby's birth provides a forum for and encourages speculation.

Fans also speculated that Claire may be a modern Rosemary from *Rosemary's Baby*. Even the series' creators admit that the film influenced a scene in "Homecoming" (1.15), in which pregnant Claire nervously waits for Ethan to come for her. Coupled with the interest in Turnip Head, officially named Aaron ("Exodus," 1.24), do fans have the right idea—that Claire's baby is somehow demonic? In the larger struggle between good and evil—not confined to any one religion—can there be something inherently evil in such an innocent-looking child? It is too early to say. In the first half of Season Two, Aaron seems to be a remarkably normal baby; he often is happily cuddled by Claire or Charlie.

Pagans and other nature enthusiasts may be dismayed that Locke is viewed by many fans (and characters) as a shady, slightly creepy man who knows more about the island than he should. As it seems, the island is Locke's religion. Locke frequently sits or stands in the rain, arms outstretched, as if being blessed by Mother Nature ("Pilot," 1.2). He knows nature so well that he accurately predicts when the sudden downbursts will occur ("All the Best Cowboys Have Daddy Issues," 1.11). He takes what he needs from the island to make weapons and tools. He understands which animal parts or plants are necessary to make items ranging from glue ("Numbers," 1.18) to medicinal salve ("Hearts and Minds," 1.13). He walks purposefully throughout the jungle and never seems to lose his way. Locke is "one" with the island. He understands and reveres it, and it returns the favor in what we perceive as mysterious ways.

In addition to well-established religions and expressions of religious beliefs, *Lost* illustrates elements of New Age philosophy and practices. Locke is most often associated with visions and a mystical understanding of the natural world usually associated with New Age or pagan practice. In effect, Locke helps Jack and Boone on vision quests. In "White Rabbit" (1.5) Jack already believes he is hallucinating when he meets Locke in the jungle. Locke guides him toward leadership of the group by pointing out that, in many ways, Jack already has taken control of situations and seems respected by others. Locke further helps Jack accept the vision/hallucination of his father; Locke does not think Jack is crazy, but just needs a sign. When Jack accepts that what he sees may be real, even if logically he cannot understand that conclusion, he is able to follow his father's apparition to the caves. Jack's discovery not only helps him deal with his father's death but provides the castaways with a much-needed water source and new shelter.

In another episode, Boone seems hopelessly bound to Shannon and tells Locke he cannot keep secrets from his sister. Locke not only knocks Boone unconscious to help him get started on his vision quest, but provides what might be a hallucination-inducing balm for Boone's head wound. Although Locke later denies his concoction is anything more than a healing salve, and indeed Boone might have had a mild concussion that causes him to see a horrific vision, there is still a hint of the mystical, and Locke alone seems to understand it ("Hearts and Minds," 1.13).

Locke also serves as a counselor or an advisor who mysteriously shows up just when someone needs guidance. He motivates Charlie with music, first to give up heroin ("The Moth," 1.7), and later to become a button pusher in the Hatch ("Everybody Hates Hugo," 2.4). He tells Sawyer a strange story about animals embodying the spirits of dead people, which causes him to question the "human" qualities of the boar he tracks ("Outlaws," 1.16). He turns up just in time to watch Sun destroy her garden in frustration ("…And Found," 2.5). He understands her anger, but more importantly tells her to stop looking for what she has lost (such as her wedding ring), because then she will find it.

Locke insists he has been "found" on the island. Locke, of all the survivors, finds redemption and salvation, not only healing and the culmination of his destiny, through belief in the island. If the island has a sinister motive rather than a predestined providence for the survivors, what does that say about Locke's character?

Good vs. Evil

Many religions teach that the basic struggle is between good and evil. Hints that such a larger battle may be shaping up on the island begin in "Man of Science, Man of Faith" (2.1). New character Desmond helps Jack when, in a pre-crash flashback, Jack injures his ankle as both men run the steps in a stadium. From their conversation we learn Desmond is training for a world run, almost became a doctor, and likely has a spiritual bent. He tells Jack to "lift it up," a double meaning to elevate the injured ankle and to pray for a miracle for accident-victim Sarah. "What would you do if a miracle were possible?" Desmond asks Jack. Is Desmond (as close to Demon as a common name can be) offering Jack a pact with the devil? After all, he notes that Jack has been running as if the devil were chasing him. Desmond also tells him they will see each other in another life, and they do encounter each other on the island, although Desmond seems less omnisciently demonic and more generally paranoid when he meets Jack in the Hatch. As with many characters struggling with inner demons in an internal war between good and evil, the struggle between Devil and God may be played out during Season Two.

The introduction of Desmond in the Hatch raises questions about the nature of a life path. Dharma, in both Hindu and Buddhist beliefs, refers to a life plan in harmony with the greater good. Only when people are in harmony with the universal power—living in balance with nature, spirit, and other people— can true happiness be realized. Those who do not spiritually follow dharma must live life on earth again, being reincarnated into a new life to learn more about following the true path. Perhaps Desmond's comment about the next life symbolically matches this aspect of dharma.

Dharma also means protection along one's spiritual path. The quarantine on the outside world indicates the Dharma Initiative means to protect what is stored or who lives down the Hatch. However, little spiritual development can take place for those who are forever sheltered from the outside world.

Spirituality is indeed an active force on the island, and as the series progresses, the castaways' belief systems will be tested. Whether they follow the tenets of a specific religion or blend concepts from the beliefs of those around them is yet to be seen. As more characters, such as Mr. Eko, apparently renounce their dark pasts and look for spiritual responses to the island's challenges, even more examples of spiritual or explicitly religious symbolism are likely to make their way into *Lost*'s multiple layers of meaning.

WHAT'S IN A NAME?

Names are often symbolic on *Lost*. Two prime examples are Jack Shephard and John Locke. (Other interesting coincidences with names are listed in part 4, "Similar Names.") Damon Lindelof conceded that "[e]very single name…has purpose and meaning." The writers' clues about characters point to Jack Shephard as the hero of *Lost*. "[Jack Shephard] is the de facto leader of the island's society, thus his appropriate surname is…one who tends the flock." Jack's father is even named Christian. Jack acts as a savior from the moment we see him open his eyes on the island. During the first fifteen minutes of the pilot episode (1.1), he frantically runs from crisis to crisis, directing the salvation of many people. Seemingly capable of saving everyone, almost by himself, he only delegates tasks once he averts danger or solves a problem. Jack, often dubbed the show's moral center, grows into his job as the survivors' leader. However, as Matthew Fox has explained, Jack becomes more human and less like a savior as the first season progresses and his beliefs come into question. According to Fox, Jack "is not always going to be good. He is going to be tested to go into very deep-gray areas." In the real world, a leader's morality or judgment is sometimes called into question, and the concept of a leader as a model of virtue is outdated. Jack seems more flawed, and thus more real, as he begins to deal with these gray areas.

Surprisingly, moral-center Jack professes no religion and is labeled a "man of science" by Locke, a self-described "man of faith," during the first season's finale ("Exodus," 1.23–24). Jack wears a key around his neck. Is he symbolically the one to open the locked secrets and bridge the gap between science and faith?

At times Jack reverts to some earlier religious training, but he keeps his spiritual beliefs, whatever they may be, to himself. He explains to Claire that he does not feel comfortable leading the memorial service for the numerous dead ("Walkabout," 1.4). Although he allows that others may need a religious context for the deed, he is not one of them. His need to make scientific, logical meaning out of island experiences makes him the opposite of Locke, who often interprets his impressions, rather than analytically assessing the information he receives.

The castaways' other (first-season) leader is John Locke, the name of a prominent British philosopher of the eighteenth century. That John Locke argued that the origin of faith is not in reason but in extraordinary communication—such as a spiritual revelation. Some things cannot be empirically proven; they cannot be known as fact. Those areas of knowledge are not based on experience but can be based on revelation. People have faith that this knowledge is correct, even though they cannot prove it by experience. (An interesting choice of title for a recap episode is "*Lost:* Revelation," shown in early January 2006 right before the U.S. debut of "The 23rd Psalm" after a long hiatus. Perhaps *Lost*'s creators want us to believe in the series, no matter how farfetched some story arcs might seem.)

As the first season progresses, the island's John Locke increasingly relies on revelation. In "Deus Ex Machina" (1.19), he follows the symbols and information provided in a dream/vision to guide him in his next actions. He tells Boone that the island will provide him with the knowledge he needs. After Boone's death ("Do No Harm," 1.20), he visits the Hatch to beseech "the island" about his lack of understanding. He has clearly done the island's bidding but is unsure why Boone needed to die. His momentary lack of confidence is restored when a light shines from the Hatch's window. This moment of revelation seems to fuel his enthusiasm for opening the Hatch and uncovering the hope he is sure is contained within ("Exodus," 1.24).

Locke seems much more interested than Jack in exploring the Hatch ("Man of Science, Man of Faith," 2.1). He wants to uncover the mystery by going inside the Hatch, even if it seems like only a long, dark drop into the unknown, with a few steps on a broken ladder leading the way. Although Kate is the first person Locke lowers into the Hatch, he quickly follows once she disappears from the end of the cable. His curiosity quickly pays off, but not in a friendly way. The Hatch's occupant, Desmond, holds Kate and Locke captive.

More clues about the Hatch—truly a misnomer because it opens into a cavernous living/working space—indicate that a government agency may be at work. Kate opens a larder filled with foodstuffs, all packed in black-and-white containers with the Dharma Initiative's label. Desmond himself is "packaged" in the same way; his uniform bears the Dharma insignia, as does the fin of a shark menacing Sawyer and Michael on the remnants of the raft ("Adrift," 2.2). If the government, perhaps a sinister Big Brother, runs the island, how will Locke react? His religion or god has been the island; to find that it is operated not by nature or a beneficent supreme being may make him question his faith.

By the end of the second season's first nine episodes, Locke often lives comfortably in the Hatch and seems to have taken Desmond's place in charge of button pushing. He sets up a schedule so that everyone must take a turn with the button.

For all practical purposes, Locke has become the Dharma Initiative's recruiter for maintaining Station Three. Locke often tells the survivors about his schedule for pushing the button. In "Orientation" (2.3), Locke tells Jack that he will set up a schedule. In "Everybody Hates Hugo" (2.4), Locke entices Charlie with promises of music in the Hatch and reminds Hurley that he has a job to do, whether he likes it or not. During "What Kate Did" (2.9), Locke explains the schedule to Michael and Mr. Eko. He sips a cup of coffee and sets up the orientation film so Mr. Eko and Michael can learn about the Dharma Initiative.

Locke seems like he has made himself at home during "The Other 48 Days" (2.7). His presence in the Hatch during "What Kate Did" (2.9) also supports his shift from boar hunter to office worker; he not only knows where everything is, but he acts comfortable with the living and working arrangements in the Hatch. He is seen increasingly often in the Hatch instead of outside in the jungle or on the beach.

However, Mr. Eko helps Locke reconnect his spiritual, or island-given, connection with his recruitment role in the castaways' society. He provides not only a missing segment from the orientation film but he also provides an Old Testament story to compare the King of Judah's actions and motivations for rebuilding the temple at Jerusalem with the castaways' recent events and possible "rebuilding" of Station Three ("What Kate Did," 2.9). For Mr. Eko and Locke, the practical and spiritual may again be reconnected. The island, through Mr. Eko, again has provided a revelation on which Locke's future actions may be based.

DEALING WITH DEATH

One purpose for spirituality is to help people deal with death. On *Lost*, as in life, there are many different reactions to death. As we noted earlier, Jack seems to believe his purpose in life is to save everyone. When he loses a patient, he takes it personally and has difficulty dealing with the finality of death. Jack lacks words at Boone's funeral, and Sayid steps forward to honor Boone when Jack and Shannon say nothing ("Exodus," 1.23). Jack does slightly better at Shannon's funeral ("Collision," 2.8) when Sayid is unable to continue the eulogy and leaves the gravesite. Jack doesn't speak, but he begins the ritual of placing a handful of earth into the grave. Dealing with funerals, including his father's planned interment, seems difficult for Jack, who as a healer wants to save his patients. He defies death frequently, and acknowledging its victory is something he is loath to do, even from a spiritual standpoint.

However, Jack takes charge of one burial. When the marshal dies, Jack calls on some type of religious upbringing to bury the man and mark the grave with a cross, the most important Christian symbol. (In "Whatever the Case May Be," Jack tells

Kate he buried the marshal.) He probably feels guilt at the marshal's death—not only is he unable to save the man from his injuries, but he apparently euthanizes him after Sawyer's botched attempt to end his suffering. Perhaps providing a Christian burial is the only way that Jack can atone for the man's untimely death.

In a similar way, Charlie seems obligated to bury Ethan, the "monster" he gladly shoots multiple times in "Homecoming" (1.15). He feels no moral dilemma over killing Ethan, but he nevertheless takes the responsibility of burying his enemy. Hurley humorously questions whether monstrous Ethan, just like the undead in horror movies, will rise from the grave to chase them. Charlie, however, does not respond to Hurley's humor. Perhaps if he keeps telling himself Ethan's death is necessary, he can keep at bay any spiritual guilt from committing murder. Perhaps he merely wants to make sure Ethan is dead and gone—out of sight forever. Whatever his motives, Charlie ensures Ethan gets a proper burial when he simply could have dumped the body elsewhere.

As the series continues, most likely the cemetery by the sea will grow. The crosses marking the graves of the marshal, Boone, and Shannon already are a touchstone image for several episodes. Before Shannon searches for Walt, she sits beside Boone's grave ("Abandoned," 2.7). When Kate questions her sanity because she fears she sees ghosts and receives messages from the dead, she is sitting at the edge of the cemetery ("What Kate Did," 2.9). Questioning the reality of images of the dead (such as ghosts or spirits) or seeking some solace by remembering the dead is becoming the focal point of scenes set in the cemetery. The ritual of burying the dead and honoring them with crosses seems to have a significant spiritual impact on the surviving castaways.

Facing the reality of loss, including death, how do *Lost*'s characters deal with impending doom? Those with strong religious beliefs, such as Rose, have faith they will have what they need to survive. However, some characters without such a belief structure feel overwhelmed when a crisis occurs.

Self-centered Shannon denies that she may not be rescued soon and relies on old patterns of behavior to manipulate others into helping her. After a few weeks, however, she develops more independence and self-esteem as she translates Rousseau's notes from French ("Whatever the Case May Be," 1.12) and builds her own shelter ("...In Translation," 1.17). As she spends more time with Sayid, she reveals she can take care of herself. But she also falls in love. This positive progression into self-reliance and openness with others abruptly ends, however, with Boone's death. She deals with this loss by returning to her manipulative ways. When Locke asks her forgiveness for his part in Boone's death, Shannon ignores him. After Sayid refuses to kill Locke for her, she takes matters (and a gun) into her hands as she attempts to kill Locke herself ("The Greater Good," 1.21). Instead, the bullet only grazes him, and Shannon becomes angry and isolated for a few episodes. Her ability to deal with loss is devoid of a spiritual context; she tries to solve problems herself, and when that does not work as she wants, she becomes bitter.

In "Exodus" (1.24), Shannon seems genuinely concerned for Sayid's welfare and relieved by his safe return after a confrontation with Rousseau; she thinks of another instead of herself. However, at times she still seems overwhelmed by grief. As the castaways retreat to the caves to hide from the Others, she struggles to haul Boone's as well as her own belongings. Sobbing, she tells Sayid she needs Boone's clothes, her only link to her brother. In agreeing to help her carry her spiritual as well as physical baggage, he helps her heal, a process she seems incapable of beginning alone. Shannon needs outside guidance and support, but she is so accustomed to manipulating others she does not know how to ask for help.

Sawyer is also self-absorbed and often finds enjoyment in tormenting other survivors. On their first night on the island, Sawyer runs into Jack as they search the fuselage (including deceased passengers and storage bins) for salvageable materials ("Tabula Rasa," 1.3). Jack looks for alcohol, medicines, and tools that might be useful to treat the survivors; Sawyer gathers whatever will make his life easier or may be useful in trade. During the first season, Sawyer's stash of goodies almost becomes a running joke; whatever is needed can be found within Sawyer's makeshift tent. The con man justifies his actions by reminding Jack they are far from civilization and truly "in the wild." Without human-made laws, each castaway theoretically can do whatever he or she chooses without consequence. Whereas Jack tells Kate each person has a clean start on the island ("Tabula Rasa," 1.3), Sawyer takes that message to mean "each person for himself" at whatever cost to the rest of the castaways. He remakes himself as the rich man who owns the few remaining luxuries and is thus more powerful.

Sawyer mellows over time, but he usually follows his own rules and cares little about anyone else, except as they affect what he does. His prime objective in his pre-crash life is to murder the man he blames for destroying his family; now he has no real purpose in life. Sawyer may suffer somewhat for being perceived as an outsider who only occasionally helps others, but he does not seek redemption. Occasionally he is magnanimous, as when he finally tells Jack about an encounter with his father in a bar in Sydney ("Exodus," 1.23). Jack has long awaited the validation the story of a father's pride in his son provides, and the fact that it comes from Sawyer, who typically keeps such information to himself, presents a redemptive moment for the con man. Nevertheless, later in the same episode, Sawyer assures Michael that he is "no hero." Sawyer seems content to rely on himself and disregard any spiritual, as well as many human, laws.

Ana Lucia seems to share Sawyer's interest in vengeance. She kills the man who shot her ("Collision," 2.8), apparently with no remorse. When she frees Sayid and reluctantly joins the now-merged society of Tailies and other castaways, she worries that Sayid will kill her because she killed his love, Shannon. Ana Lucia's understanding of life is more of a Biblical "eye for an eye" worldview, and she doesn't expect to be treated well, to put it mildly, by Shannon's group of friends. Without a spiritual foundation, Ana Lucia, like Sawyer and Shannon, has trouble believing in herself and others. They fail to trust people in part because they don't place their trust in a higher being.

Traditional expressions of religious belief provide solace to the faithful, but the castaways on *Lost* without a belief system often are shown having difficulty dealing with crises. Characters like Claire and Charlie move toward a heightened spirituality, a shift from their recent pre-crash lives. Although belief in a higher power doesn't seem to protect anyone on the island, those with a spiritual foundation, such as Rose and Mr. Eko, are portrayed as less lost and more likely to emotionally survive the island's challenges.

CHAPTER FIVE

LARGER SPIRITUAL CONCEPTS

Like the castaways, we must learn to live with fear and loss, just as the castaways do. The stakes on the island are high, just as in real life. The characters have as many different ways of dealing with uncertainty as we do. However, *Lost* also illustrates larger values that help people deal with life's chaos. Hope, faith, redemption, rebirth, fate, and destiny transcend a single religion and express the universality of spiritual and philosophical beliefs.

Series creator Damon Lindelof calls the episodes "redemptive stories. We show character flaws in the past, and explore ways these people can evolve on the island and redeem themselves." The series' themes force characters to change as they struggle to find their way in their new environment. Some characters grow spiritually, whereas others find their beliefs tested and ultimately begin to question them.

HOPE

Hope is one of the words, like faith, fate, and destiny, repeated in many episodes by different characters:

- Sayid mentions that hope is dangerous to lose ("Tabula Rasa," 1.3)
- Christian Shephard suggests Jack give hope, even false hope,

to his patients ("Do No Harm," 1.20)

- Kate refuses to move to the caves because to do so would be to give up hope that help will arrive ("House of the Rising Sun," 1.6)
- Locke believes hope is at the bottom of the Hatch ("Exodus," 1.24)

Hope is on shakier spiritual ground than faith, because hope is unsubstantiated. The cliché is that people cling to hope as a last resort, an undying response to a dire situation. Hope may be more vague than faith, but it is sustaining nevertheless.

Faith

A certainty that something as yet scientifically unproven exists or is true, usually faith has a spiritual connotation, but this strong belief can motivate characters outside a religious context. Some characters, such as Rose, express religious faith. Rose's unshakable faith keeps her going. Faith also reveals itself in a secular context. Jack, for example, places his faith in science and technology but sometimes loses faith in himself, especially during his first days as the group's leader and again after Boone's death.

Faith is more than a strong belief or even denial of reality. In *Lost*, faith frequently takes two forms: spiritual faith in the island and secular faith in oneself.

Locke maintains the strongest faith in the island. Of course, he also has the greatest reason to believe in the island's power and to trust its beneficence. When Locke boards the plane, he is a paraplegic and has been unable to walk for several years. Locke is shown in a wheelchair in Sydney during "Exodus." In an earlier episode's backstory, "Walkabout," Locke comes to Australia, although wheelchair-bound, to participate in a walkabout. He explains that he has been in a wheelchair for a few years. (At the time of writing, the cause of his paralysis has not been revealed.) When he wakes up—when he is reborn on the island—he wiggles his toes in disbelief. Moments later Locke struggles to his feet, and as Jack calls on him to help move an injured man, he runs to help ("Pilot," 1.1). For Locke, the island offers not only the experience he has sought in an Australian walkabout but the healing that traditional medicine could not provide.

Locke's faith may have a deeper spiritual underpinning, at least symbolically. In the pilot episode, Locke is shown shoeless until his "rebirth" with the ability to walk again. Then he ties on his shoes and gets to work helping others. An interesting detail in "Man of Science, Man of Faith" (2.1) is the camera's, and Jack's, lingering look at a pair of shoes neatly placed outside the entrance to Desmond's underground living/working quarters. If this were not a significant detail, why would the camera pause long enough for Jack—and us—to notice the shoes? Jack soon hears Locke's voice and realizes that he is being held prisoner; seeing the nondescript shoes is really not a clue about the identity of the person who owns them. The following episode shows Locke without his shoes—he removes them before he encounters Desmond ("Adrift," 2.2). Is he walking on holy ground, the mecca where his pilgrimage has led him? Or does being shoeless mean that inside the Hatch, Locke himself is "dead" again? In Western funereal practices, people are buried without shoes.

What is clear, though, is that Locke has faith that even difficult decisions, such as sacrificing Boone, offer worthwhile outcomes, because the island will not mislead him. Locke does not fear the castaways' dark sides but rather accepts the good and the bad without judgment. Because he feels comfortable with all aspects of the island, Locke lives more naturally and functions effectively. He can enjoy his new life because he now knows who he is.

Life on the island requires flexibility and acceptance of sudden change. Midway through the first season, Locke receives his calling to a greater challenge—uncovering and opening the Hatch ("All the Best Cowboys Have Daddy Issues," 1.11). Locke dedicates himself to this quest, but for once, the MacGyverish Locke fails in a task. He cannot open the Hatch, even though he uses sharp tools and the trebuchet he builds ("Deus Ex Machina," 1.19). The Hatch seems lifeless, an unexplained relic. Nevertheless, it compels Locke to open it; day after day he returns to figure out the riddle. During this time, Locke befriends Boone and acts as a surrogate father/mentor. Boone becomes so rabid in his defense of Locke he occasionally acts like a zealot; Locke becomes a spiritual leader with a single devout follower.

Even when Locke lashes out in frustration at his inability to open the Hatch, he senses a greater purpose at work. His faith is being tested. He tells Boone, "The island will give a sign" ("Deus Ex Machina"). Finally, Locke receives his vision. Although the images seem fragmented to us, the vision provides Locke with information to convince his disciple the sign is real. Locke's vision foreshadows Boone's injury and the discovery of the Beechcraft. Convinced he is now on the right path, Locke forges ahead. An injury to his leg debilitates him, and Boone must climb into the plane alone. When the Beechcraft tumbles from its perch on the cliff, Boone suffers severe, eventually fatal, injuries. Locke sacrifices his "son" during his spiritual quest on behalf of the island.

After Boone's death, Locke again finds his faith in the island tested. Covered in Boone's blood, Locke returns to the Hatch and uselessly smashes his fists against its lone window. "I've done everything you wanted me to do," he laments. "So why did you do this? Why?" Just when Locke's faith in the island, its many mysteries and omens, hits bottom, a light shines from the Hatch's window ("Do No Harm," 1.20). Locke still has not opened the Hatch, but he sees the light—quite literally—and knows that he is back on the right track. His faith is restored, so much so that in the final episodes of the first season, Locke once more is comfortable with himself and confident around the other survivors.

During "Exodus" (1.24), Locke passionately tells a disbelieving Jack that Boone's sacrifice is important as part of a series of events culminating in opening the Hatch. Although Locke needs dynamite and assistance from Rousseau and others, he feels that his spiritual purpose has been accomplished. We may question the cost of Locke's spirituality, but he clearly does not.

Whereas Locke may not seem to be inherently good, he does help the other castaways. Early in the first season, for example, Locke leads boar hunts and brings back meat for the others ("Walkabout," 1.4). Without Locke, the survivors would have had a more difficult first forty days. However, we have difficulty knowing if he always has the best interest of the others at heart.

Even the series' cast and crew question whether Locke is good or evil. In a March 2005 gathering at the William Paley Festival, J. J. Abrams and several actors from *Lost* discussed Locke's character. Abrams asked who thought Locke was a good guy. Ironically, only Ian Somerhalder (Boone) raised his hand. Is Locke just human, with good and bad qualities like any other character, or is there something sinister going on? Should the castaways—should we?—be concerned that Locke is dubbed the man of faith? Should such faithful leaders be suspected or followed? Even faith becomes a debatable topic as we unlock *Lost*'s secrets.

Whatever his morality, Locke is both a mystical and symbolic character. He knows how to find his way without a compass; he obviously knows where he is going and feels comfortable navigating the island. When he gives Sayid the compass the older man declares he no longer needs, Sayid discovers that north is not where it is supposed to be on the device ("Hearts and Minds," 1.13). If Locke's moral compass is indeed off kilter, it could help explain why he feels at home on the mysterious island.

As a mentor, Locke embodies tough love along with his faith in others, even when they lose faith in themselves. Charlie initially exchanges his drugs for Locke's information about the location of his guitar. Locke, however, gives Charlie three chances to ask for the drugs; on the third request, they will be returned. Each time Charlie begs for drugs, Locke expresses his faith in the addict's ability to give them up. Upon the last request, Locke hands over the baggie, which Charlie tosses into the campfire. Locke restates his faith in the shaky young man ("The Moth," 1.7).

In "Hearts and Minds" (1.13), Locke knocks his next mentee Boone unconscious and then smears a salve on his wound that seems to promote a gruesome hallucination, in which Boone believes the Monster mutilates Shannon. Tormented by the vision, he attacks Locke, who shows him that the vision is not real but can motivate him to start a new life. Because Locke never questions the information given by the island or his role as the only one who understands its true nature, he feels confident in dispensing wisdom, even in painful ways. In his own style, he shows his faith in others' ability to make the right decision.

Until the final episode of the first season ("Exodus," 1.24), only one character sees the Monster—Locke. Early in the first season, in "Walkabout" (1.4), Locke comes face to face with it, but it does not harm him. He later tells Jack that he has looked into the island's eye, and it is beautiful. Locke is so attuned to the natural world, with its healing grace as well as horrific dangers, that what is frightening to others is empowering to him. Unlike the other castaways, who often seem frightened by the natural world and want to escape from it, Locke lives at peace on the island. He has faith in and respects the island's power.

On *Lost*, faith requires confidence that one's actions are necessary and right, because they are firmly grounded in one's belief system. Jack and Locke, the survivors' most likely leaders in the second season, place their faith in very different ideals. In any future split among the castaways, characters may have to decide which leader to follow and subsequently place their faith in his beliefs.

REDEMPTION

Although any character might be ripe for redemption, some characters seek redemption more than others. Their arrival on the island and subsequent relationships with other survivors force them to look at themselves and change. As Damon Lindelof told *Entertainment Weekly* in April 2005, *Lost* is like other well-done character-driven shows in that it is about individuals "searching for redemption in the face of their flaws and struggles."

During the first season, the best overt example of redemption is Charlie. A U.S. television commercial for the second season shows Charlie playing his guitar on the beach while musing about the possibility of having a second chance. He asks if there can be redemption. An ongoing reason for Charlie's need for redemption is his addictive personality. He must deal with his drug addiction as well as his personality, which requires even longer-term changes and intermittently drives him to seek spiritual solutions to his problems. "Pace" is another accurate surname: one of Charlie's challenges is to pace himself instead of veering madly from one extreme to another.

Charlie often seems at the mercy of the warring sides of his nature—to be spiritual, as in his pre-DriveShaft past, or to succumb to temptation in a weak moment. In a May 2005 interview for *E!Online*, Dominic Monaghan explained that he plays Charlie as a "bad good guy at this point, but he could very easily become a good bad guy." Like many people, he selflessly helps others one moment but selfishly lashes out the next. For every tender moment spent caring for Claire and her baby, there is another where Charlie lies, punches, or, in one memorable situation, commits murder.

Charlie's temptations range from international fame and fortune, to sex and drugs and rock 'n' roll, to something as simple as Claire's diary. In one of *Lost*'s humorous scenes, Charlie mightily struggles between desire to read the diary and self-loathing that he would stoop so low. He peeks at a page, then abruptly closes the book. He fidgets a moment, reaches for the diary again, and finally stashes it out of sight in Claire's bag. But that does not keep him away for long. Soon he tells Jack and Sayid what he read ("Special," 1.14).

When Charlie sticks with what he thinks is right or moral, he seems strong. When he admits to the priest that giving up DriveShaft is preferable to the casual group sex to which he just confessed, he seems sincere and committed. However, temptation comes immediately in the form of Liam, Charlie's adored but untrustworthy older brother, who offers Charlie not only a recording contract but his approval and good will. Charlie gives up God—or his belief in what is right—for fame, money, women, and the entrapments of false power. However, such power is fleeting. Charlie loses first Liam and then himself to the fast lifestyle that accompanies the band's rise to fame ("The Moth," 1.7).

On the island, once free of drugs, Charlie seems to be on the right path to a better life. He feels so capable and strong that he blurts during Claire's (false) labor that "I gave up drugs, so I can deliver a baby" ("All the Best Cowboys Have Daddy Issues," 1.11). Charlie's strength lasts until he and Claire are kidnapped by Ethan. In the aftermath of his near-death experience, and plagued with guilt over his inability to protect Claire, Charlie needs something stronger than himself. Once she returns, he again becomes confident. He tries to help amnesiac Claire by talking with her and vowing to protect her. However, his protection once again takes a destructive turn when he lies to Claire, destroying her trust in him, and he then shoots Ethan ("Homecoming," 1.15).

Charlie's frequent promise to Claire that he will take care of her and her baby sends a warning signal to us. In backstories, Charlie's relationships with women are at best one-sided and at worst predatory ("Homecoming"). Seeing him as a caretaker for mother and child is easy as long as no real danger threatens, but on *Lost* it always does.

When Rousseau absconds with Claire's baby, Charlie insists on accompanying Sayid to retrieve the child. After running headfirst into Rousseau's trap and sustaining a head injury, he refuses to return to Claire without the baby. Although eventually present for the child's safe return, it is Sayid who finds the child and coaxes Rousseau into handing him over.

Charlie's return to Claire is another redemptive moment. The young man basks in the castaways' praise and Claire's joy in being reunited with her son. She chastely kisses Charlie and tends his head wound. Nevertheless, a close-up of Charlie's backpack reveals a Madonna statue within ("Exodus," 1.24). Which mother and child ultimately will claim his devotion? Can he permanently be redeemed?

"Fire + Water" provides some answers, when Charlie himself poses a threat to Aaron. As a result of a dream full of religious icons and an overwhelming feeling that the baby is endangered (e.g., trapped in a piano, washed out to sea), Charlie twice kidnaps him. Claire recently has packed Charlie's bags after he lies to her about the drug-filled Madonna, and her trust in him is destroyed by his aberrant behavior. Charlie admits to Jack that he has been tempted to use heroin again, but he claims that he resists. He believes that recent events, such as discovery of more heroin, are his test. However, passing this, or other, spiritual tests isn't a guarantee of a happy ending. At the end of the episode, Charlie is shunned and seems to have no hope for regaining his surrogate family or even the friendship of other castaways.

Especially in this episode, *Lost* illustrates that redemption is less a happily ever after, single-episode plotline than a never-ending rollercoaster. The larger issue is whether without a quick payoff, or conversely, with the continuing perils and problems on the island, Charlie (or other characters) will seek to live a good life just for goodness' sake.

REBIRTH

Each character symbolically dies in the crash and is reborn on the island. Other scenes of death and rebirth are sprinkled throughout the first season's episodes, perhaps most blatantly in "The Moth"

(1.7). In this episode, Locke, in his role as Charlie's temporary spiritual advisor, provides the parable of the moth, explaining that butterflies are flashy and get everyone's attention, but moths are stronger and more valuable because they spin silk. If the cocoon is opened prematurely, the moth will be too weak to survive. But the moth that struggles out of the cocoon on its own is able to survive in the world. Locke clearly believes Charlie is a moth and slowly convinces him he is much stronger than he believes.

When Charlie is entombed with Jack during a cave-in, Charlie sees a moth flying toward the top of the cave. He follows the moth toward the light and pushes his way through the earth into the sunlight. The camera focuses on Charlie's forearm struggling through the soil until it pushes free, looking very much like a horror movie shot of the undead rising from a fresh grave. The heavy-handed symbolism illustrates Charlie's growing faith in himself without drugs; he is able to save himself and Jack by finding another way out of the caves. Charlie the addict "dies," and a drug-free man struggles to be reborn.

Charlie also is the focus of another death/rebirth scenario in "Raised by Another" (1.10). Jack and Kate find Charlie hanging, apparently left for dead by Ethan. Jack desperately performs CPR for so long and with such violence that Kate begs Jack to stop. Charlie appears long dead, and Kate sobs not only for his loss but for Jack's inability to let go. With a final effort, Jack pounds life into the young man, whose loud gasp again suggests the undead coming back to life.

Jack also facilitates Rose's rebirth. In the pilot episode (1.1), Jack corrects Boone's CPR technique. Rose also seems beyond help, but through Jack's persistent efforts comes back to life and suffers no permanent damage from her brush with death.

In Season Two, even Sawyer is the catalyst for rebirth. When Michael nearly drowns, Sawyer performs CPR and mouth-to-mouth resuscitation until Michael comes back to life ("Adrift," 2.2).

Even the death of the first main character parallels a birth. Boone's death scene is intercut with scenes of the birth of Claire's baby. As Jack cries over Boone's body, Claire's face shines with tears of joy ("Do No Harm," 1.20). The cycle of life continues, with birth and death being closely related.

The Christian concept of being born again, or "saved," even affects characters who do not seek redemption and most likely doubt that they are spiritually saved. When self-proclaimed sinner Sawyer awakens from delirium to find himself in a bunk bed inside the Hatch, he believes the castaways have been rescued. Kate assures him that they are still on the island and finally takes him outside the Hatch to prove it. "We're not saved?" Sawyer mournfully asks. "Not yet," Kate replies. Although the two outlaws have not yet sought redemption, *Lost*'s writers imply that spiritual rebirth—being saved—is possible even for those who so far have not embraced their second chance for a new life.

Lost emphasizes that these people, armed with knowledge of their past mistakes, have been given a second chance. They do not have to share their past indiscretions with other survivors; they need only reveal what they wish others to know. As they learn even from their experiences since the crash, they continue to grow spiritually. Nevertheless, many survivors return to old behavioral patterns. Rebirth, like other spiritual events, is not easy; it requires struggle for a new life to survive.

FATE AND DESTINY

How much independence do humans have in their actions? How much is determined by fate? Does each person have a destiny only he or she can fulfill? In some religions, fate and destiny are key components, although these concepts are more abstract to most Westerners. Jin, Sun, and Sayid, however, find such questions particularly important to their growth, and Jin and Sun especially wrestle with these spiritual concepts as the couple part.

In Sun's and Jin's backstories ("...In Translation" [1.17] and "House of the Rising Sun" [1.6]) we see the couple lose their way in an increasingly tense marriage. Although they love each other and overcome differences in social standing in order to marry, their relationship rapidly deteriorates once Jin begins working for Sun's father. As an employee of the ruthless Mr. Paik, Jin finds himself beating a man and delivering threatening messages. Even when he plans to escape his father-in-law's tyranny, he learns that he is being followed and must remain enslaved in the family business ("Exodus," 1.23). If he does anything else, he will lose Sun. Jin faces a terrible dilemma: if he runs away with Sun, they will be tracked and separated permanently; if he continues working for his father-in-law, he becomes tainted by the tasks given to him and also will lose his wife. Jin believes that being isolated on the island is his fated punishment for being a bad husband, and he longs to save Sun from the misery he continues to cause her.

Sun wonders if the survivors are being punished for past actions or secrets. She has kept secrets from Jin—such as her plan to abandon him once she learned English and start a new life in a new land. She knows he is shamed when she reveals her language skills. Once Jin sails on the raft and Sun is left behind, she asks Shannon if fate could be punishing them. Claire responds that fate does not have any bearing on their situation, but Sun and Shannon look far less certain ("Exodus," 1.24). Fate, in Sun's estimation, could be the great equalizer to balance past misdeeds with current punishment. Only when fate is satisfied can the survivors truly start a new life free from their pasts.

As alluded to in the series, fate is also part of devout Muslim belief. When Sayid infiltrates a terrorist cell in Sydney, his friend, a member of the cell, tells the others that Sayid was a communications officer and has valuable skills they can use. The group's leader declares that Sayid's reunion with his college roommate is no coincidence; fate intervenes to provide the terrorists with just the new member they need ("The Greater

Good," 1.21). This scene sets up two very different possible interpretations, depending on one's belief in the power of fate. Those who do not believe fate is a controlling force can interpret the terrorist's comment as naïve; Australian and American intelligence agencies have provided Sayid with his friend's whereabouts and coerced him to spy on the group. Those who accept that fate plays an important role in human interaction realize the intelligence agents merely provide Sayid with the opportunity to fulfill fate's mission. Part of *Lost*'s successful storytelling is its ability to layer meanings into simple dialogue; the words can take on different meanings for different members of its audience.

When Sayid is later held prisoner by Ana Lucia, she asks him if she should let him go. Her belief is that if Sayid is truly a good man, she should not kill him. Sayid explains that he has done terrible deeds in the past. He suggests that perhaps Ana Lucia is meant to kill him ("Collision," 2.8). Ana Lucia's belief system indicates that good people should be saved. Sayid believes that whatever is meant to happen will happen.

Even Mr. Eko seems to value fate. Locke marvels at the coincidence that Eko would find the missing segment of the Dharma Initiative's orientation film, bring it with him to the other side of the island, see the film, and be able to splice the missing segment back into the film. Mr. Eko tells Locke not to confuse coincidence with fate. Perhaps something more powerful than random chance is at work on the island.

Destiny, often associated with fate, is another recurring theme. Locke clearly believes in destiny and shares his belief with others, especially Jack. In a commercial on U.S. television for the second season, Locke explains what brought him to the island; destiny is his keyword. Even the tagline used in television and print promotions touts the destiny-friendly pronouncement that "everything happens for a reason" ("The Moth," 1.7).

The significance of character names hints at further predestined connections among the survivors. Although "Thomas" is a common Western name, its repetition probably is not coincidental: Kate's love, Tom; Charlie's dealer, Tommy; Claire's lover, Thomas. "Beth" pops up in a conversation about Kate's friend and a backstory involving a deceased patient. Even "Jack" is a variation of "John," so that the castaways' most likely leaders share the same first name. (See "Similar Names.")

Familiar faces also show up in different episodes. As only one example, the actor who plays Charlie's parish priest rides the scooter Hurley buys at the Sydney airport ("Exodus," 1.24).

The survivors' lives are "intertwined before they all got on that plane," Damon Lindelof told *TV Guide* in October 2004. Hurley appears on the Korean television program seen in the house where Jin threatens his boss's wayward client ("House of the Rising Sun," 1.6). A handcuffed Sawyer is led through the Sydney police station where Boone talks with an officer ("Hearts and Minds," 1.13). (See "Character Connections" for more common experiences.)

This episode also indicates that *destiny* might be another word for *curse*, at least in Hurley's case. The mystical Numbers pop up throughout the scenes of Hurley rushing to the airport. His car breaks down, the speedometer falling from one lottery number to the next. He goes to the wrong terminal and must run to the international area, passing a soccer team clad in jerseys bearing the lottery numbers. When he finally makes it to the correct gate—23, of course—the door is closed. Hurley's plaintive insistence on getting on this flight compels an attendant to ensure that he is allowed on the plane. Destiny in these scenes is humorous, an entertaining way for us to learn about the characters' interconnectedness.

Locke, however, takes destiny much more seriously. Although Sun perceives fate as a punishing force and likely fears destiny, Locke sees fate as beneficent and destiny a powerful force for good. He believes that each survivor is chosen for an important purpose on the island. Locke explains to Jack that everything—all messages from the island, all visions, all events, including Boone's death—leads to the opening of the Hatch ("Exodus," 1.24). Jack refuses to believe in destiny and tells Locke as much. "That's just because you don't know it yet," Locke assures him, confident that destiny is the operative force.

As the first season closes, a split not only philosophically but spiritually divides the castaways' leadership between Jack and Locke. Jack questions himself and seems less morally sound after his forty days of "tests." Locke seems the stronger power; however creepy he may seem, he clearly feels confident in himself and his beliefs. He has a strong foundation from which to act.

The second season opener emphasizes the shift in belief systems. Once the Hatch is opened, Jack, to his dismay, thinks that the small entry and broken ladder make the Hatch an impossible hiding place from the Others. Jack then abandons the Hatch and tells Locke to do the same. Locke, however, is more than merely curious and returns to go down the Hatch. He wants to know what is there and feels there is purpose in exploring it ("Man of Science, Man of Faith," 2.1). He has faith that the exploration will be safe; after all, destiny has guided him to opening the Hatch. It would be unthinkable to abandon destiny once the Hatch is open.

Jack bases his reactions on facts and observations; Locke bases his on feelings and instincts. Jack relies on his own judgment to determine what is real or true; Locke interprets signs and trusts in destiny to steer his actions. If Jack makes a mistake, he blames himself. If Locke errs, he has misinterpreted destiny. Jack believes in free will and self-determination; Locke searches for meaning in a grand preordained plan in which each person must play a special role.

As we have already discussed, writer David Fury recalls that during the first season ABC did not want to label the show as science fiction. Because of the network's reticence in having mystical or supernatural explanations for the island's mysteries, the writers tried to create a logical answer for every question, even if such answers have not yet been provided. We can choose whether to believe a mystical or a logical reason for strange happenings.

Perhaps a strength in *Lost* is that there are no clear-cut answers. Either on the show or in life, the questions invite myriad interpretations. We, as well as characters, discuss and analyze the meaning of life through a series of question-raising situations, but individually determine what forces are in play and how they affect human behavior and beliefs.

The castaways undoubtedly will find their beliefs tested as they continue to seek redemption or enjoy the possibilities of a new life. For some, spirituality may be the only calm eye in the island's barrage of emotional and physical storms.

PART FOUR:

KEYS TO UNLOCKING THE MEANING OF *LOST*

CHAPTER SIX

LOST ANCESTORS

Books, film, music, television, as well as other manifestations of both low and high culture—to borrow the witty formulation of film scholar Robert Stam—are governed by the same principle as sexually transmitted diseases. To have sex with another is to have had sex with all of his or her other sexual partners, and every text—every new novel or short story, song, or movie, or television series—is far from innocent; each potentially carries the "contagion" of every other text it, and its creators, have "slept with."

According to the literary critic and bestselling author Harold Bloom, every great writer (and, by extension, every work of the imagination) must struggle to escape from the influence of the writers (and works) that came before. In order to be original, the newcomer must simultaneously borrow from its "ancestor texts" and depart from them in order to become unique and innovative.

What Bloom says about books and writers is true of television as well. A series like *Lost* has a variety of ancestors to which it is indebted, but if the creators of *Lost* must break free from their hold on its imagination it is to become a one-of-a-kind television series. The following is a comprehensive though by no means complete catalog of *Lost* ancestors.

THE ADVENTURES OF BRISCO COUNTY, JR.

For a brief discussion of this television series, see chapter 1, "Creating Lost," pages 15–16.

ALIAS

J. J. Abrams's spy drama, *Alias* (2001–2006) has whisked its audience to a thousand and one exotic locations with main character and series heroine, Sydney Bristow (Jennifer Garner) in an array of flashy (and often revealing) costumes and disguises. But the premise of *Alias* isn't just about the couture: Abrams has said the original concept came from his WB network semi-hit *Felicity*, which inspired him to concoct a storyline that centered around a college student who just happened to be a spy. (*Alias*, according to Abrams, "was the result of wanting to do 'something with dramatic stakes a few notches higher than the romantic turmoil of a college coed'" [Dilmore 22].) Add a mythos concerning prophetic Renaissance inventor Rambaldi, who created devices that can destroy the world, and a dysfunctional father-daughter relationship, and a new cult hit was born.

The series was initially dependent on standard cliff-hanger endings that prevailed through much of the first season, while Sydney tried to keep her secret lives secret: she juggled working as a double agent for the CIA against the nefarious SD-6, which she'd previously thought was a black ops division of the CIA. Her best friends, roommate Francie (Merrin Dungey) and reporter Will Tippin (Bradley Cooper), were kept in the dark, thinking that she worked for an international bank, Credit Dauphine. Her boss at SD-6, Arvin Sloane (Ron Rifkin), has functioned as Sydney's prime nemesis for the duration of the series, and her relationship with her father, fellow Season One double agent Jack Bristow (Victor Garber) has traveled through a dizzying array of up and down emotionality.

Sydney endures the loss of her fiancé, Danny, in the pilot episode after revealing her spy status to him (he is killed by SD-6). She witnesses her best friends, Will and Francie, destroyed as a result of her secret life—Francie is killed and cloned by the second and third season baddie, the Covenant, and Will is put into the Witness Protection Program. She learns that her mother (Lena

Olin) was a traitor—a spy for the Russians against the U.S.—and that her death when Sydney was a child was a lie told to protect her. In the five seasons of *Alias*, Sydney has found out her dead mother is actually alive; lost her memory; worked as an assassin for the government; saved the world—repeatedly; fallen in love with her CIA handler; taken down SD-6, the Alliance of Twelve, and the Covenant; discovered a long-lost pair of aunts (one evil, one semi-evil); and had all of her eggs stolen. Add to the mix that she's a key figure in the apocalypse predicted by Rambaldi, whose creepy inventions and even creepier designs on the future world somehow always manage to figure into each season's story arc.

The connections between *Alias* and *Lost* are manifold. Despite the action-packed drama on each series, both are primarily character driven. In both *Alias* and *Lost*, intrigue and mystery imbue the characters. The taciturn and occasionally brutal Jack Bristow may remind viewers of both shows of the hard-edged but tender Sayid. The quirky techno-hip geek Marshall (Kevin Weisman) might be seen as a (slightly smaller) mirror image of the funny (yet cursed) Hurley, or maybe even Charlie Pace. The characters of both J. J. Abrams series share depths unusual for these kinds of shows. Without their inner turmoil, neither show would have much of a life expectancy.

Sydney's emotional trials and tribulations are often set against the backdrop of life-or-death situations not unlike the challenges the castaways of *Lost* face. Sydney has had to MacGyver herself out of many situations while in spy mode, requiring the audience to suspend disbelief in a way occasionally required by *Lost* as well. The mythology of *Alias* enlists fans to become experts on all things CIA, spy or black ops, and the existence of a prophecy involving the series' heroine has engaged more than one fan on wild goose chases, solving the Rambaldi prophecy—futile quests well-known to the zealous *Lost* fan. Other tie-ins between the two series include the destination city of Sydney, Australia, and the number forty-seven—a prominent fixture in *Alias* that makes a brief appearance on *Lost* in the pilot episode (a tally number of survivors). Terry O'Quinn (John Locke) spent two seasons on *Alias* as FBI assistant director Kendall, and *Alias* regular Greg Grunberg made an appearance as the short-lived, pulled-out-of-the-cockpit-by-the-Monster pilot in the series pilot. (He's very briefly visible in "Exodus" as well.)

Never a big success in the ratings, *Alias* benefited greatly in its fourth season from having the more successful *Lost* as its lead-in. *Alias*'s better Season Four numbers were in part the result of viewers who tuned in for the new Abrams series and stuck around for the older one. If they didn't budge from their seats, even at the end of each show, they got to see twice that rapidly moving, red cartoon automaton and hear the children's voices scold "Bad Robot"—the name of J. J. Abrams's production company, responsible for both shows. Even without that signature the careful viewer might well have guessed *Lost*'s and *Alias*'s shared genesis.

Talking about his two Bad Robots with *Cinefantastique*, Abrams had a lot to say about his more successful younger child:

> If eight or nine million people are watching *Alias* and sixteen or seventeen million people are watching *Lost*, then it says that *Lost* is doing better than *Alias*. But if a show is doing well enough to stay on the air, the experience from my point of view is fairly the same on both shows. As long as you're on the air and doing well enough to sustain, you don't really experience an enormous difference in the creation or the reception of the show.

In fact, from Abrams's perspective as executive producer, "The job is exactly the same. The numbers are different, but you're still trying to do a good show. I've always been really proud of *Alias* and of the viewership of the show. There's something special about it being a cult show. I'm not saying I wouldn't love it if it broke out in the fourth season and found a bigger audience, that would be awesome. But if it doesn't happen, that's okay, too. I think the audience we have is terrific."

ALICE IN WONDERLAND

A strange literary ancestor of *Lost* is Lewis Carroll's 1865 *Alice in Wonderland*. The series' writers borrowed a character for the episode title "White Rabbit" (1.5) but exactly who is the White Rabbit in *Lost*'s wonderland?

"White Rabbit" provides Jack's first backstory, in which viewers see the frazzled doctor reach a breaking point. Although he has saved many lives since the plane crash, he also has lost a few, most notably the marshal and, at the beginning of this episode, a young woman caught swimming in a rip current. In his peripheral vision, Jack begins seeing a man in a black suit, but when he turns to get a closer look, the man disappears. Viewers, and Jack, don't know if the vision is real or only a hallucination. Locke later convinces Jack it doesn't really matter if the vision is real or not. What is important is what Jack does when he sees the vision.

As in Carroll's Wonderland, *Lost*'s jungle is full of hidden marvels and dangers. Jack's introduction to the surreal nature of the island comes from the vision of, it turns out, his father. This White Rabbit guides Jack into the jungle and over a cliff, instead of down a rabbit hole. Instead of a pocket watch, Christian Shephard carries a nearly empty drink in his hand, clinking the ice cubes against the glass as he walks. This aural cue reminds Jack of a dominant image from his childhood and a recurring theme in his father's life—alcohol.

During the flashback sequences, we learn that Jack's father was a demanding man who always found his son lacking. Jack didn't "have what it takes" to make tough decisions and live with the sometimes tragic consequences of his actions. During "White Rabbit," Jack confronts his troubled memories of his father and follows the apparition/hallucination through the jungle until he finally discovers caves with a limitless supply of fresh water. There Jack's awe-filled entry into this wonderland ends.

Even within the serene beauty of the caves is mystery and intrigue; among the wreckage littering the entrance is an empty casket. Jack's father's body is missing, leaving Jack once more to confront his anger not only at his father's death, but his inability to find closure in their relationship. Like Carroll's White Rabbit, Jack's father acts as a guide into a mysterious and confounding world full of contradictions. The apparition appears and disappears suddenly to get the story (flashbacks) moving again, just as Alice's rabbit does throughout the novel.

Like father, like son. Although Jack and his father have very different personalities and priorities, both at times become a White Rabbit. Alice's White Rabbit is often nervous and flighty, rushing from task to task with a never-ending fear of being late. Christian Shephard, as shown in this episode and sequences of Jack's other backstory episodes, seems unhurried and confident— or at least that is his mask for his colleagues and family. However, Jack's actions in the beginning of the first season align him more closely to the White Rabbit's personality. In the pilot episode, for example, Jack runs from one injured survivor to another, and although he is confident in his medical knowledge, he also lacks the time he needs to make a difference. In the opening segment of "White Rabbit," Jack needs more time to swim first to Boone's rescue and then to return to save Joanna. Time unfortunately runs out, and Joanna drowns before Jack can reach her. Jack seems compelled to do everything himself, and he rushes from one crisis to another. He doesn't carry a pocket watch, but he does recognize the demands of time. (In a side story during "White Rabbit," a timepiece does play a major role. Michael and Jin come to blows over an expensive watch.)

In a later episode, Jack also acts like the White Rabbit, the character who stands up to the king (an authority figure like Jack's father) and demands that Alice be allowed to testify at her trial.

In a flashback we see Jack finally stand up to his father during a medical inquiry into actions during a botched operation. Jack's testimony leads to Christian's dismissal as chief of surgery. The court in *Alice and Wonderland* parallels the board of inquiry in "All the Best Cowboys Have Daddy Issues" (1.11). Although that episode takes place later in the season, Jack's ability to stand up for what he believes is right is a White Rabbit moment.

Several *Lost* episodes are titled with a song title or lyric (e.g., "All the Best Cowboys Have Daddy Issues" [1.11], "House of the Rising Sun" [1.6]), and "White Rabbit" is one of these. Jefferson Airplane's Grace Slick wrote "White Rabbit in Wonderland" in 1967, and the trippy lyrics echo not only Carroll's Wonderland but Jack's as well. "If you go chasing rabbits, and you know you're going to fall" is one line, and that is what Jack does. He blindly chases the vision of his father into the jungle and over a cliff. Only Locke's timely arrival saves him from a deadly fall. By the end of the episode, Jack apparently agrees with Slick to "feed your head" and follows Locke's advice to stand up as the survivors' leader. He also has followed the vision in his head to find a water supply so crucial to the group's survival. Viewers know that, like Alice, Jack's adventures in this strange new place have only begun.

BUFFY THE VAMPIRE SLAYER, ANGEL, FIREFLY

Episodic television in the first decade of the twenty-first century owes a substantial debt to the critically acclaimed series created by Joss Whedon: *Buffy the Vampire Slayer* (1997–2003), *Angel* (1999–2004), and *Firefly* (2003–2004). Though never big Nielsen successes, they made possible multi-genre, character-driven shows with fantastic themes.

Lost cannot be said to be directly under the influence of the Whedonverse; so far, *Lost* has given us no chosen ones, no demons, no vampires, no spaceships. Still, its credits are studded with the names of key writers and directors who came to the series with the experience of working for Whedon still fresh in their minds. Major Whedon collaborator David Grossman, director of twenty-one episodes of *Buffy* and *Angel*, did *Lost*'s "The Greater Good." *Buffy* director (and television veteran) Tucker Gates directed "Confidence Man" (1.8) and "Born to Run" (1.22). Marita Grabiak, who worked on all three Whedon series, directed "Raised by Another" (1.10). Daniel Attias, who helmed two Season Five episodes of *Buffy*, directed the pivotal episode "Numbers" (1.18), cowritten by David Fury—another key Whedon collaborator, both as a writer and director, on *Buffy* and *Angel*—and Brent Fletcher, who had written a Season Five *Angel*. Fury also authored "Walkabout" (1.4), "Solitary" (1.9), and "Special" (1.4). Drew Goddard, author of three episodes of *Buffy*'s final season, wrote "Outlaws" (1.16) for *Lost*.

No single episode exemplifies the Whedon touch better than "Numbers," both written and directed by Whedon alums. Its comedic attention to detail (the chicken on Hurley's fast-food work shirt in the first flashback, for example), its dark, absurdist humor (the dispassionate death of his grandfather during Hurley's appearance on TV as the lottery winner), its mixing of pathos and humor in the same scene, its self-referentiality (Hurley complains to Rousseau about the island's perplexing mysteries, especially the Monster, with a kind of impatience that suggests he might just be a regular watcher of the series in which he appears: "I want some freakin' answers!")—all of these are Whedon signatures.

CAST AWAY

Cast Away (2000) must have played a role in the chain of inspiration for *Lost*. An Oceanic Airlines plane (FedEx plane) crashes after a terrifying in-flight incident on (near by) an island in the South Pacific; the story then tracks the struggles of the survivors (the only survivor) of the disaster to survive on the island. Was Lloyd Braun's bare-bones idea for the series in fact a case of what is now sometimes called "kleptonesia," a convenient forgetful borrowing, from the Zemeckis/Hanks film? Perhaps, but the basic idea, in whatever form, is not exactly high concept nor terribly innovative.

Tom Hanks—who purportedly brought the idea for the film to Robert Zemeckis—plays Chuck Noland (No-land), a FedEx efficiency expert, whose life is ruled by the clock. Jetting all over the world to spread the company gospel of on-time delivery (the film opens in Moscow in what *Slate* critic David Edelstein has deemed "an overture that plays like an especially grandiose Federal Express commercial"), Noland is sent off to Asia on Christmas day to deal with an emergency but never arrives. The air cargo plane on which he's the only passenger goes down over the ocean in what Edelstein rightly describes as "the most harrowing plane crash ever filmed (or computer-generated)," and he makes it, thanks to a life raft, to a nearby island where he spends four years. Except for a volleyball, a fellow survivor he names Wilson (he gives it a face painted with his own blood), Noland goes it alone, and the film follows his solitary struggles: to crack coconuts, make fire, stay sane, build a raft. He makes it to sea and is rescued. The film's ineffective final act shows Noland trying to reenter a world where the love of his life (Helen Hunt) has married another man and he is now an alien.

By multiplying the number of survivors to forty-eight (with fourteen the center of focus)—a move that was a necessity for an ongoing series, *Lost*, of course, radically alters *Cast Away*'s subject matter. In just over forty days of *Lost* time, exponentially more has happened to the *Lost*aways than transpired in Noland's four years. With no fellow survivors, nor Others, on his island, Noland's interactions can only be with the contents of washed-ashore FedEx parcels (including the one containing his Fridayish volleyball), nature (like *Lost*, *Cast Away* is full of beautiful seascapes), and, most importantly, himself. As Stephanie Zacharek would observe in *Salon*, "Hanks might have taken the easy way out and played this lost man as a blank, a character outside of ourselves to be observed from afar and pitied. Instead, he works the miracle of inviting us inside his troubled shell, where loneliness sounds like the rush of the sea, and feels like company." *Cast Away* is more *Robinson Crusoe* than *Lost* or *Lord of the Flies*.

Watching *Cast Away* again after *Lost*, we can't help but wonder. Will we, one day, perhaps years in the future, be tuning in to see the return of the *Lost*aways to civilization? What will have happened to Hurley's millions in his absence? Will Charlie have a new hit album (and record "The Monster Ate the Pilot")? Will Turnip Head grow up happy and well-adjusted in his post-island life? Will Jin escape his servitude to Mr. Paik? Will Kate go to prison? *Cast Away* is at its best when Hanks goes solo, but director Robert Zemeckis is "out of his depth" (Edelstein) in the scenes of human interaction, particularly those that follow Noland's return to Memphis. *Lost*, for all its wonderful, tantalizing mysteries, is at its best in its human interactions. *Lost, The Return* is likely to be riveting.

One final sharp contrast between *Cast Away* and *Lost* makes vividly apparent the difference between movie and television storytelling. In his review of the movie, Roger Ebert found *Cast Away*'s full-of-spoilers marketing disconcerting: "I would have preferred knowing much less about *Cast Away*," Ebert writes. Previews of the movie, in fact, left no doubt about Noland's survival. Such spoilage, Ebert shows, was not the result of "the 20th Century Fox marketing department [giving] away the secrets over the dead body" of director Zemeckis:

> Zemeckis apparently prefers to reveal his surprises in the trailers. He got a lot of flak earlier this year when the ads for his previous film, *What Lies Beneath*, let you know Harrison Ford was the bad guy, there was a ghost, etc. At that time he was quoted in David Poland's Web column: "We know from studying the marketing of movies, people really want to know exactly every thing

that they are going to see before they go see the movie. It's just one of those things. To me, being a movie lover and film student and a film scholar and a director, I don't. What I relate it to is McDonald's. The reason McDonald's is a tremendous success is that you don't have any surprises. You know exactly what it is going to taste like. Everybody knows the menu."

Setting aside the huge question raised by such a statement about Zemeckis' fast-food artistic morals, we might at least ponder the implications of such an attitude for the respective media of film and TV. Zemeckis may be right that moviegoers expect the expected, but surely no one could reach such a conclusion about the small screen? Do *Lost*'s obsessed viewers want to know in advance the answers to any of those questions asked above? Do they want the real nature of the Monster to be revealed in "Next Time on *Lost*"? Do they want the enigma of the Hatch resolved in a tease? Should the coming attractions demystify the Others? "Life," a Zemeckis/Hanks character used to say, is "like a box of chocolates. You never know what you're gonna get." The best of television, including *Lost*, must remains faithful to that Gumpism.

GILLIGAN'S ISLAND
Imagine, if you will, a television series in which the following events transpire:
- Marooned on a Pacific island, castaways try to retool a radio into a transmitter.
- One of the island's new residents is fabulously wealthy. Another is certain he has won millions in a sweepstakes.
- An airplane is discovered in the jungle.
- The new residents are besieged by recurring strange dreams.
- The islanders construct a golf course.
- The newcomers discover that the island is already inhabited by another castaway from a foreign land.

- The island turns out to be inhabited by mysterious others.
- One of the survivors is afflicted with amnesia.
- Another survivor is expected to perform surgery under primitive conditions.
- Plans are made to build a vessel in order to escape.
- A member of a rock group is on the island.
- One of the castaways is believed to be a criminal, perhaps a murderer.
- The islanders discover that their paths have crossed before their fateful journey.
- A mystery attaché case is found.

As a reader of a book on *Lost*, no doubt you are rolling your eyes at such belaboring of the obvious. Even an honorable mention winner in a *Lost* trivia contest can probably identify each of them, chapter and verse. But they were not original with *Lost*. Each of these narrative events can be found as well in a series often considered to be one of the most idiotic in the history of television: *Gilligan's Island*, a half-hour sitcom about a seven-member sight-seeing party on the charter boat *S. S. Minnow* shipwrecked on a South Pacific island.

Running on CBS from 1964 to 1967, *Gilligan's* cast included the Skipper (Alan Hale), a burly, usually jovial, former navy officer; Thurston Howell III (Jim Backus), a supercilious billionaire, who made his fortune on Wall Street; Lovey Howell (Natalie Schafer), his snobbish wife; Ginger Grant (Tina Louise), a beautiful, flirtatious, self-important, and vapid actress; Mary Ann Summers (Dawn Wells), a beautiful, honest, down-to-earth girl-next-door from Kansas; the Professor (Russell Johnson), a high school teacher with a PhD, who possessed an extraordinary breadth of scientific knowledge and was fluent in multiple languages as well; and, of course, Gilligan (Bob Denver), the *Minnow's* second mate, the Skipper's "Little Buddy" and all purpose screw-up (his comedy of errors deep-sixes every possibility of rescue), who finds himself quite happy in his new home.

Some of the *Gilligan* seven likewise share traits in common with the *Lost* fourteen. When the *Gilligan's Island* Fan Club website describes one of the characters as "display[ing] little tact, blam[ing] the Skipper for the shipwreck, and…always trying to break the castaways' laws and bribe others…sneaky, untrustworthy, conniving, greedy, and corrupt," the *Lost* fan might well think, if we substitute Sayid for the Skipper as the recipient of blame, that is (all together now!) Sawyer being described. The Professor certainly reappears in *Lost* as well, although his functions are divided among several different characters: Jack and Leslie Arzt (however briefly) exhibit some of his scientific knowledge, Sayid and Locke inherit his Mr. Fix-it-ness and Locke his survival skills, and at least a trace of his felicity for language emerges in Shannon. The Howells' wealth is passed on to the far more "dudely," far less pretentious, far less wealthy Hurley.

But, thanks to the ever-evolving, deliberate revelations of their backstories, *Lost*'s central characters escape their types and become complex moral human beings we find difficult to judge. The "stupendous stupidity" of *Gilligan's Island* asked nothing from us. Most laughable of all (not meant as a compliment) were the series' preposterous plots. For being a "desert island," *Gilligan's* location was a primary destination for a wide variety of strange visitors. An eccentric pilot drops in. A bank robber makes the island his hideout. A World War II Japanese sailor turns up— twice. An exiled dictator arrives. Two Russian cosmonauts land. A rock group makes the island a hideout from their fans. A mad scientist finds the island a perfect locale for his mad science. A film producer crash lands and wackiness ensues. Other visitors include a surfer, an eccentric painter, a butterfly collector, a game-show contestant, and a big-game hunter. In a 1981 *Gilligan's Island* special that ran fourteen years after the series was cancelled (aka, "put out of its misery"), even The Harlem Globetrotters showed up. The voracious need of television to acquire programs somehow transformed Gilligan's island from a land of the lost into a magnet for the farcical and the inane. If the writers of *Lost* decide to import a lepidopterist just to liven things up, fans and critics will proclaim immediately, loudly, and with one voice that their beloved show has jumped the shark.

Strangely, *Gilligan*, like *Lost*, was full of elements of the fantastic and science fiction. *Gilligan* would offer us episodes in which characters become mind readers, are turned into zombies, switch bodies, and become robots. A robot plummets from the sky and lands on the island. The castaways acquire a rocket pack; find a space capsule; and discover a meteor that causes premature aging. A NASA satellite bound for Mars mistakenly lands on the island and sends back to Houston pictures of the castaways thought to be proof of extraterrestrial life. Every other episode of *Gilligan's* third season makes use of bizarre dream sequences, in which Gilligan becomes an on-trial Jekyll and Hyde, Mrs. Howell is Mary Poppins, and Mary Ann plays Eliza Doolittle. *Gilligan* resorted to such motifs not because of a true generic affinity for them but because they made the generation of new stories possible. Finding new material was a special challenge for *Gilligan's* makers, who had to churn out, in keeping with the network demands of the day, over thirty episodes—thirty-six, thirty-two, thirty—in the show's three seasons. But for all their shared plot and character elements, *Gilligan's Island* can hardly claim to be a true *Lost* ancestor. *Gilligan* was always lost at sea, devoid of any direction, never for a moment aspiring to be anything more than silly rubbish. *Lost* aspires to be suspenseful, mind-blowing, engaging, inventive, memorable. The islands of *Lost* and *Gilligan* are not even in the same archipelago of the imagination.

JURASSIC PARK

Michael Crichton's novel now seems almost prehistoric as an ancestor to *Lost*. The "don't mess with Mother Nature" or even sterner "playing God with species creates problems you can't begin to imagine" theme has been used many times, and the special effects that once seemed innovative in Steven Spielberg's cinematic version seem, well, Jurassic in comparison to *Lost*'s capability to create the moving smoke/Monster, much less the level of dinosaur effects showcased in films like Peter Jackson's *King Kong*. Nevertheless, *Jurassic Park* and *Lost* share an island setting in which scientific "breakthroughs" run amok and frighten the island's inhabitants. In *Jurassic Park*, nature defies scientists' expectations, and dinosaurs take matters (and people) into their own claws. With *Lost*'s Season Two inclusion of the Dharma Initiative and the likelihood that research has indeed gone awry, *Lost* moves closer to *Jurassic Park* in this theme. Spielberg's movie version similarly plays with us through unexpected scares (e.g., in both *Lost* and *Jurassic Park* people are unexpectedly snatched by monsters, whether dinosaurs or the Others) and scenes of growing tension (e.g., a raptor stalks a child in *Jurassic Park*, *Lost*'s Shannon runs toward the unsuspecting Tailies and Ana Lucia's gun). Whereas the temporary visitors to Jurassic Park are able to leave, and new visitors won't likely be invited to this scientific theme park, *Lost*'s castaways aren't that lucky. In fact, they'd probably much rather deal with one consistent reptilian threat than the variety of terrors on their island.

THE LANGOLIERS

As a science fiction novella about a bizarre airline flight, later adapted as a 1995 made-for-TV movie, Stephen King's *The Langoliers* naturally makes the short list of *Lost* ancestor texts. The nine passengers include a British secret agent, a blind psychic girl, a deranged corporate type, a mystery writer, and, conveniently, an off-duty pilot, all bringing with them substantial extra-baggage. They awake on board an American Pride flight from Los Angeles to Boston to discover they are the only people left on a previously full but now pilotless plane. Thanks to the mystery writer, they figure out they have gone through a time warp that (for some reason) obliterates anyone not asleep. At the Bangor, Maine, airport, now existing in a time-outside-of-time, they encounter the Langoliers, ravenous beings (and laughable CGI effects in the movie) that eat up yesterday in order to make room for tomorrow. Retracing their steps, passing this time intentionally through the time warp, they make it back to LAX, and five of the original nine live happily ever after.

If the characters on *Lost* had been as badly developed as *The Langoliers'* depthless stock figures, if its mysteries had been as cheesily probed and explicated, *Lost* would probably have been cancelled by mid-season rather than becoming one of 2004–2005's biggest hits. Still, superficial connections do exist. When Nick Hopewell (the secret agent) makes the obvious observation, in conversation with Brian Engle, the pilot, that all the passengers "were going to Boston for different reasons," the far more interesting backstories of the survivors of Ocean 815 come to mind. When Bob Jenkins, the mystery writer, speculates about possible explanations for the disappearance of their fellow passengers, and later Nick Hopewell recalls all the science fiction he has read and wonders if they might now be in the middle of a sci-fi scenario, we can't help but think of all the fan-generated conspiracy theories and speculations inspired by *Lost's* enigmatic first season. And, at the Bangor Airport, Nick exclaims, in a moment of anger and desperation, a line that might be uttered by any *Lost*away: "I'm starting to feel like Robinson Bloody Crusoe."

LORD OF THE FLIES

Because *Lord of the Flies* (1954) has been one of the most often-read books in American secondary schools for more than thirty years, it would be surprising if it had not influenced the creators of an American television series about the survivors of a plane crash on a desert island.

Written by British novelist and Nobel laureate (1983) William Golding (1911–1993), *Lord of the Flies*, of course, had its own ancestor text. Golding's novel can be read as a revision/repudiation of R. M. Ballantyne's popular Victorian novel, *The Coral Island* (1857), in which shipwrecked proper little subjects of the queen build themselves the very model of a modern British society on a desert island.

As every reader of *Lord of the Flies* (or its CliffNotes) knows, Golding's English schoolboys don't fare quite as well as *The Coral Island*-ers. Survivors of a plane crash and of some distant war they appear to be fleeing (Golding quite intentionally never makes the context clear), the boys must choose between two possible leaders:

- The quiet and serious Ralph, who would establish, with the advice and counsel of pudgy, thoughtful, bookish, bespectacled, asthmatic Piggy, a fledgling democracy on the island
- The aggressive, cruel, and hedonistic Jack.

Lured by the attraction of becoming boys-run-wild—painting their faces, hunting wild boar, enjoying the pleasures of the tribe—Jack and his followers triumph. The only thing they need from Jack and Piggy is the occasional use of the latter's glasses in order to focus the sun's rays to start a fire.

Early on, fear spreads that there is a "Beast" on the loose. And even though the fabled monster is only an air force pilot who crashed and died on the island, Jack finds it convenient to keep the myth alive in order to maintain control over his subjects. A final encounter between Jack and his hunters and Ralph and Piggy results in Piggy's murder with a deliberately toppled boulder. As the forces of Jack stalk Ralph, all are saved by the deus ex machina of the British Navy. At the end, a naval officer inquires whether the boys have put on a "Jolly good show. Like the Coral Island."

A few micro-similarities between *Lord of the Flies* and *Lost* exist (though hardly as many as *Gilligan's Island/Lost*). Both islands have an asthmatic inhabitant: *Lord of the Flies'* Piggy ("Sucks to your ass-mar," repeated by friend and foe alike, is one of the book's most familiar lines) and *Lost's* Shannon. Glasses play a role on each: Piggy's broken, then stolen, lenses not only mark his character but help to drive the plot; on *Lost*, Jack (with an assist from Sayid), provides glasses for the headache-afflicted but constantly reading Sawyer. Both in *Lord of the Flies* and on *Lost*, the desert islanders hunt boar for food. Both narratives have a resident Monster (the real nature of which on *Lost* remains, at the time of writing, unknown).

In its approach to the formation of a new society apart from civilization, however, *Lost* follows a middle road between *The Coral Island* and *Lord of the Flies*. By the end of Season One, the *Lost*aways have not reverted to barbarism, but they have not yet built a stable social order, either. For much of the season, after all, they lived apart as two enclaves, those who remained on the beach and those who had moved to the caves. Though we have yet to see a severance anything like that of Ralph/Jack, we do find oppositions developing clashes between several pairs:

- Jack and Sawyer (over Shannon's missing inhalers, who should keep the marshal's guns)
- Michael and Jin (over Sun)
- Kate and Sawyer (over a discovered briefcase and a place on the raft)
- Sayid and Sawyer (over Sawyer's accusation of Sayid's involvement in the crash and, later, over Sayid's torture of Sawyer)
- Boone and Locke (over Shannon and the Hatch)
- Jack and Locke (over Locke's involvement in Boone's death and their increasingly opposite world views)

In "Exodus" (1.24), Jack himself predicts that the Lostaways may well face a "Locke problem." If that suggestion proves prophetic, *Lost* could well become more like *Lord of the Flies*, as the forces of science and rationality (*Lord of the Flies'* Ralph and Piggy; *Lost's* Jack) do battle with the forces of irrationality (*Lord of the Flies'* animalistic Jack; *Lost's* mystical Locke).

Lord of the Flies' critics have often charged the novel, perhaps justifiably, with being too heavy handed and too allegorical. It does seem to be one of those books John Keats once told us to distrust because it has "a palpable design upon us." At this point in the unfolding narrative of *Lost* it is impossible to conceive of anyone making a similar charge. There may well be a design—its creators insist there is—but we can only barely imagine what it may be and where we are being led. Yet even if it is by a not-yet-perceptible ring in our nose, do we not still go willingly?

LOST HORIZON

Not only does the series share "Lost" in the title, but James Hilton's novel and two resulting films (one a musical) have a plane crash in common. Frank Capra brought the novel to the screen in 1937, a much more dramatic and true-to-the-book version than a 1970s musical remake. However, all versions use a plane crash in a mysterious location as the plot device for the survivors to change their lives.

Capra's film tracks the story of five Westerners stranded in a remote region of mountainous China who are rescued by the inhabitants of the utopian Shangri-La. Hidden from the rest of the world by high mountains, the inhabitants live in a mystical harmony. The visitors undergo profound changes as they spend time in the Valley of the Blue Moon.

Whereas the cause of *Lost*'s plane crash has not yet been revealed, the plane in *Lost Horizon* is hijacked for an unknown reason and flown into Asia. When the plane crashes into the mountains and the pilot is killed, the survivors must figure out where they are and how they are going to survive. In this way, both groups of survivors face similar problems.

As in *Lost*, the survivors are not alone. However, the inhabitants of Shangri-La are friendlier than, if equally mysterious, as the island's Others, Ethan Rom, or Danielle Rousseau.

Lost Horizon's characters often parallel those who are *Lost*. Robert Conway is a respected British diplomat who helped citizens escape China during the 1935 revolution. He is most like Jack, also a well-respected professional, in his ability to lead the survivors and in his search for answers about the plane crash.

Henry Barnard displays many of Sawyer's characteristics; both are criminals trying to get away from the police, enjoy being obnoxious to the other survivors, and are interested in getting their share of life's wealth. Barnard, like Sawyer, is not as bad as his past might indicate. When he discovers gold in the Valley of the Blue Moon, he plans to get at least his share. Like Sawyer, he is out for himself. However, also like Sawyer, the more time he spends in Shangri-La, the less the gold appeals to him. Eventually he begins to work for the greater good instead of looking after only his own interests. Sawyer, at the end of the first season, seems to be moving in a similar direction, although his motivations are still primarily to put himself first, even as he works to help others along the way. This may change as he spends more time on the island (to which he eventually returns in the second season).

Lost Horizon's Alexander Lovett is both suspicious of the mysterious inhabitants and curious about his surroundings. His character often provides humorous insights, and his comments echo the ironic and very human humor that Hurley provides to the island's survivors. Whereas Lovett is sensitive about his more effeminate nature, especially when compared to a strong, manly leader like Conway, Hurley is sensitive about his weight when compared to other men on the island.

Even Chang, the Chinese leader of Shangri-La, parallels Locke in his approach to life. Both characters have a spiritual understanding of and interest in the mysteries of their environment, and both hold back significant pieces of information. They embrace the spiritual elements and seem to understand more about what is going on than they care to share. They are content to remain where they are.

Lost Horizon's crash survivors learn that Shangri-La can provide them with long life; the valley intends to keep them there, and bad things happen to those who try to leave. Although *Lost's* survivors do not know of any benefits provided by the island (Locke is the only exception so far), they find that bad things happen to those who try to leave. The raftaways are attacked by the Others, their craft burned, Walt kidnapped, and Sawyer, Jin, and Michael shot at and abandoned in the ocean. Perhaps, like the refugees who make Shangri-La their permanent home, they will eventually find that living on the island is not as bad as it originally seems.

ROBINSON CRUSOE

Daniel Defoe's 1719 book about a man shipwrecked for twenty-eight years on an island is an obvious ancestor text for *Lost*. The original story has been popular for nearly three hundred years and so is the ancestor of several films and television shows.

Defoe's hero may have written the book for *Lost*'s castaways' behavior; they all seem determined to survive after a wreck, whether ship or plane, and they approach life on the island in remarkably similar ways. Crusoe is the only survivor from his ship and must rely only on himself for several years, until he saves the man he dubs Friday from cannibals and thus gains a companion for the remainder of his stay on the island. It remains to be seen if the *Lost*aways will live on their island as long as Crusoe or have as many encounters with people visiting the island. On the surface, though, Crusoe and the modern castaways share a game plan: 1) Salvage goods from the vessel; 2) find food and water; 3) build a shelter; 4) set up camp for the long haul.

During *Lost*'s first season, the large group of survivors accomplishes these tasks. Like Crusoe returning to his ship, Sawyer and Jack return to the fuselage to gather the supplies each needs, whether *Playboy* magazines and cigarettes for Sawyer or medicine Jack plans to use for the wounded. The other survivors also take what they can from the crash site, making shelter from tarps and metal debris, finding usable clothes in the luggage, picking up whatever items might make their lives more comfortable. Crusoe has the same idea; after painstakingly making his way into the grounded ship, he searches for suitable clothing to take with him, gathers firearms and ammunition, and locates the remaining unspoiled food. He even builds a raft from the ship's planks and masts so that he can float his supplies to shore. Whereas Michael builds a raft on *Lost* in an attempt to escape the island, not return to it, Raft Building 101 seems a must for anyone stranded on an island.

Crusoe easily finds a pure water source and soon begins to hunt birds and fish. Only a few days after the crash, Jack stumbles upon a pure water source in the caves. When the prepackaged food has been eaten, Locke begins to hunt boar, and Jin fishes and prepares food, such as sea urchin, from the ocean. Crusoe digs caves instead of finding them, but both he and *Lost*'s castaways rely on caves for safety and storage.

Fear of wild animals and wild men drives Crusoe to build a fort as his first home. Although the castaways first build flimsy shelters on the beach, several people soon move to the more easily defended caves. Whereas Crusoe discovers human bones on a beach and becomes wary of cannibals who sometimes roam the island, the modern castaways attribute the bones they find in the caves to ritually prepared bodies laid to rest. They only begin to fear the Others on the island when Sayid reports the Frenchwoman's lair and simultaneously Claire and Charlie go missing. Then the level of the castaways' fear of others matches Crusoe's, and they too begin to spend more time building defenses.

With the necessities under control, Crusoe builds a raft so he can explore the island. During *Lost*'s second season, the survivors begin to explore their environment. Jin, Sawyer, and Michael wash ashore on the island and discover "new" people (the Tailies) living there. The progression of events for castaways in general follows an established path, and *Lost*'s survivors seem to walk in the steps of Robinson Crusoe during their first days on the island.

Robinson Crusoe shares other minor plot points with characters from *Lost:*

- Crusoe thankfully has scavenged goods from the ship before the wreckage is washed to sea. The castaways abandon the fuselage, after it has been stripped of usable parts and materials, because a rapidly rising tide begins to wash away the wreckage.

- Crusoe's masted wooden ship may have looked similar to the Black Rock beached miles inland on *Lost*'s mysterious island.
- Like Crusoe, whose family name originally is Kreutznaer, Sawyer changes his name (Ford to Sawyer).
- "Father issues" come into play. Robinson Crusoe fails to take his father's advice and live a comfortable, safe, middle-class life in England. Instead, he chooses to go against his father's wishes and take up a life of adventuring. The senior Crusoe warns his son that he will live a miserable life if he insists on going to sea, but Robinson disregards this warning. Later stranded on the island, Robinson remembers his father's words and wonders if God is punishing him. Several *Lost* characters have disagreed with their fathers and gone their own way; later, on the island, they recall these disagreements. Claire receives a warning from a psychic, but his prediction encourages her to leave home, instead of staying. The psychic tells Claire that her son's life is doomed if she fails to heed the warning to raise her child herself, and this spooky "father figure" seems accurate in his prediction.
- Crusoe keeps a journal of his life on the island, as does Claire.
- While on the island, Robinson Crusoe talks to God and becomes more spiritual. Locke also finds that the island provides him with a miracle; he establishes his own dialogue with the island, his deity.
- Eventually Crusoe is rescued after an encounter with pirates. The Others who take Walt from the raft look like pirates, but rescue by or from anyone hasn't occurred yet.

Defoe's *Robinson Crusoe* became a popular novel in its time and in succeeding centuries because it offered escapist fare that allowed readers to wonder what they might do in a similar situation. It put readers in an exotic location very different from their homeland and gave them the vicarious freedom to do exactly as they pleased. In part, *Lost*'s popularity may be attributed to our interest in the survivor scenario; *Lost* offers us the same opportunity to identify with the castaways while wondering how they would react to island life.

The Stand

The writers and creators of *Lost* have specifically stated on several occasions that Stephen King's 1977 novel *The Stand* never leaves the writers' room. On podcasts and in interviews, Abrams, Lindelof, and Cuse repeatedly hint at the importance of the book, its characters, and storyline. "We took *The Stand*," Cuse has insisted, for example, "and put it on an island." The parallels are indeed remarkable.

King's novel opens with an outbreak of a weapons-grade influenza virus in a secret government weapons facility in the California desert. When the quarantine protocol fails, one man is able to escape along with his wife and child, effectively exposing the rest of the United States population to a super flu popularly known as Captain Tripps, which kills off 99 percent of the population. The novel chronicles the virus' effects and the plight of the immune as they struggle to find potable water and uncontaminated food in a post-flu world. They are involved in a deeper battle as well—one of good versus evil, God versus Satan, as survivors are divided into two distinct camps based on dreams and their inherent goodness (or evilness) as they travel to either Mother Abigail's camp in Boulder, Colorado (the "Free Zone"), or Randall Flagg's in Las Vegas, Nevada.

The threat of disease exists in both *The Stand* and *Lost*. In King's work, disease is the catalyst for all the novel's action. In *Lost* we first hear of its presence on the island when mentioned by Rousseau in "Solitary." The presence of disease reappears when Kate finds "Quarantine" stamped on the inner hull of the Hatch ("Man of Science, Man of Faith," 2.1)—Desmond inoculates himself daily and the mural on the Swan station hatch wall pictorially depicts a deadly sickness. Whatever the disease is, Rousseau explicitly defines it as dangerous—dangerous enough to cause her to kill a crew of researchers that included her husband.

The most obvious parallels between *The Stand* and *Lost* exist in the characters. Several share similar traits and attitudes.

FRANNIE GOLDSMITH AND CLAIRE LITTLETON

The first and most apparent is King's Francis "Frannie" Goldsmith and Claire Littleton. Both women are young and pregnant and struggle with the realities of their pregnancy in less than optimal conditions. Both keep a diary, exhibit similar fears about motherhood and raising their children, and have psychic experiences through dreams. Frannie repeatedly dreams of Mother Abigail, the emissary of goodness who beckons the survivors first to her old homestead in Nebraska and later to Boulder, Colorado. Claire dreams of the *Black Rock* and fuzzy details of her capture. Both are carrying children that have extreme significance. Frannie's child will be the first born in a post-flu world and will let the survivors know if the human race can hope for long-term survival. Claire's child is born on an island that is in quarantine for an unknown disease. Eventually, both Frannie and Claire give birth to male children that do survive: Frannie's Peter fights off Captain Tripps, and Claire's Aaron survives a kidnapping initiated by Rousseau.

LARRY UNDERWOOD, HAROLD LAUDER, AND CHARLIE PACE

Charlie can be seen as a combination of two characters in *The Stand*: Larry Underwood and Harold Emery Lauder. Larry is a one-hit-wonder guitarist and singer with a history of cocaine use who has never been an all-around nice guy. He has let several people down in his life, including his religiously pious mother. At the novel's beginning, as Captain Tripps claims its first victims, Larry is on the run from California after blowing his advance from the record company and owing debt collectors forty thousand dollars. He journeys to New York to hide out with his mother. Larry's quasi-hit, "Baby Can You Dig Your Man," appears throughout the novel, sung by Larry and other characters as an ephemeral thread between the characters and the old world (not unlike DriveShaft's "You All Everybody"). Selfish and self-absorbed before the flu, he only gradually achieves redemption, mostly acquired through witnessing the horrific deaths of his mother and a traveling companion. Charlie, of course, mirrors Larry in his rock star status and his drug use.

But he also calls to mind King's Harold Lauder as well, an inveterate loser devoted to Frannie Goldsmith. When the two are the only survivors in Quantagnut, Maine, Harold positions himself in the role of protector for Frannie in a way similar to Charlie's desire to protect Claire. Mild-mannered and apparently harmless, Harold exhibits a streak of violence that is unexpected and uncontrollable—much like Charlie when he takes revenge on Ethan Rom for kidnapping Claire. In addition, both Harold and Charlie read their beloved's diaries.

STUART REDMAN AND JACK SHEPHARD

Stuart, or "Stu" Redman is a rough-and-tumble East Texan who escapes from the disease control center in Stovington, Vermont. Despite their obvious difference in education and a country drawl that might remind some of Sawyer, Stu most resembles Jack. Like him, Stu becomes a reluctant leader, forced into his role because no one else is there to do it. He uses deadly force only when necessary, a policy Jack also follows. And both serve as shepherds for their wayward flocks, placed in control of the group without requesting the position.

When Stu's traveling party is joined by a man with appendicitis, Stu finds a medical textbook and attempts to save the man by performing an impromptu appendectomy—a surgery that mirrors Jack's futile effort to save Boone. Stu exhibits the same degree of stubborn control that Jack aspires to have, and does not want to give up—even after his patient has died from blood loss.

Named marshal of the Free Zone following Mother Abigail's death, Stu becomes a psychic superconductor, receiving prophetic visions from the beyond. Jack takes on the role of the island's only doctor and its unconventional leader, delegating responsibilities such as burial of the dead, finding a water source, and ushering the survivors to the caves, eventually warming to his role as protector and leader. But Stu and Jack are both coaxed into this role by others, Glen Bateman and John Locke, respectively, who suggest that good, strong leadership is central to the continuity of the new society that they hope to form.

GLEN BATEMAN, TRASHCAN MAN, AND JOHN LOCKE

Locke's character can be understood as an interesting (and conflicting) combination of *The Stand's* Glen Bateman and the "Trashcan Man."

Glen Bateman is a retired sociologist, painter, and all-around philosophical good guy. Accompanied by an Irish Setter (named Kojak) that he found post-flu, Bateman is both practical and realistic. He sees the promise in the social and psychological realities brought about by the flu, the capacity to build a new world in place of the old, predicts the coming order of things, attempts to explain away the supernatural elements all the survivors are experiencing, and remains benevolent throughout the course of the novel. Like Glen, Locke contemplates the needs of their new society long before the other survivors. Like him, he is a counselor and spiritual facilitator for others (see part 3).

Unlike Locke, however, Glen is not a firm believer in the spiritual elements of the survivor's experiences. Locke's profound and unblinking faith in the island does resemble the strange religiosity of *The Stand's* Trashcan Man, who receives visions and dreams that fuel his manic allegiance to Randall Flagg. The Trashcan Man commonly recites the mantra "My life for you!" to Flagg to assure him of his unwavering belief in redemption through facilitating Flagg's dark plans, not unlike Locke's zealous belief that the island will provide the answers to all things and that those answers are "beautiful." The Trashcan Man's obsession with fire leads him to procure an A-Bomb in the desert and bring it back to Flagg's headquarters in Vegas, where it is detonated. Locke exhibits a similar degree of obsession when faced with the challenge of opening the Hatch, and his fondness for collecting—and storing—evidence of the island's more dangerous mysteries (including the Virgin Mary statues packed with heroin) may prove to be his eventual undoing.

RITA BLAKEMOORE AND SHANNON RUTHERFORD

King's Rita Blakemoore is rich and insufferable, and it is only through Larry Underwood's help that she is able to make it out of New York City alive. Rita is accustomed to the finer things in life, has a frivolous attitude, and has no idea how to take care of herself—all characteristics shared by Shannon Rutherford. Rita tries to hike in stylish heeled boots, pops a Valium when reality is too much for her, and is constantly nostalgic about the life she once had. Shannon sunbathes in a bikini and gives herself a pedicure while others seek to recover from the crash. And both Shannon and Rita prove themselves to be extraneous to their stories: Rita kills herself (a drug overdose); Shannon is shot by Ana Lucia.

KATE AND NADINE CROSS

Nadine Cross in *The Stand* struggles with the teeter-totter of good versus evil. She tries to make good by joining up with Larry Underwood, for she sees the capacity for transformation in him and knows he is a good man. But Nadine is drawn inexplicably to the west and Randall Flagg. She is to be his bride, his intended, and in that respect believes herself to be evil. Nadine is attracted to both Larry and Randall in a way that mirrors Kate's attraction for both Jack and Sawyer. As much as Kate wants goodness for herself, and possibly believes that Jack's good nature might finally redeem her, she is drawn to Sawyer. Ultimately Nadine chooses

Flagg and regrets her choice, eventually killing herself in a final attempt to repent.

MOTHER ABIGAIL, MR. EKO, AND ROSE

Although the similarities are minimal, comparisons can be made between *The Stand*'s Mother Abigail and *Lost*'s Mr. Eko and Rose. Mother Abigail is the ultimate good character in *The Stand*. She is 108 years old, communicates with the other survivors through psychic dreams, and has pipeline access to the word of God. She is benevolent and warm and good—all qualities that inspire others to travel across the country to join her. The African American Mother Abigail has traits similar to both Rose and Mr. Eko on *Lost*. Rose, after all, is spiritual and has unwavering faith in her husband's survival, despite his being in the tail section. She prefers to dry her laundry on a clothesline (as does Mother Abigail), and appears to exhibit certain psychic tendencies similar to Mother Abigail's.

In the first half of Season Two, Mr. Eko appears to be religious or spiritual to some extent. He observes forty days of silence to pay penance for those that perished in the crash and the Others he killed on their first night on the island. He carries a stick that he carves as he makes his journey across the island. And he tells Locke an obscure Old Testament story about the long-forgotten King Josiah. Eko's references to scripture are similar to Mother Abigail's—the elderly mother often references scripture in the course of the book, occasionally as hidden clues.

JOE/LEO AND WALT LLOYD PORTER

In *The Stand*, Nadine Cross and "Joe" find Larry following the death of Rita Blakemoore, and Larry spends a great deal of time helping to care for the two. Nadine found Joe in a grocery store, abandoned, mute, and feral. The child cannot communicate and often reacts with a predatory anger toward those who try to touch or confine him, and it is only with careful provocation that he emerges from his silent shell. When the boy finally becomes comfortable with Nadine and Larry, he informs them that his name is Leo, and from that moment on, Leo acts as a psychic conductor, knowing things about people that no ordinary child would know. Leo is first to notice Harold's deceit, and perceives Nadine's darkness as soon as she commits herself to her destiny as the Dark Man's bride.

Leo's psychic ability is similar to Walt's on *Lost*: both boys are able to perceive the thoughts and feelings of others, and both can read the goodness or badness inherent in others. The boys also share an interesting vengeful streak: Leo attempts to stab Larry several times as he sleeps; Walt burns down his father's first raft so they cannot leave the island. Seeking mentors, they both form relationships with men other than their father: Leo seeks out and bonds with Larry, and Walt grows close to Locke.

THE BLACK ROCK

A black rock exists in both *The Stand* and *Lost*. Randall Flagg's symbol, worn by his followers, is a black stone marked with a red flaw, on more than one occasion is referred to as "the Black Rock." The Black Rock in *The Stand* is able to change shape and meaning. Flagg turns it into a key on more than one occasion—the key to the demonic kingdom that all his followers are promised.

The *Black Rock* in *Lost*, first mentioned in the paranoid mumblings of Rousseau, is a marked location on her map and a place on the island that she avoids. By the end of Season One, we learn that the *Black Rock* is a run-aground, masted slave ship of unknown age and origin that, among other things, houses some very old dynamite. Rousseau's hesitation to go on board the ship indicates that the place is more frightening and sinister than she is willing to say. The ambiguity of the ship's name (and unanswered questions about its meaning or how it got on the island) closely parallel the ephemeral concept of the black rock that Randall Flagg's followers wear.

ANIMALS

Animals appear as symbolic in both *The Stand* and *Lost*: Randall Flagg often appears as a crow or sends out packs of gray wolves to do his bidding and spying. Rats swarm the cornfields in front of Mother Abigail's homestead, and she attributes the rodents to "the Devil's Imp"—Randall Flagg.

On the island, the Others have sharks and polar bears that appear to display significance—especially the shark emblazoned with a Dharma logo. A black horse may be the animal embodiment of Kate's dead father, and Charlie is inspired to break his heroin addiction thanks to a magnificent moth.

Kojak in *The Stand* and Vincent on *Lost* are both extraordinary dogs. Kojak survives a few encounters with the Dark Man's wolves and tracks across the country looking for his owner, Glen Bateman. Vincent goes missing on several occasions in Seasons One and Two, most notably his disappearance and reappearance following the crash. Kojak is even the point of view character for a passage in the course of *The Stand*, a dog's-eye-view of his journey and all the perils encountered along the way. Damon Lindelof admits that he had initially hoped to close out the first season with an episode from Vincent's perspective, but discarded the idea after news of the concept leaked out onto the Internet.

SPIES AND SPYING

Spying is pivotal to the narrative of *The Stand*, as the Free Zone elects to send out three spies to explore the west and learn more about Randall Flagg. The Others in *Lost* have also used at least one spy, Goodwin, to ascertain the "good" and "bad" survivors from Oceanic Flight 815 before he is killed by Ana Lucia. Although the writers have never established Ethan Rom or Nathan as Others, the audience has collectively assumed them to be spies.

THE STAND MINISERIES

The filmed version of *The Stand* was a network television miniseries event in 1994, starring Rob Lowe, Molly Ringwald, and Gary Sinese. Some notable additions to the filmic text appear to influence *Lost*. The dog Kojak is a yellow Labrador retriever in the miniseries, not an Irish setter, and truly resembles Vincent. The black rock necklace Flagg's followers wear is completely black, without the red flaw described in the book.

In the miniseries Harold delivers two lines that are not in the book but echo with *Lost* significance. He says to Frannie that their survival of the flu is as lucky as winning the Megabucks Lottery. Hurley's winning lottery ticket on *Lost* was from none other than Megabucks. When Harold turns against the committee in the Free Zone and makes a bomb with dynamite, he explains that dynamite sweats nitroglycerin—a line that Arzt echoes prior to his death in "Exodus" (1.23).

Until the end of the series, it is impossible to know every parallel between *The Stand* and *Lost*. Several characters, most notably Sawyer, Ana Lucia, and Michael, have no clear ancestors in *The Stand*. In time, these connections may appear, as well as even greater resonance between the two texts.

SURVIVOR

Mark Burnett's inventive castaway reality series *Survivor* premiered in the U.S. on CBS in 2000. The original premise: sixteen castaways are forced to "outwit, outlast, and outplay" fellow contestants while creating a "new society" on a deserted island as they are competing for a million-dollar reward. The series secured a several-season reign at the top of the Nielsen's and has consistently remained in the top ten during new-run episodes.

Separated into two tribes of eight, the contestants spend thirty-nine to forty-one days roughing it in the middle of nowhere, without any modern conveniences or potable water. The castaways forage for their own food (many of the early seasons included a tin of rice for sustenance, but viewer demand for harsher conditions eventually led to full deprivation); locate a water source, build a shelter, start a fire, and compete in bi-weekly challenges for both reward and immunity. Every three days, the losing team has to face the dreaded Tribal Council, where one is ceremoniously voted off the island.

When Steve McPherson, former head of programming for ABC television, suggested a drama with *Survivor*-like undertones—the show that would eventually become *Lost*—the reception was less than warm. *Survivor's* appeal to audiences is based on the dramatic component of the challenges and tribal council sessions; group dynamics were simply a sideshow. Marrying *Survivor's* high concept to drama and suspense required a significant outside force—in the case of *Lost* a big-island mystery that could keep the emotions running high and the audience hooked.

Lost is often linked to *Survivor* in the print media; the first season was often described as *"Survivor* meets *Lord of the Flies* meets *The X-Files."* Mid-Season One, Fox's *Mad TV* offered a parody of the series, where the *Lost* castaways journey through the dense jungle to discover Jeff Probst, who prompts them to participate in a reward challenge.

THE THIRD POLICEMAN

When Desmond hurriedly packs a few belongings before he bolts from his underground home ("Orientation," 2.3), the camera briefly shows a copy of Flann O'Brien's novel, *The Third Policeman*. Prior to the episode's first airing, rumors circulated that this book is important to understanding what is happening on *Lost*, especially during the second season. Fans rushed to order the book to learn about any similarities between O'Brien's dark tale of life after death and the castaways' fate.

At first glance, *The Third Policeman* seems to go against what *Lost*'s creators have assured fans is *not* going on: O'Brien's main character, the story's narrator, is dead, although he fails to understand that for most of the novel. *Lost*'s creators have insisted in numerous interviews that the castaways are not dead or living in some kind of purgatory.

The narrator's journey involves a strange visit with two policemen at their station and on their rounds. Along the way, the student-turned-writer-turned-thief-turned-murder-victim learns about the absurd nature of the world he now inhabits. Bicycles, for example, not only meld with their owners physically and emotionally after they spend so much time riding together, but they also have a mind of their own. They are an excellent example of the way "atomic theory" works; the atoms of humans and machines interact and eventually merge. Even more interesting, a mysterious vault contains whatever riches the policemen and the narrator can imagine; whatever can be desired or imagined is provided. However, there is one catch: the goods cannot be taken above ground.

This last point may hold clues about *Lost*'s Hatch. After all, Desmond has been living below ground apparently for a long time, and before him, Kelvin manned Station Three; the walls bear the marks of someone counting off scores of days. Still, without regular deliveries of supplies, the Hatch's pantry is marvelously stocked with everything from food to candy to shampoo. The Hatch already provides the castaways who learn about it with what they want. (Locke and Hurley find it difficult to keep secrets about what they have seen.) Kate has a shower and washes her hair. Charlie finally gets real peanut butter for Claire and perks up when he hears that Desmond has a record player. Locke finds purpose in button pushing. Hurley, however, takes the pantry's remaining goodies to distribute among the castaways on the beach—O'Brien's rule about not taking the wealth out of the Hatch does not seem to apply on *Lost*.

By the end of O'Brien's novel, the narrator finally meets the third policeman, who reveals to him the strange nature of time and space. They are not what living people presume, and the narrator discovers that what seems to have taken place only moments or hours before actually occurred in real time several years ago. He now can travel through walls or even back to his old home to visit with the partner who did him in for his share of pilfered wealth. O'Brien does more than create a good ghost story; he develops a "real" surreal world that plays with our notions of space and time, life and death.

If *The Third Policeman* really contains clues about the nature of *Lost*'s mysterious island, the island is not so mysterious after all; it merely operates under a different set of rules for a different reality. Already we might question how such a large island can be off the rest of the world's GPS finder; Sawyer says as much in "Exodus" (1.23) and the number of inhabitants revealed in later second season episodes also alludes to a much larger island than the castaways previously explored. Time also is an issue—how long has the Dharma Initiative been operational? Could the castaways really have been on the island much longer than forty days during the first season's episodes? Damon Lindelof suggests that time may not be what we think; time should be measured pre- and post-crash, not in terms of 2004 or 2005 dates.

O'Brien's novel has been called "darkly comedic" in critical reviews. If it does not contain as many clues as rumored, perhaps *Lost*'s creators and writers are having the last laugh as we are left clueless but more literate after reading *The Third Policeman*.

THE TURN OF THE SCREW

As Locke looks for the Dharma Initiative orientation video just where Desmond told him it would be—"top shelf, right behind *The Turn of the Screw*"—for just a moment the Dover edition of the classic Henry James's ghost story fills the left half of the screen. Set in a country house called Bly, not on a desert island, James's story is really the diary of a young governess who has become convinced that the two small children she cares for, Miles and Flora, are demonically controlled by their former governess, Miss Jessel, and her lover, a servant names Peter Quint. The book has inspired a variety of readings since its publication in 1898, with some critics taking it to be a true tale of the supernatural and others convinced everything is in the mind of the young governess, who has projected the haunting out of her own repressed sexuality.

Other than serving (like *The Third Policeman*) as Desmond's reading material, is *The Turn of the Screw* a *Lost* ancestor text? Mysterious children under the thrall of "Others"; the presence of ghosts—or are they?; an indecipherable text, capable of multiple interpretations. These factors make *The Turn of the Screw* a must for the Hatch bookshelf, but it is clearly not a major source.

THE TWILIGHT ZONE

During the pilot episode of *Lost*, the camera pans to a dark sky teeming with stars. The shot lingers as the stars twinkle over the castaways. The scene emphasizes just how alone the survivors really are, so far from any human-made lights, so small in the scope of the universe. According to series' cocreator Damon Lindelof, this scene also welcomes the castaways to *The Twilight Zone*.

When *Lost*'s writers and creators were growing up, they loved TV series like Rod Serling's masterpiece. How fitting for their own creepy crawly series to include in the very first episode a fond salute to the master. *The Twilight Zone* opens with Serling's narration of the week's episode and a slow pan to the starry night as viewers, and that week's cast of characters, are welcomed. Like *Lost*'s island, the *Zone* is a familiar land with weird twists that play with and prey on the imagination.

Although Serling is often solely credited with *The Twilight Zone*'s development and success, much as J. J. Abrams often is singularly praised for *Lost*, Serling worked with two other writers to craft what many viewers and critics believe is one of the finest science fiction shows ever. Charles Beaumont and Richard Matheson shared writing credits with Serling for the series' episodes. These writers are well known in their own right; in fact, Stephen King, among other writers, has noted Matheson's influence on his writing. (Beyond his connection to *The Twilight Zone*, Matheson adapted Edgar Allan Poe's works in scripts for films such as *The Pit and the Pendulum*, and his original book *I Am Legend* was immortalized on film twice: *The Last Man on Earth* and *The Omega Man*.) In a six degrees of separation way, Matheson influenced King who also, in turn, influenced Abrams, Lindelof, and other *Lost* writers through *The Stand*. The science fiction community is, indeed, an incestuous place.

Although Matheson, Beaumont, and Serling wrote the episodes, the idea for *The Twilight Zone* came from Serling. Unlike Abrams and company, who were encouraged to produce *Lost*'s pilot episode, which was quickly bought upon viewing and put into production by ABC, Serling had a tougher time convincing CBS executives of *Twilight Zone*'s merits.

Serling wrote "The Time Element" as the first *Twilight Zone* episode—an hour-long drama about a man traveling to Pearl Harbor just before the attack in December 1941. To the man's frustration, his knowledge from the future fails to persuade Hawaiian residents and officials that a disaster is imminent. Ironically, the time traveler dies during the bombing, and therefore all evidence of his life after 1941 is erased.

This episode was produced by Desilu, the production company established by Desi Arnaz Sr. and Lucille Ball. After this first *Twilight Zone* aired, Arnaz appeared on stage (after all, the broadcast was live) to provide a logical explanation for the plot: the time traveler is merely a dreaming scientist, and the visit to the past a figment of his dream. *The Twilight Zone* provided a different kind of television viewing in the 1950s and early 1960s; audiences were accustomed to linear story lines enacted live like a televised play. Science fiction with possibly multiple interpretations offered a new experience, and many viewers apparently were not quite ready.

Lost also faces this dilemma—whether to embrace its science fiction nature (at the peril of network executives' displeasure and possible ratings decline) or to hedge the writers' meaning within layers of possible explanations for each event on the island. As with *The Twilight Zone*, hardcore viewers watch just to unravel the many possible meanings and to discuss what might be interpreted logically or mystically.

This "second pilot," or first aired episode within the framework of the regular series, is far less complicated than "The Time Element." A man finds himself alone in a deserted town; the loneliness is oppressive. When he presses the traffic button at a crosswalk, he inadvertently pushes a panic button, and the experiment in which he is participating ends. In reality, the man is an astronaut in training; he has been hallucinating in an isolation booth.

The theme of loneliness or isolation crops up frequently in *The Twilight Zone*, and isolation, whether from the world at large or other castaways, also is prominent on *Lost*. Many other common themes link the two series:

- *The characters' journey is the audience's journey*: The opening narration to "Where Is Everybody?" explains that "the journey into the shadows that we're about to watch could be our journey." *The Twilight Zone* can be found anywhere; anyone can stumble into it. So it is with *Lost*. Their journey could be our journey on an ill-fated flight, but more importantly, their personal struggles with themselves and each other are very much like our daily concerns. We could venture into *The Twilight Zone* just as easily as we could be *Lost* in our lives or the larger world.

- *Paranoia resulting in misunderstandings or violence*: Although episodes like "The Shelter," in which neighbors fight over the lone homemade bomb shelter, emphasize mistrust between people who should know each other well, Serling's classic episode "The Monsters Are Due on Maple Street" shows urban paranoia at its finest. The anticipated Monsters lead neighbors to fear and suspect each other, leading to gunfire between friends. Even in *Lost*'s pilot episode, Sawyer calls Sayid a terrorist, instigating a fight. In "Abandoned"

(2.6) Ana Lucia mistakes Shannon as one of the Others and shoots her. Characters frequently suspect each other's motives (or misinterpret information) and jump to conclusions, sometimes with violent results.

- *Second chances, or the ability to start a new life*: In "A Passage for Trumpet," a musician gets a second chance at life; a guardian angel starts the day over for a better result in "Mr. Bevis." Throughout several *Lost* episodes, characters, most notably Jack and Locke, remind each other that life on the island allows them all a chance to start over, to become new (and possibly improved) people.

- *The ability to create a personal reality, or the power to make something happen*: Both *Lost* and *The Twilight Zone* explore the possibilities that people create—or visualize and then materialize—what they need. Walt, deemed "Special" (1.14) by the "fathers" in his life (stepdad Brian, Michael, and mentor Locke), may be able to create the reality he wants. After all, a bird and a polar bear seem to appear shortly after Walt reads about them; Locke teaches Walt to visualize throwing a knife into a bullseye, and the boy succeeds on his first try after seeing it happen in his mind. In "The Mind and The Matter," Serling gives a man who reads a book about thought the ability to create his own world. A playwright's characters come to life as he writes about them in "A World of His Own." The closest link to Walt, however, takes place in another classic episode, "It's a Good Life." A young boy, demonically portrayed by freckle-faced Billy Mumy, has the power to change people and objects into whatever he wants; adults quickly learn to praise the boy for these changes, for fear that he will turn them into something bad if he becomes unhappy. If the Others believe Walt has such power, the castaways may have much to fear in the future.

- *Mysterious flights*: *Lost*'s survivors beat incredible odds when their plane breaks up midair. The aircraft's rear section falls away, as do the cockpit and first class section. During the first season, we follow the adventures of people from the middle section that lands roughly in one piece on the beach. Mysteriously, most of the forty-eight survivors have only minor injuries, when no one logically should have survived. Earlier flights of Serling's fancy include "The Odyssey of Flight 33," in which a plane breaks the time barrier and lands in a prehistoric past, and "The Arrival" of a plane whose passengers mysteriously vanished, leaving an empty plane to land. Perhaps a closer connection between Oceanic 815's flight with one or more of Serling's airborne episodes will be revealed, as Lindelof promises that *Lost*'s flight has not been downed by any terrorist action. Something else, possibly mysterious, caused the plane's destruction.

- Other themes, including time travel, space travel, nuclear war, death and the afterlife, and sentient machines, may be tangentially linked to *Lost*. For example, at the end of the first season, the Monster increasingly seems to have a mechanical basis. If so, *Lost* echoes *Twilight Zone*'s many episodes in which machines of all types think and act, often to the peril of the people around them.

Lost shares common themes and values with *The Twilight Zone*. The best episodes make viewers think; they scramble audiences' perceptions of the way the universe works; they have a message, although they seldom are heavy handed in delivering it. They bring in elements of the fantastic, but, as characters and viewers discover, the worst monsters come from their imaginations. People are often the monsters that other people should fear most, and human acts resulting from fear, paranoia, and "group think" often provide the greatest terror.

TWIN PEAKS

The ABC television series *Twin Peaks* (1990–1991) would count as a *Lost* ancestral text even if it hadn't figured prominently in the thinking of both the network executives and show creators who put *Lost* on the air in the fall of 2004. Virtually every important maker of end-of-the-millennium and early twenty-first-century TV, from Joss Whedon to David Chase to J. J. Abrams, has spoken of their debt to David Lynch and Mark Frost's bizarre tale of Special Agent Dale Cooper's investigation of the murder of prom queen Laura Palmer in the small Northwestern town of Twin Peaks. ABC knew full well to expect something out of the ordinary from Lynch (director of *Eraserhead*, *Elephant Man*, and *Blue Velvet*) and Frost (*Hill Street Blues*), though they may not have anticipated a woman who communed with her log, a dancing dwarf, unforgettable dream sequences, crime-solving through Tibetan rock throwing, and a supernatural parasitic being named BOB. Described in one early press story as the "show that will change TV," *Twin Peaks* quickly became a cultural event but flamed out early in its second season, abandoned by a once-huge audience that quickly grew weary of its difficult-to-follow metaphysics and over-the-top quirkiness.

But the thoroughly postmodern (it riffed on/sampled scores of movies, TV shows, and works of literature, from *Double Indemnity* to Arthurian legends) and genre-mixing (was it a soap opera? a sitcom? a police procedural? an FBI drama? a coffee commercial?) *Twin Peaks* did make it possible for television creators to think outside the box. It is hard to imagine ABC allowing J. J. Abrams to morph the basic "plane crashes on an island" idea into the series *Lost* has become without the splendid failure of *Twin Peaks* in its collective past.

Though not nearly as postmodern as *Twin Peaks*—it is not often self-referential, nor strongly intertextual, nor is it fond of quoting from other shows—*Lost* certainly is genre bending. As we watch, we are never quite certain which genre-spectacles to don in order to facilitate our close reading of either its present tense or backstory narratives. An old Sufi tale describes how several men touching different parts of an elephant offer dissimilar reports on the reality before them. Depending on where we encounter the *Lost* elephant, we too might well make very different genre reports.

As Jack operates (in present and past tense) we may think we are watching a medical drama. When Boone sleeps with his stepsister Shannon or Sun and Jin's marriage goes awry, we may think melodrama. As terrifying noises fill the night and a mysterious Monster roams the island, we are afraid *Lost* may turn out to be horror. In the aftermath of Oceanic 815's crash (and in the frighteningly realistic flashbacks to the catastrophic event that broke the plane apart), we might well think we are watching a disaster movie. Flashback after flashback incrementally revealing the backgrounds of all the major characters might mislead us into thinking *Lost* is really an anthology drama. Its many mysteries— Locke's inexplicable ability to walk, the baffling appearance on the island of Jack's father, Walt's psychic ability, the magical power of the numbers that have altered Hurley's life—might make us think *Lost* is some kind of supernatural tale, an exercise in what is sometimes called the fantastic. *Lost*, of course, damn it, never insists on how we should understand it, and in this openness to mystery lies its greatest debt to *Twin Peaks* and its most significant heir, *The X-Files*.

Later in this book (in chapter 7) we detail the many conspiracy theories *Lost* has inspired in its avid fans. That too, we should note in closing, is *Twin Peaks'* legacy. One of the first television series to truly energize its fan base (see Henry Jenkins's essay in *Full of Secrets*), *Twin Peaks* inspired obsessive theorizing; its long-delayed answer to its central question (Who Killed Laura Palmer?) only fed the flames. In addition to nominating all the usual subjects, fanatics would also suggest that Laura's murderer was (a) an often-used-as-a-transitional-image traffic light and (b) the ceiling fan in Laura Palmer's house. Crazy people enjoy TV, too. But then again, we did learn in *Twin Peaks: Fire Walk with Me*, the series' feature film prequel, that BOB, Laura's actual killer (using her father as his agent), traveled throughout weirdsville via the electrical system, including that ceiling fan at the top of the stairs...

WATERSHIP DOWN

As Sawyer puts it in "Confidence Man" (1.8), Richard Adams's *Watership Down* is a nice little story about bunnies. So what does it have to do with *Lost*? At the story level, *Watership Down* creates turmoil among the castaways when Boone sees Sawyer reading the book. Boone assumes the book is his. He placed a copy in his checked luggage, which leads him to the conclusion that Sawyer must have found the bag and confiscated his belongings. Therefore, Shannon's medication also should be in the luggage, because Boone always packed extra inhalers for his sister. When Shannon suffers an asthma attack, there is little Boone won't do to case her suffering. Ransacking Sawyer's belongings and being beaten as a result seem a small price—if the medication can be found. The inhalers are nowhere near, and Sawyer is accused of hiding the medication.

Of course, as with most plot points in the *Lost* world, the book is a misleading clue. Sawyer claims, even after torture, that he picked up the book on the beach. If indeed this copy comes from Boone's luggage, the rest of the bag's contents are scattered. Perhaps the copy came from another passenger, although it's questionable just how many people would bring *Watership Down* on a flight more than thirty years after the book's publication and even long past the release of a filmed version.

The series' fans quickly picked up on *Watership Down* as a possible ancestor text that could provide clues about the writers' direction for *Lost*'s upcoming scripts. After all, the rabbits face danger in their familiar world and escape toward what they hope will be a safer place. Although *Lost*'s castaways are forced to live on the island instead of choosing to leave their homes, their encounters with dangerous monsters often parallel the rabbits.'

When rabbit leader Hazel finds what seems to be a secure place with plenty of food, friendly rabbits, and few predators, this paradise quickly proves to be too good to be true. Just as the survivors of Oceanic 815 find threats within their Eden, Hazel discovers that his paradise hides deadly traps. The newly arrived rabbits discover for themselves the dangers lurking within the lush fields. Cowslip, a spokesrabbit for the group already ensnared in this environment, knows about the deadly wire snares. He not only fails to share that information but refuses to help free a trapped newcomer. It seems that a few casualties are to be expected as a fair trade for plenty of food and relative safety from such monsters as dogs and birds. Perhaps Rousseau is the island's Cowslip, who is aware of the dangers and traps but only shares knowledge reluctantly once Sayid infiltrates her camp.

The rabbits face many monsters and dangers on their trek to a new home, just as the castaways discover ever more perils await them as they explore the island. Not everyone survives, but those who do are stronger for their struggles. As the rabbits band together during their journey, they develop a new society, with leaders and visionaries to guide the way and help them fend off rival groups.

The castaways do the same. Jack is given, rather than demands, leadership; he guides the survivors toward safe shelter and develops strategies to protect his people from the Others. The same is true of Hazel, who recognizes danger and formulates plans for keeping the rabbits safe. *Watership Down*'s Fiver seems to have a sixth sense; his dreams often provide knowledge of current or future events beyond his experience. As a visionary, Fiver rivals Locke, who also seems to have mystical knowledge of current and future events.

Part of the enjoyment of reading *Watership Down* is understanding the larger world from a rabbit's eye view. When Bigwig is nearly run down by a car one afternoon, he glories in the feel of wind rushing through his fur. He isn't afraid of the monster when it drives past. Bigwig believes the car can't hurt him during daylight. When the other rabbits point out roadkill, Bigwig explains that the monster only kills at night. Then its large, bright eyes lure animals into its path of destruction.

In a similar way, during "Exodus" (1.24), Locke courts what Jack perceives as disaster when the older man allows himself to be dragged away and into a hole. Locke tells Jack that he'll be all right, but Jack insists that Kate blow up the Monster in order to free Locke, an act that Locke finds unnecessary. Locke firmly believes that he will not be hurt, but only tested, by the Monster. Perhaps those who understand the nature of the island (at the end of Season One, their identity remains unknown) might smile at Locke's description of the Monster just as human readers understand more than rabbits do about cars.

Watership Down also parallels *Lost* with a common title. In the chapter "Deus ex Machina," Hazel is saved from certain death by a cat when the cat's owner, a young girl, discovers her pet poised to kill the injured rabbit. The girl cuffs the cat and carries Hazel into the house, where Hazel's injuries can be tended. In the episode "Deus Ex Machina" (1.19) Locke is saved from possible death when he is disabled and can't climb into the plane that he and Boone find in the jungle. Instead, Boone climbs into the plane and, moments later, tumbles to what will be his death.

Watership Down's deus ex machina is truer to the original theatrical definition of a god swooping down to save the day, often carrying off the hero in the process. The girl suddenly appears, gets rid of the cat in the nick of time, and lifts Hazel to safety. True to its premise of "what you see may not be at all what you get," *Lost's* deus ex machina has flown in years before, and instead of lifting a hero out of harm's way, crashes him to earth (and death). However, the plot device does radically change the direction of the story. As Locke explains to Jack during "Exodus," everything after the discovery of the plane leads to the opening of the Hatch, the event that Locke feels is most significant to their life on the island.

Although *Watership Down* can't be used as a blueprint for *Lost*'s plotlines, it does provide some similarities in characters and story. Perhaps more importantly, it provides Sawyer with another framework for making sense of his and the other castaways' experiences on the island.

A WRINKLE IN TIME

Madeleine L'Engle's Newberry Award-winning young adult science fiction action-adventure was published in 1962 and is widely considered a classic. The book focuses on the Murry family, primarily Meg, who goes on a journey across space, time, and alternate dimensions to find her missing father, a physicist named Alex. Alex had been working on a theory involving a tesseract as a way to travel through time, and one day had gone missing mysteriously, effectively abandoning his family.

Early in Season One, Sawyer is seen reading the book on the beach, his follow-up choice to *Watership Down*. *A Wrinkle in Time* is an ancestor text not only due to its appearance in the series, but also because of interesting parallel connections between central characters and themes throughout the book. Meg's youngest brother, Charles Wallace, is described to readers as "different"— a difference not unlike Walt's. Both Charles Wallace and Walt, extremely perceptive, if not psychic, appear to know things before they happen.

Meg encounters Mrs. Whatsit, an interesting figure who informs Meg, Charles Wallace, and Mrs. Murry that "there *is* such a thing as a tesseract." Meg and Charles Wallace pair up with Calvin O'Keefe, one of Meg's schoolmates, and travel to another dimension with the help of Mrs. Whatsit and her two equally eccentric sisters, Mrs. Who and Mrs. Which. They utilize the tesseract to "wrinkle," or travel across dimensions, so that they can overcome a mysterious darkness. The darkness is a shadow that is described in *A Wrinkle in Time* as "not even as tangible as a cloud," a cloud that seems similar in description to the shadowy black *thing* seen over the exploding engine in the Pilot (1.1) and again in "Exodus" (1.24). Since tesseracts make travel to other dimensions possible, the idea proved convenient for fans seeking a "scientific" explanation for the castaways' appearance on an uncharted island.

Other parallels exist: Mrs. Who loans the children her magical glasses to help them see the "reality" of their situation, not unlike the glasses that are crafted for Sawyer so he can be relieved of headaches caused by his far-sightedness. Charles Wallace is even abducted in the course of the novel by the sinister force behind the ominous CENTRAL Central intelligence—IT, a being whose thirst for control and domination had resulted in populating the universe, in the name of science, with emotionless, thoughtless creatures. The similarities between *Wrinkle's* IT and the Others are obvious. When Charles Wallace, under IT's control, states, "Perhaps you do not realize that on Camazotz we have conquered all illness, all deformity," we cannot help but think of the Hanso foundation, whose mission statement includes its goal "to further the evolution of the human race and provide technological solutions to the most pressing problems of our time."

THE X-FILES

One of *Lost's* key characters, Hurley, does share a last name with Agent Monica Reyes (Annabeth Gish) from *The X-Files'* final season (2001–2002), and Robert Patrick (Agent John Doggett on the series [2000–2002]) and Terry O'Quinn (who appeared in a second season episode ["Aubrey," 2.2] and in *The X-Files* movie [1998]) do show up on *Lost*—as Hibbs, the man who sets up Sawyer to kill his namesake in Australia in "Outlaws" (1.16), and Locke, respectively. Unlike *Gilligan's Island* or even *Lord of the Flies*, however, the Fox Television series *The X-Files* (1993–2002) shared few if any story elements with *Lost*, and yet it stands as a key ancestor text in many respects.

Created by Chris Carter, *The X-Files* followed the investigations of two FBI special agents: the "I want to believe," open-to-all-things-occult, convinced "the truth is out there" Fox Mulder (David Duchovny) and the medical doctor and skeptic Dana Scully (Gillian Anderson), assigned to investigate the agency's most "out there" cases. (The series had its own ancestor texts, of course: the Watergate hearings, television programs like *The Night Stalker* [ABC, 1972–1975] and *Twin Peaks*, books like John Mack's *Abduction: Human Encounters with Aliens* [1994].) The show became first a cult hit and then a mainstream success that played a pivotal role in the establishment of Fox as a bona fide network.

Its fan base was rabid, producing some of the most brilliant, comprehensive, and ingenious websites to date and penning tons of fanfiction that not only consummated (at last!) the PST (Prolonged Sexual Tension) of Mulder/Scully but "relation-shipped" all sort of other characters as well, including Mulder and Director Walter Skinner. But Fox was not kind to its fans, often shutting down websites for copyright infringement when they were contributing mightily to the series' growing populari-ty. In a later century, the creators of *Lost* would stroke the very fans Fox would counterproductively alienate.

Though *Lost* has no FBI agents and offers no police procedural, it does replicate several *X-Files* traits: its pairing of believer and doubter (on *Lost*, Locke and Jack, respectively); its casting of relative unknowns in its key roles, with Matthew Fox as Jack and Evangeline Lilly as Kate replicating the Duchovny/Anderson pairing (both the male leads were somewhat better known, both the women were complete unknowns); but perhaps the greatest similarity between the two series lies in their similar openness to the mystery.

The X-Files was a show so resistant to closure—to satisfactory resolution of the myriad questions each individual story and its overarching mythology episodes introduced—that it even self-referentially joked about it. "Whatever 'out there' truth Mulder and Scully discovered in the hour—whatever evidence they accu-mulated, by means of his intuitions or her careful science, of the existence of the paranormal or the supernatural or of vast conspiracies—dissipated or evaporated before the closing credits." In *Lost*'s *Black Rock*, Dark Territory, Others, polar bears, Monster, and Hatch, we find echoes of *The X-Files*' reliance on its own recurring mysteries: the alien bounty hunter, the black oil, the Cigarette-Smoking Man, the Syndicate, the Well-Manicured Man, the bees, the alien rebels, supersoldiers... By the end of its run, however, many, if not most, *X-Files* regulars had grown tired of its mysteries without end. Marketing, on TV and in print, constantly promised that our questions would be answered, but they never were, and even more were raised.

Writing recently about *The X-Files*' unhappy end in the *Chicago Tribune*, Joshua Klein would, not surprisingly, think of *Lost*: "TV watchers may currently sense a similar situation in the mysterious *Lost*, the finale of which angered viewers by failing to answer any of the many questions raised during its first season." Klein asked the man himself, *X-Files* creator Chris Carter, what he thinks of *Lost*.

> I'm a big fan of J .J. Abrams. I think he's really creative, and I'm a big fan of what he does. But I know there are pits to fall into, and you've got to avoid them every step of the way. It takes a lot of thought and gut instinct. I can tell you that with mythology shows, if you stumble, you fall.

Lost's makers are well aware of the dilemma, and they don't anticipate stumbling anytime soon.

No doubt *Lost* will itself soon become an influential ancestor text for other narratives, in the process spreading not only its unique seeds but those of the books, movies, and television series to which it is indebted.

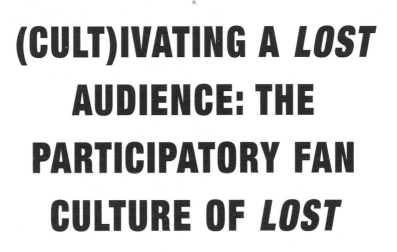

CHAPTER SEVEN

(CULT)IVATING A *LOST* AUDIENCE: THE PARTICIPATORY FAN CULTURE OF *LOST*

"[Lost fans are] like Talmudic scholars. They have created a body of scholarship about every episode."
—JAVIER GRILLO-MARXUACH

The first decade of the twenty-first century has been a golden age for television fans. Once routinely portrayed as obsessive losers in need of a life, fans have now come out of the closet, flocking to conventions where they can meet their favorite show's actors, actresses, and prime movers, trawling the Internet in search of the latest information (including, for some, spoilers—advance knowledge of future developments), writing fanfiction, and TiVoing episodes for later frame-by-frame inspection. No series has inspired fans more than *Lost*, and no television show has done more to actively feed their appetites and respond to their passions.

FANDOMS

Every new pilot on network television must overcome similar obstacles and navigate the same stepping stones in order to succeed—gaining widespread support from programming executives, generating interest from a potential viewing audience through well-placed marketing and advertising, and securing a viewer-friendly timeslot. But no challenge is as precarious as the formulation of a solid, appointment-viewing fan base. Creating a series with lasting power in the ratings market is challenge enough, and *Lost* has apparently accomplished that feat. But it has inspired as well the buying and promotional power of viewers who not only engage in regular watching but actively engage in the text of the series. *Lost*'s creators and writers have given fans an interactive environment that draws on multiple levels of audience participation, enticing viewers to decipher the hidden clues and secret symbols that might lend insight into the complicated mythology of the series.

In doing so, *Lost* has redefined the concept of the cult audience. *Lost* fans are neither small in number nor are they remotely obscure. They are a community of tens of thousands of like-minded individuals, a network of engaged, active viewers who invest time, money, and effort into a text they love for its innovation, capacity for game play, and broad appeal. In addition, the diverse cast offers at least one character every viewer can identify with, thereby securing a diverse, international viewership.

In cultivating its audience and fandom, *Lost* faced several challenges: the original concept (plane crashes on island; *Survivor* meets *Lord of the Flies)* was questionable, the price tag on the pilot was hefty, and the timeframe between greenlight, casting, production, and broadcast was drastic, even by television standards. Series creators J. J. Abrams and Damon Lindelof shared in the network's skepticism until they penned a script that offered much more than just a group of survivors on a desert island. They worked together to craft a series that had a mythology that offered fear and suspense in a mystery/action/adventure that could easily hook an audience and activate a fan base. Casting and auditions, as we learn from the Bonus Features on the *Lost: The Complete First Season* DVDs, inspired an influx of creative ideas, and original characters mutated while others were added, eventually expanding the number of series' regulars to sixteen. From early on, the creators' ever-evolving, ever-innovative vision of *Lost*, backed by a small band of vigilant supporters at ABC, drove a series that would, within less than a year, be declared a major primetime success in the United States and an international hit as well.

Following casting in spring of 2004, news of the series, cast, and concept filtered out on the Internet. *Zap2it.com*, *Hollywood Reporter* and *Variety* reported on cast members being signed, including Dominic Monaghan, Matthew Fox, and Terry O'Quinn. Monaghan's participation may have been the first catalyst for fan activity. Best known for his involvement in the *Lord of the Rings* film trilogy as the hobbit Merry, the actor already had a solid fan following. Our survey of 117 *Lost* fans (conducted in the summer of 2005) reflected that 73 percent of respondents reported Monaghan's involvement influenced their initial viewing. A visit to MTV in May 2004 by Monaghan added more fuel to *Lost*'s fire, as he revealed on *Total Request Live* that the pilot was one of if not the most expensive in television history. His appearance coincided with a spoiler that circulated on the Internet that a polar bear would appear in the first episode, which began the trend of fan speculation that would later become trademark.

By May 2004, fans became convinced the series had potential for early (and possibly preemptive) cancellation. In response, they organized a pledge drive in support of the series and publicized a letter-writing campaign to ABC and Touchstone. The campaign originated on one of the earliest fan sites, *Lost-TV.com*, and sixty-nine potential fans had signed up as supporters by the time the pilot was screened by test audiences. At the same time, a variety of Internet news sites reported that the pilot had randomly aired on cable television networks, including the Game Show Network (GSN). These impromptu screenings, aired commercial free, increased the buzz surrounding *Lost*. Soon after the encouraging test runs, ABC officially picked up the pilot plus eleven episodes, toying with the idea of the series serving as a mid-season replacement for *Alias*. Clips from the pilot airing on Entertainment News Network and several media outlets either touted ABC's creativity or condemned the series to an early death due to its expense and genre limitation. After a month of consistently positive feedback, however, ABC officially assigned an 8/7 p.m. timeslot on Wednesdays.

The early formation of the fandom as a network of interconnected individuals planning to become regular viewers gave a preliminary indication of future trends in the intensity of fan activity and engagement. ABC decided early on to take action steps to initiate a *Lost* fan base. Fans cited the promotional materials based on the premise as a significant (35 percent) influence on their viewership. Word-of-mouth also played a role: 17 percent of fans responded that they initially viewed the series based on the recommendation of a friend, family member, or through a third party Internet source. *E!Online*'s entertainment gossip series *Watch with Kristin* continually promoted the series throughout June 2004, as the popular host gushed that the series was one of the most anticipated of the fall premieres. The weekly Internet talk show airs exclusive interviews with actors and series' creators, holds interactive chats, and provides spoiler information on a host of shows with heavy Internet fandom activity, including *Gilmore Girls*, *Smallville*, and *Alias*. *Watch with Kristin*'s promotion of the show as having a mythology grounded in science fiction and fantasy, along with frequent mention of series creators J. J. Abrams and Damon Lindelof, aided in a cross-pollination effect that occurred across several interrelated fandoms.

In June 2004, trade magazines announced David Fury's plans to join the creative team as writer and coproducer. Fury had previously written for Joss Whedon's *Buffy the Vampire Slayer* and *Angel*, both series with active fan bases. The addition to *Lost*'s creative team of Javier Grillo-Marxuach, who had been involved in *Jake 2.0* and *Pretender* and had an adoring (if small) fan base, inspired additional interest. Intentional or not, the addition of writers with existing fan bases further secured active initial support for the series.

Early visibility continued to generate popular interest after cast and creators attended the Comic-Con convention in San Diego (July 2004), which featured posters depicting characters with "Help me—I'm Lost" beneath grainy black-and-white "Wanted"-style photos. During Labor Day weekend, only weeks before *Lost*'s television debut, ABC placed one thousand message-in-a-bottle advertisements for the series along popular coastlines, a creative marketing campaign that hoped to entice beachgoers to get *Lost*.

The Lost-TV site was still collecting petitions and drumming up interest for the freshman series throughout the summer as official marketing efforts continued. The site secured a telephone interview with Lindelof to discuss the way the show had evolved from premise to reality and the creator's feelings regarding the importance of listening to a fan base. This interview cemented the value ascribed to the fan base by the series' creators and the commitment of the marketing and creative team that fans were already important to them, even if still relatively small in number. Lindelof self-identified as a fan of both his collaborator Abrams and *Alias*, and as a former student of sociology and psychology. His comments in the interview, which focus on the nature of forming fan bases and the psychology of viewing, indicate that Lindelof is acutely aware of the support of fandom.

In July 2004, DavidFury.net interviewed Fury about his involvement with *Lost*. The interviewer (referencing his writing for *Buffy* and *Angel*) asked if Fury planned to "terrorize the *Lost* Net fandom." He jokingly responded that he hoped to create a "*Lost* fan fight club"—a broad ambition for a series three weeks before its premiere. Fury understood the value of his fans as potential viewers, and a promise to engage his present fan base in a new environment was a motivation for some of his more skeptical fans to tune in to the ABC drama.

The key players of *Lost*'s creative team had experienced both the positive and negative influence of fandom. The Alias fan base, Abrams was well aware, had helped to keep the ratings-struggling series afloat in the third and fourth seasons. Writers David Fury and Drew Goddard realized the influence of fandom from working with Joss Whedon on Nielsen bottom-feeders *Buffy the Vampire Slayer* and *Angel*. Fans can help make or break a series, and the writers, creators, and actors of *Lost* were acutely aware of the precarious nature of consciously attempting to construct a fan base. Cultivating—and maintaining—a positive relationship with the fans was especially important to Abrams, who had experienced fan backlash resulting from the plot and lack of character-driven storylines in the third year of *Alias*. He admitted in a May 2005 interview that "The Internet has really changed the way we watch TV. Instantaneously, thousands of people are reacting and creating a consensus on what they like and don't like. The scrutiny is mind-blowing, and you'd be moronic not to listen to the fans."

The first season of *Lost* premiered with some of the highest ratings of any ABC debut, earning ninth place in the ratings overall for the week. Following the premiere, Lost-TV's webmaster, Xander, emailed a congratulatory message, and Lindelof was quick to respond with: "We're obviously in shock over how well the show did...but what really thrills us is the fan response. Thank you so much for your continued dedication to *Lost*—we'll keep doing our best to earn the love...Hugs, Damon." The focus of the email is not on the ratings the premiere achieved but on the viewers and fans themselves. The language cements the relevance of that relationship—the affectionate "hugs, Damon" exudes familiarity. What's more, Lindelof has not forgotten the role Lost-TV played in development of the fan base: he sent a thank you card from all the writers and creators of the series on the one-year anniversary of the website in March 2005.

Listening to—and understanding—the fan base fell on the shoulders of the creative and marketing teams working together in order to create a distinctly unique experience for the *Lost* viewer. Interactivity continues to play a critical role in the sustained development of the fandom.

Actual online gaming environments and hidden clues and Easter eggs distributed within the episodes of the series have fueled development of the fan base. (The term is borrowed, of course, from the video game industry practice of hiding, in the game's architecture, secret items, unessential to the overall success or comprehension of the game as a whole, but a bonus adding to the player's overall enjoyment. The Easter eggs in *Lost* work in similar fashion: they enhance viewer enjoyment—if the viewer is so inclined to explore in deeper detail.) In the week of the premiere, for example, Internet-savvy fans were granted access to the hide-and-seek game I-am-lost.com. The Flash-based game allowed players to scavenge through virtual plane wreckage and tropical undergrowth for clues about their favorite cast members—clues that included Kate's handcuffs, Jack's medicine, and a blinking red light, marking the location of the plane's transceiver. (Tie-in games and websites were not new for an Abrams series: the first year of *Alias* saw the launch of a dummy website for the fictional Credit Dauphine, Sydney Bristow's cover job; later seasons brought an interactive online game acting as a precursor for a live-action gaming console release.) In October 2004, *Lost* message boards were abuzz with news of the game, which acted as a gateway for series information: each week, the content of the game coincided with the show's narrative development and clues for upcoming episodes.

I-am-lost.com set an important precedent for the level of textual involvement by *Lost* fans. The game became more and more complex each week, with new stages and items to explore without posted rules or guidelines. The lack of official information about how to play the game created a need for discussion on the Internet with other fans. Bouncing off ideas about new developments in the game and the series creates initiated fans who might not have otherwise been interested in engaging with a community of online *Lost* enthusiasts. The Internet worked to fuel the speculation of fans, as more and more people tuned in each week to "get lost." Fans also took their watercooler discussions about the series to the Internet, which opened up additional new avenues for speculation and community building. More and more websites devoted to the series, its actors, fanfiction, and art populated the Internet throughout the first year of the series. Fans, it seemed, could not get enough of the mysterious island and even more mysterious castaways.

The online game was not the only interactive element of the series. Beginning with the first episode, *Lost*'s multiple, creepy enigmas teased viewers. What is the monster? "Where are we?" (Charlie's panicked question at the end of the pilot). And 4, 8, 15, 16, 23, and 42 would soon prove to be more than just Hurley's accursed lottery winners; they became inscrutable signifiers that somehow held the key to *Lost*. The successful integration of the numbers stemmed from the initial concept of interweaving characters into flashback scenes, sometimes for foreshadowing. Such moments marked the start of the intertextual Easter eggs of the show.

The numbers clued a large number of viewers in that there was more than meets the eye to the text of *Lost*. The first tip off was the flight number: Oceanic 815 contained two of Hurley's numbers in succession, and supported the theory that the numbers were cursed. The introduction of the numbers in episode eight piqued the interest of enough fans who were interested to see if the numbers had made an appearance in earlier episodes. They had. A flurry of interactivity began as information about the numbers spread across the Internet and has continued to grow more complex. The numbers continue to play a crucial role, either in combination or alone. Near the end of "Exodus, Part 2" (1.24), Hurley realizes the outer door of the Hatch has been stamped with the sequence, and they are discovered, in Season Two, to be the code which must be input into the computer within the Hatch every 108 minutes—or 4+8+15+16+23+42 minutes.

Knowing the numbers proved integral during the break between the first and second seasons. During this time, the Oceanic Airlines website was introduced, which for the first month of operation required that visitors entered the numbers, in proper succession, in order to navigate an Easter egg-laden website that included a hidden link to the theory and speculation boards of OceanicFlight815.com.

Complex discussion has always been at the heart of the *Lost* fandom. LiveJournals and blogs dedicated to theory and speculation only augmented the intense conversations already underway on message board across the Web. The "official" ABC boards for the show quickly grew in membership numbers and traffic, and as fans sought new information, they stumbled upon already existing or newly created websites that seemed designed for their particular fan discourse. Premiere fan site Lost-Media.com launched in September 2004 with a small collection of links to other fan sites; by the close of the year it had an active and engaging message board community. Other message boards flourished as well, as people joined to discuss their own concepts and theories about the show. Attuned to this trend, the Abrams-supported message board website, The Fuselage, appeared, an innovative community where fans are invited to ask the creative team (including the creators and executive producers) and actors questions, as well as discuss theories, speculations, and spoiler content. Part of the continued efforts of *Lost*'s makers, The Fuselage indicates that the Powers That Be are actively interested in what fans think and feel about the series and the direction it is taking.

Fan activity extends beyond official game play or theory and speculation. Websites circulated on the Internet devoted to the translation of conversations between Korean-speaking Jin and Sun and the French distress transmission picked up by Sayid's transceiver. Fans calculated the exact number of years the message had been broadcast, challenging the sixteen-year calculation put forward in the pilot. Screenshots of Rousseau's maps made their way online as fans speculated what, and where, the Black Rock was. As the season neared a winter break, fans began to converse about the mysterious "whispers" heard in several episodes. The first documented discussion of whispers followed the Sayid backstory-based episode, "Solitary" (1.9), in which the former Iraqi soldier is captured by Rousseau during his trek in the jungle. A transcript of the whispers from Lost Links detailed what fans heard after repeated careful listening:

> MAN'S VOICE: Just get him out of here.
> MAN'S VOICE 2: He's seen too much already.
> MAN'S VOICE: What if he tells?
> WOMAN'S VOICE: …Could just speak to him.
> MAN'S VOICE: No.

An intense discussion began among fans about the validity of the whispers and the accuracy of the transcription of the voices. Those who could hear the whispers began to speculate about the existence of underground tunnels and other experiments on the island, while other fans claimed the whispers were simply auditory hallucinations. When the whispers reappeared during "Outlaws" (1.16)—heard this time by Sawyer, fans claimed to detect the following dialogue (also from Lost Links):

> WOMAN'S VOICE: Maybe we should just talk to him.
> MAN'S VOICE: No, if he sees us it will ruin everything.
> MAN'S VOICE: What did he see?

WOMAN'S VOICE: They could help us.
MAN'S VOICE: Can't trust…Come back around.

In the episode, Sawyer pauses, causing the audience to question if he can hear the whispers.

MAN'S VOICE: What did he see?
MAN'S VOICE: Nothing, he was following it.
WOMAN'S VOICE: Speak.
MAN'S VOICE: Nothing.

For several months following the first airing of these episodes, the validity of the whispers generated a great deal of contention among fans. On The Fuselage, fans banded together and formed the group W.H.I.S.P.E.R.S—an acronym that stood for "We Hear Interesting Sounds Per Episode Replay" (new members had to testify to hearing, and believing in, the whispers)—which garnered a great deal of negative response from "non-believers." The most interesting aspect of this development within the theory and speculation fandom was not that the whispers actually did exist, but the way supporters organized themselves.

The existence of "shippers" (or "relationshippers"—fans who believe certain characters belong together romantically; often, shippers refer to their pairings as OTP: One True Pairing, or one true love) within fandom has dated back at least to *Star Trek* Kirk and Spock enthusiasts who wished to see the two men engaged in something more than a professional relationship. The use of the term shipper is well documented within *X-Files* fandom (shippers longed for a romantic relationship between Fox Mulder and Dana Scully). From the start of fandom, the dynamic of romance and relationships has been a distinctive, even dominant, element of fan behavior. *Lost*, too, has its traditional relationship-centered fans, but the whisper-centric segment of the fandom has created something new: a highly specialized "ship" of their own.

Whisper shippers set up camp in the relationships area of The Fuselage message boards and began to recruit what they termed as "converts." Many of the enthusiasts attested their involvement in the pursuit of whispers as a direct response to the lack of updates in the I-am-Lost game. This led, in turn, to the repeated watching of previously aired episodes, in the hope that clues could be found that included whispers. The listening trend has continued, and since the start of the second season the investigative nature of *Lost* fans has been pushed to new limits: in the premiere episode, "Man of Science, Man of Faith," Shannon encounters a spectral Walt, who whispers incoherently. When played backward, Walt seems to be saying either "Don't push the button, No, the button's bad," or "Push the Button, No Button's Bad." Each has decidedly different implications, and message board fans have been in an uproar arguing over the articulation.

Although this particular level of interactivity—with fans recording sound clips and digitally reversing them—is initially accessible only to the digerati, the fandom can become engaged on any level and as consciously as they want. They can research the origins of the characters' names—theorizing the significance of Rousseau and Locke, count the recurrences (and combinations) of the numbers and speculate on their significance, plot the possible geographic location of the *Lost* island, analyze the images of the mural found in the Hatch, catalogue all of *Lost's* many intertexts and references, create transcripts of episodes, or explore the origins of backgammon.

The audience is welcome to take from the series what they want: fans who only want to watch the series and enjoy the pleasure of a continuing serial each week can do that; those who revel in hours spent plumbing the show's hidden mysteries will not be disappointed. *Lost* does not prescribe in advance levels of access or forms of enjoyment.

FAN ACTIVITIES

Like all major fandoms, *Lost*'s does more than surf the Web. A variety of fan gatherings and conventions have also enticed and inspired fans. On March 12, 2005, for example, the series became the subject of a panel at the William S. Paley festival, which honors breakthrough television shows. One of the first Paley events to sell out, it featured a majority of the cast and creative team: J. J. Abrams, Naveen Andrews, Bryan Burk, Carlton Cuse, Emilie de Ravin, Matthew Fox, Maggie Grace, Jorge Garcia, Josh Holloway, Malcolm David Kelley, Daniel Dae Kim, Yunjin Kim, Evangeline Lilly, Dominic Monaghan, Terry O'Quinn, Harold Perrineau, and Ian Somerhalder all attended. Cuse asked the attendees and audiences if they thought Locke was good or evil, receiving a mixed response, and opened the floor to Q&A. Notable responses included Andrews's comment that the show didn't insult the intelligence of its viewers and Abrams's confirmation that one of the series regulars would die in Season One.

Following the success of the Paley festival, fans themselves organized a fundraising event convention titled "Destination: LA. A Party for *Lost* Fans" organized by E.M.A. Fan Geek Productions. ("M" [Maya] and "A" [Allyson] were both grassroots fan-supportive organizers who had hosted several "Save Our Show" and fundraising silent auctions in the past.) Organizers auctioned a lunch with supervising producer Javier Grillo-Marxuach, various autographed *Alias* and *Lost* scripts, autographed *TV Guide* covers featuring the cast, and an exclusive memento from Grillo-Marxuach: his first script, "House of the Rising Sun." The entire cast and creative team were invited, and Kim, Abrams, Perrineau, and Greg Grunberg, among others, made appearances.

Touchtone Television and ABC would hire Creation Entertainment (well-known within sci-fi fandoms for their fan conventions for shows like *Xena*, *The X-Files*, and *Star Trek*) to host a series of *Lost* conventions, the first in June 2004 in Burbank, California. In a press release announcing the event, Bruce Gersh, senior vice president of business development for ABC entertainment, explained: "*Lost* has a tremendous fan following, and it is time we gave back to the fans." At the convention an upcoming bi-monthly glossy fan magazine and fan club were announced, and the event sold a variety of merchandise, including clothing (T-shirts and $130 *Lost* jackets), character banners, and signed photographs. Three lucky winners enjoyed lunch with de Ravin and Terry.

Expanding *Lost's* "reality" has been a constant within the *Lost* fandom. Early in the first season, two fans created a DriveShaft website (www.driveshaftband.com) mourning the missing Charlie Pace and providing a history of the band (complete with a cohesive backstory, discography, and concert history), critic reviews of their albums, and transcribed articles detailing the tragedy of Oceanic 815. The well-designed site led a majority of the fandom to assume it had been created by ABC and Touchstone. The site was so successful that the ABC website offered a DriveShaft video for "You All Everybody" and suggested the possibility of a DriveShaft CD.

Our *Lost* fan survey offers insight into the amount of time and dedication hardcore fans commit to the series. While a modest 35 percent stated that they spent between one to two hours per week, the average amount of time spent on *Lost* activity was eleven hours. The longest reported amount was seventy-five hours per week, and 16 percent devoted twenty-five hours or more. Fan activities included visiting fan and speculation sites, participating in message boards, writing and reading blogs, and writing and reading fanfiction. In addition, 60 percent indicated that they spent a majority of their time developing theories to explain the complicated mythology of the show, and 66 percent admitted to seeking out storyline spoilers.

While the creative team repeatedly asserts (and even has a disclaimer on The Fuselage site) that they are prohibited from reading fanfiction while working on the series, they do support it. In an interview with PopGurls.com, supervising producer and writer Grillo-Marxuach confessed to being a big fan of fanfiction, and that "I'm a big supporter and admirer of fanfic...I encourage everybody to write it at all times." *Lost* fanfic writers face challenges not known to those who sought to tell their own *X-Files* or *Buffy* stories. "Fanfic seems to be difficult, with the way the plot twists every episode," one *Lost* fan, vampiresetsuna, reflects. "It seems the prevalent activities in this fandom are icon making, theory-speculating, and analyzing screen captures for relationshipping quality."

The writing of critiques or essays, made popular within the *Buffy the Vampire Slayer, Angel,* and other fandoms, seems a prevalent fan activity for *Lost*. Episode reviews are also a popular practice, with most of the reviews appearing on blogs and LiveJournals. Most of these contain humorous or insightful anecdotes from the characters in the show.

The level of fan activity for *Lost* on LiveJournal alone results in the need for icons—user created pictures in 100x100 format that allow bloggers to express their identities and interests through characters or scenes. Fan art includes the creation of these icons for personal use, as well as screensavers, backgrounds, instant message skins, and layouts for diaries and online journals. Groups of fans with like sub-interests join LiveJournal communities and share their creations with other fans. The interaction in a community-based format allows for a chain of activities to occur, as some fans devote their creative activities to taking detailed screenshots from episodes and hosting them online for the use of artists who wish to make icons or other graphics from the captures.

The behavior of *Lost* fans is not, of course, wholly unique: all fandoms, at some level, actively engage with the source text of their fandom. What makes *Lost* fans different is that they have formed a discourse community or knowledge network—a group of individuals devoting time and effort into discussing, analyzing, and investigating their favorite series as though it were a distinct discipline of study. Their behaviors mesh well with Matt Hills's theory of the fan-scholar, or fans that study the object of their fandom in discursive fashion. In some large-scale fandoms, the creation of derivative works, from fanfiction to art, is the most prevalent activity. The *Lost* fandom, however, is more likely to be engaged in discussion, research, and synthesis of ideas presented within the series:

- 77 percent of fans reported spending time discussing the series on message boards
- 65 percent regularly visited blogs that focus on the show
- 42 percent self-published their thoughts on their own blog
- 17 wrote essays, critiques, or reviews of the series

These numbers are interesting when compared to the derivative activities of the fandom:

- 30 percent wrote fanfiction
- 34 percent created art
- 18 percent created or watched videos

Serious fan engagement requires a level of commitment to the series far beyond casual appointment viewing. The establishment of the Society for the Study of Lost—a website that houses scholarly essays on the series and publishes a peer-reviewed Internet journal—further illustrates the dedication and commitment of fan-scholars to explore the series in full detail. The website also hosts archived message-board posts from Lost-TV.com by category ("literary allusions," "psychology 101," "astronomy," and "physics").

What inspires such an incredibly active community? When asked to evaluate the appealing elements of the series, 88 percent of fans indicated aspects directly related to the writing and narrative of the series—from the premise of a plane crashing on an island to the interconnected backstories and flashbacks, characterization, mythology, and mystery. Characters and characterizations were continually represented favorably. As one fan explains: "Because the show's main group of characters reflect such a large panel of people, beliefs, and backgrounds, it makes their situation actually possible to identify with. Every one of them is a full-fledged three-dimensional character with a rich backstory, and that's the kind of writing that appeals to me."

The highly speculative elements of *Lost*—those that lend themselves to theorizing, reading spoilers, and analyzing data (60 percent of responding fans regularly engage in such)—appear to be key factors in the continued interest of fans in the series and are often the objects of fan scholarship. Hidden Easter eggs on official websites, within the series, and on the Season One DVDs provide additional thrills for secret-seeking viewers. Each episode reveals new and different mysteries, and the devotion of fans to rewatch episodes fuels the fire. The Season One finale, the three-part "Exodus," revealed on careful examination a link to the Oceanic Airlines website, and the fan-detectives found a full-of-goodies website devoted to the ill-fated airline. Oceanic-Air.com not only provided fans with material to discuss in relation to the series' unique mythology but also fostered the sense of continued community investment.

Conspiring with a *Lost* Audience

As discussed previously, *Lost*'s creators envisioned the series from the beginning as a kind of game its audience would actively play. But as they have indicated in interviews, they probably did not anticipate either the intensity or wackiness of the speculation their series would instigate. Both fans and the media (often following fan-initiated theories) have spent a great deal of time constructing complex theories about Oceanic 815, its survivors, and the mysterious island on which they crash. Is it possible that the *Lost*aways are really dead and in purgatory? Could they be victims of an alien abduction? Is the island located within the Bermuda Triangle? Is Mystery Island really the lost continent of Atlantis? or MU? Are the Adam and Eve Jack finds in the caves ("House of the Rising Sun") really Amelia Earhart and Fred Noonan, lost on a round-the-world flight in 1937? Is the island a site for a complex cloning experiment? Is the island overrun with nanotechnology? These and many, many more conspiracy theories have been proposed.

A cornucopia of mysteries, *Lost* spins off theories as naturally as sparks from a fire. Even before the Hatch was opened and we learned about the Dharma Initiative, the island was populated with numerous "invitations" (if you will) to conspiracy thinking: the Monster, the polar bear, Locke's miraculous rejuvenation, the ghost of Jack's father, the Others, the disease, the cable stretching from the island into the Pacific, the crash itself, the whispers, Walt's mysterious powers, the possibly cursed numbers. Each of these is, in itself, a "riddle wrapped in a mystery inside an enigma." Taken together they positively demand conspiratorial thinking.

The opening of the Hatch, of course, hatched other theories. Now that we have watched the Dharma Initiative's (dis)orientation film, eaten Apollo bars, looked at the mural, found a man (Desmond) Jack met in LA trapped in the Hatch, met the Tailies, learned that the Others only kidnap "good" people, seen the Dharma logo on a shark (and, retrospectively, on Oceanic 815), and seen a horse (from Iowa) loose on the island, conspiracy theories seem to be completely legitimate, entirely essential, weapons in our ever-challenging engagement with *Lost*'s narrative power.

The "Orientation" video, first viewed during the Season Two episode with the same title (2.3), briefly discusses the role of the Dharma Initiative. Filmstrip host Dr. Marvin Candle—a mysterious, white-coated scientist with a prosthetic hand—briefly outlines the work of the initiative, which includes research in meteorology, psychology, parapsychology, zoology, electromagnetism, and utopian societies. In a heavily spliced video, the survivors of flight 815 learn what Desmond had tried to explain: that a code must be entered into the central terminal of the computer every 108 minutes—or else. Without any other explanation, the video concludes and Locke says in bewilderment, *"We'll have to watch that again"*—a recommendation taken to heart by TiVo and VCR users worldwide and web users when the filmstrip appeared on the Hansofoundation.org website.

Although weekly developments in watched and rewatched broadcast episodes serve as the main conspiracy generators, official websites and the Easter eggs planted there have certainly aided and abetted conspiracy theorists. Oceanic-Airlines.com launched immediately following the Season One finale with imbedded messages (a script page, for example) and hidden "message in a bottle"-style letters, presumably from the Flight 815 survivors. From May through mid-July 2005, the site featured a banner that proclaimed "Taking you places you never imagined," with an island shot of a perfect blue sky and clear, unoccupied water. In July, the banner was replaced with an image depicting a ship that resembled the *Black Rock* and a swirling column of smoke that seemed unremarkable, until compared to another interesting switch. The original site invited visitors to "Visit Mysterious Australia," but switched in July to "Visit Ancient Australia."

The layer-embedded seating chart on the site offered Easter eggs such as Danielle's maps and Kate's arrest information (dated 7/17/2004). Late July, visitors that entered "The" and "Boy" on the flight tracker information screen were treated to pencil drawings of New York—the Statue of Liberty and World Trade Towers in plain sight—and the self-portrait Michael drew during his recovery (dated 2003). Appearing on an official site, each of these items took on, at least potentially, extra significance and fueled fan speculation.

Another official web location, the Disney-owned Hanso Foundation Website, offered additional portentous goodies, including the orientation film originally viewed in the eponymous episode. We are also given a brief biography of Alvar Hanso, foundation financial backer who has an aversion to showing a full view of his facial features. The mission statement reads: "The Hanso Foundation: a commitment to encouraging excellence in science and technology and furthering the cause of human development." This development includes the Hanso life extension project, electromagnetic research, the quest for extraterrestrial life forces, mathematical forecasting, cryogenics development, juxtapositional eugenics, and accelerated remote viewing. While most of the website links are dead ends, some reveal a series of memos that allude to the work—and progress—of the foundation.

Dated September 21, 2005, a memo celebrating the eugenics experiments of the foundation appears under the life extension project link and cites the longevity of a chimp named Joop (he was 105). Clicking at the bottom of the memo reveals a password-protected backdoor site, that with the word "Copenhagen" gives access to a letter from the GHO (Global Health Organization) ordering a cease and desist for activities occurring at the Hanso Foundation's off-shore facility near Zanzibar, dated two days before the triumphant accounts of Joop's lifespan. The letter references an outbreak of a meningococcal-type disease in the region of Tanzania.

Alvar Hanso's biographical information on the website adds complexity to an already mysterious individual—we learn that he delivered munitions in World War II and served as "the leading purveyor of high technology armaments to NATO." Linking from his biography photo—shadowy, as always—a mouseover effect reveals that the picture is more than meets the eye. A hidden computer message—mimicking the scene from "What Kate Did" in which Michael seemingly makes contact with the outside world—identifies the person at the terminal as simply "mole." From there, another letter appears from the GHO thanking the foundation for their generous donation and encouraging the continuation of "important work" at the Zanzibar facility.

For those who seek them out, such "paratexts" (as media scholars call them) feed back into *Lost* proper and become, at least for that segment of the audience engaged in active interpretation of the "text," important elements in their deeper understanding.

Keep in mind that at root the word "conspire" means to "breathe together." *Lost* conspiracy theories are distinctive ways of thinking about the show's many puzzles that bring together not only numerous individual mysteries but like-minded fans smitten, at least temporarily, with particular theories that help make sense of what they are watching, and ready to share them—at the watercooler, on discussion boards, or by means of websites. *Lost* conspiracy nuts have engaged in a wide variety of suppositions. The following are but a few.

STRING THEORY/TESSERACTS

Hypotheses concerning alternate universes, and/or time travel, and/or other dimensions have swirled about since *Lost* began. How else to explain the existence of a giant uncharted island in the middle of nowhere? String theory got a boost in popularity following the Creation convention in the summer of 2005, when actor John Terry (Christian Shephard) suggested reading Brian Greene's *The Elegant Universe: Superstrings, Hidden Dimensions, and the Quest for the Ultimate Theory* as a possible clue. (String Theory, a physics model often used to justify the theory of the universe's interconnectedness, argues that the universe is built on one-dimensional vibrating "strings" instead of non-dimensional point particles.) When Lindelof, Cuse, and Abrams have discussed the reveals of the island mystery, they repeatedly suggest that everything on the island can be explained with rational science. This tip-off has allowed theories like String Theory and Chaos Theory to come to the fore in theoretical discussion. While these theories are abstract concepts, they do have scientific grounding.

The idea of the tesseract and the ability to jump dimensions first surfaced as a result of Sawyer's reading Madeleine L'Engle's *A Wrinkle in Time* (for more on this book see chapter 6), a work of fiction which nevertheless offers an eloquent theory of time travel, and the existence of a tesseract on the ABC Oceanic 815 website has offered confirmation for some and another red herring for others.

THE TWO PLANE THEORY

The concept of an alternate universe or reality supports the theory of two planes from alternate universes. The Oceanic Airlines website's seating chart game first spurred the idea of the existence of two planes. This speculation was initially based on Flight 815 being listed both as 815 and 777 on the flash game website. Fans began to research the possibilities and found that two planes were used for filming the pilot and "Exodus" (probably due to the lack of availability of the same plane for both episodes). Fans who had taken the images from the pilot as canonical were piqued when logically the seats and rows in the two episodes did not seem to mesh. That some characters are only seen with certain others—Hurley, for instance, is only shown with Walt and Michael and not with Jack and Locke—provoked further intrigue for two-plane theorists.

THE 2009 THEORY

Evidence for the 2009 theory—the hypothesis that the events of *Lost* take place not in the present day but in 2009—can be found both in the show and official websites (especially Oceanic-Air.com). Michael's backstory is key to the theory. We know that Michael's son Walt is ten years old at the time of the crash, but in Michael's history ("Raised by Another") he is hit by a car on a New York street and spends several months convalescing in a hospital room, where a calendar indicates that the year is 2001. Michael leaves the hospital to attend a custody hearing in September of that year. When Michael meets with Susan at a lawyer's office for a custody hearing, the World Trade Towers, destroyed in 2001, are still visible in the large picture window.

On the luggage tags pictured on the Oceanic 815 website (in the section labeled "Rousseau's bunker") the date of the plane's departure is listed (using European date format) as 09Sep21—September 21, 2009.

Additional clues come from the Hatch. On Desmond's bookshelf there is a magazine dated 2003, a book published in 2005, a kettle design produced in 2005, and a 2004 version of a washing machine. While these may well be prop errors, *Lost* is a series that prides itself on consistency, and the creators have never committed to a specific real time date or timeline for the events of the series. The 2009 theory is possibly disproved by official correspondence that discusses the discontinuation of the search and rescue for Oceanic Flight 815, dated November 4, 2004, located on the Oceanic-Air site.

THE COLLECTIVE CONSCIOUSNESS THEORY

First proposed on the 4815162342.com forums by poster Andrew Smith, this theory postulates that survivors are pressing the button inside the Hatch every 108 minutes to download information about Earth's magnetic fields. The abnormality of the magnetic fields on the island has affected the psychic abilities of all the island's inhabitants, and the Others' long residence has given them the power to manipulate the thoughts of others (helped, in part, by remote viewing research).

THE COPENHAGEN PHOTO

Rumor has it that this image appeared on the Hansofoundation.org website for an hour as a hidden Easter egg before disappearing. Several fans with the presence of mind made the image available by posting it, but several outlets soon lost the bandwidth capacities to display the image. Fans that were able to obtain the image and download it found a photo that showed several letters, one from Marvin Candle to Ray Mullen, and another from the Global Health Organization referencing the outbreak of meningococcal disease and the successful (albeit temporary) treatment with electromagnetic pulse therapy. A dharma symbol posted on the wall is marked with initials that appear to match up to several of the survivors. A copy of *Heart of Darkness* appears, as well as several cards.

Fans uncovered hidden messages in the image with the aid of steganography, revealing layers of Morse code and hidden text that references the Zanzibar facility (citing it as a "total loss") and indicates that the virus from the test facility is being sent through Virgin Mary statues.

FABRICATED CONSPIRACIES

One of the best-done and most elaborate fan fabrications was the illegitimate Dharma Initiative Classification Video that outlined the different areas of study and featured several look-alikes to the DeGroots and Alvar Hanso as seen in the original orientation filmstrip.

The mpeg "Classifications" video hit the Internet in October of 2005, with a post originating on The Fuselage message boards by a Samuel DeGroot. The authenticity of the video was eventually disproven by *Lost* writer Javier Grillo-Marxuach on The Fuselage message boards.

The majority of fabricated content comes from the creation of websites that enhance the continuity of the series while adding to theory and speculation discussions. When asked about the websites on The Fuselage website, Marxuach offered: "There are things on the Web that are ours and others that are not….There are a lot of great fansites that take a speculative approach to the mythology—and I think that is a cool thing, but overall, I'd rather neither confirm nor deny!"

In 2005, twenty-four-hour news networks began covering what bloggers were saying as if they were all real journalists. In a comparable, watershed development, publications like *Entertainment Weekly* and *TV Guide* began in the fall of 2006 to regularly cite and discuss fan speculation—especially conspiracy theories—about *Lost* and other shows. Conspiracy theories, it seems, weren't just for nuts anymore.

SUPPORTING THE *LOST* FANDOM

Midway through the first season, ABC aired a catch-up episode for *Lost* for the unenlightened few who were not tuning in to the hit series. The basic premise was recounted, characters were introduced, and a brief summation of the action up to the present point in the March hiatus was disclosed. What the catch-up episode did not offer was all of the hidden subtexts, creepy subplots, and continuing mysteries that true fans already knew intimately. A similar episode was shown in January 2006 before new second season episodes aired after more than a month's hiatus. It, too, offered only the highlights of plots and character development but failed to reveal any carefully gathered information from months of previous online interaction.

The conscious exclusion of the more subtle elements of the show served a dual purpose. It allowed the interested viewer to enter the show with a surface accumulation of knowledge while granting them the opportunity to become enchanted later by the subtleties. And the catch-up episodes preserved as well the status of the "true" fan in relation to the show: none of the information fans had worked so hard to recover—through repeated viewings, discussion board marathon sessions, or LiveJournal posts—had been disclosed to the "outside" audience. Fans maintained the level of access the creators have repeatedly praised and supported. Entrée to the *Lost* fandom was through initiation only.

ABC's sponsorship of the Oceanic-Air.com site following the Season One finale likewise fed fan hunger and kept them busy. Visitors could find a host of clues and a second season trailer—if they knew the numbers and discovered embedded hidden messages in the source code and even a page from a "secret" script. The site launched at the close of May, and while news spread across the Internet about its existence, fans had to decipher the clues on their own. Entering the numbers in specific order allowed access to a seating chart for Oceanic flight 815, along with embedded Flash components that generated further speculation. And, in typical *Lost* fandom fashion, intrepid fans were allowed access to a new message board dedicated solely to theory and speculation. Traffic on the Oceanic-air website increased as the link circulated on the Internet and an article appeared in

Newsweek on June 10. "With this show, everything happens for a reason, and it's the same with this site," Mike Benson, senior vice president of marketing at ABC disclosed in the interview.

The *Lost* Cult?

While labeled by the network and media news as a "cult," the *Lost* fandom extends beyond the traditional label of the term, which often carries a negative connotation. Cult fans usually operate in small circles of reference and often must act as anchors and advocates for a rating-challenged program's continuation. With an average viewership for a new episode between twenty to twenty-two million in the U.S. alone, *Lost* fandom is anything but small. Perhaps we should think of *Lost* not as a cult program but as a mythology show. Like *The X Files, Buffy the Vampire Slayer,* and *Twin Peaks,* cousins in the mythology genre, *Lost* has attracted a devoted following of cultish fans.

Lost fans are hardly the small minority group of outsiders typical of cult fandom. Puzzling *Lost's* deep mysteries has become mainstream as millions upon millions of viewers—*Lost*ies, *Lost*aways, *Lost* fanatics—tune in worldwide to create a unique phenomenon. Yet no one, concrete label captures the *Lost* fan. The variety of engagement within the fandom poses a unique question: how do you define a cult audience that has extended beyond the typical definition of the term? A majority of the media articles published during the first season of *Lost* centered on trying to either define the show or create parallels to other series, generally those in the mythology bracket.

A *Boston Globe* article in October of 2004 categorizes mythology shows as those that attract a "lively, game audience"; mythology shows make their "viewers into cosmic Sherlocks....Mythology writers expect rigorous, un-couch potato like viewing—and they get it." No fandom has asked more from a series' mythology than *Lost's*.

LOST GLOSSARY

Aaron—Claire finally names her baby Aaron in "Exodus, Part 2." In a "missing scene" in the Season One DVD, she reveals that she only names her son when she feels he is relatively safe from the Others.

Abed-Jazeem, Noor—In "Solitary," Sayid's childhood friend is held by the Iraqi government as an insurgent, but he helps her escape. He calls her Nadia and travels the world to find her. A CIA agent later tells him that she lives in California ("The Greater Good").

Adam and Eve—The skeletons dubbed Adam and Eve by the castaways are found in the caves during "House of the Rising Sun." Jack determines that a man and a woman were "buried" or ritually placed in the caves.

Aguilar, Father—Hurley's family's priest dies when struck by lightning during Hurley's grandfather's funeral. In "Numbers," Hurley attributes the shocking death to the curse of the lottery numbers.

airplane (model)—In a backstory, Kate robs a bank in order to retrieve a tiny model airplane from a safety deposit box ("Whatever the Case May Be"). She later tells Jack that the plane belonged to the man she loved—and killed. In "Born to Run," the airplane belongs to Tom Brennan, her childhood love. The marshal shows her the toy in Sydney before she is extradited ("Exodus," Part 1). The same size model, this time in a series of little planes forming a mobile over a baby's crib, appears in Claire's frightening dream about her baby in "Raised by Another."

Alex—*See* Rousseau, Alex.

Ana Lucia—*See* Cortez, Ana Lucia.

Annie—In "Tabula Rasa," Kate uses this alias when she works at a sheep station in Australia while claiming to be a traveling Canadian student.

"Are You Sure"—The lyrics to this Willie Nelson/Bobby Emmons song ("Are you sure this is where you want to be?") fit each castaway, especially during the final moments of "...In Translation," when the survivors begin to realize just how long they might be on the island.

artist—In the backstory of "Special," Michael is a struggling artist who cannot make enough money to support his family. Thomas, the father of Claire's baby, is a struggling artist ("Raised by Another"), whose painting mysteriously reappears as part of the mural in the Hatch.

Arzt—The high school science teacher, first introduced in "Born to Run," goes by his last name; his first name is Leslie. He explodes during a dynamite-handling lesson ("Exodus").

asthma—According to Boone ("Confidence Man"), Shannon has suffered with asthma throughout her life and normally carries an inhaler. When the inhalers are gone, Jack guides her through a breathing exercise until she can overcome an attack, but Sun provides a longer-lasting remedy made from eucalyptus.

astrology—Claire believes in astrology and can develop astrologic charts. She guesses Kate's sign as Gemini and offers to do a chart for her, but Kate declines ("Pilot, Part 2"). In Claire's backstory episode ("Raised by Another"), she seems hesitant to visit a psychic, but a girlfriend tells her that she should enjoy the experience because she likes astrology.

Austen, Kate—Kate's childhood name is Kate Austen ("Born to Run"), although she is prone to use aliases. Although she knows that her biological father isn't Sam Austen ("What Kate Did"), she keeps his name and respects him as her father of choice.

Australia—Oceanic Flight 815 originates in Sydney but goes off course en route to Los Angeles ("Pilot," "Exodus"). Jack's father dies in Sydney ("White Rabbit"), and he travels there to bring his father home. Charlie's brother Liam lives with his family in Sydney ("The Moth"), and he journeys down under to persuade him to re-join DriveShaft ("The Moth"). Claire is from Australia ("Raised by Another"). Sawyer tracks the man he believes is responsible for his parents' deaths to Australia and kills a man in Sydney ("Outlaws"). Kate hides from the law in Australia and works on a sheep station before being turned in by the rancher. She is apprehended by a marshal and extradited from Australia ("Tabula Rasa"). Shannon lives with an Australian lover before she attempts to swindle money from Boone ("Hearts and Minds"), and he travels there to save his stepsister, both from herself and her supposedly abusive boyfriend ("Hearts and Minds"). Sun plans to leave Jin in Australia and disappear, making her absence look like an abduction ("…In Translation"). Jin leaves Sydney for Los Angeles to deliver a watch for his employer and father-in-law, Mr. Paik. Walt lives with his mother and adoptive father in Australia. Vincent, Brian's dog, accompanies Walt and Michael on the flight from Australia ("Special"). Scott, who is apparently murdered by Ethan in "Homecoming," wins a round trip, all expenses paid vacation from San Diego to Sydney when he is named his software company's prize-winning salesperson. Locke travels to Australia to participate in a walkabout. Sayid infiltrates a terrorist cell in Sydney and is rewarded by intelligence agencies with a trip to the U.S. so he can find Nadia, a friend he helped escape from Iraq ("The Greater Good"). Hurley travels to the outback in search of more information about the mysterious numbers ("Numbers").

baby—The concept of a baby comes up frequently: In several first season episodes, Rousseau talks about the loss of her "baby," now a grown woman. Claire finally gives birth to a baby (*See* Aaron) in "Do No Harm," and Aaron plays an important role in

"Exodus." In "Collision," Ana Lucia tells her psychiatrist that the "screaming baby" next door has moved, is aware of a screaming baby during a domestic disturbance call, and is herself pregnant at the time she is shot on the job as a police officer (she loses her baby).

backgammon—In the pilot episode, Locke teaches Walt to play backgammon. He becomes a backgammon prodigy and beats Hurley at several games, although Hurley placed ninth in an important backgammon tournament and has difficulty believing that a novice player can beat him ("Homecoming"). Several characters discuss life and recent island events while they play backgammon. For example, Locke and Charlie discuss Claire's and Charlie's recent argument, and Charlie's ongoing recovery from addiction, over a game in "Abandoned."

bank robbery—Kate masterminds a bank robbery in Taos, New Mexico ("Whatever the Case May Be"). Although her gang commits the robbery for money, Kate only wants to open safety deposit box 815 to retrieve a model airplane.

baptism—Mr. Eko baptizes Claire and Aaron to provide "religious insurance," as Locke explains it, in case something happens to either mother or child. Charlie's vivid (and he believes prophetic) dreams prompt him to convince Claire to have Aaron baptized ("Fire + Water").

bassist—Charlie is the bassist for DriveShaft. Although he frequently talks about the band and is seen playing guitar or composing songs on the island, "Homecoming" showcases Charlie's true role in the band.

battery—In the pilot episode, Sayid tries to save the battery needed to send a distress call, or receive a transmission, until a group of survivors reach high ground, where he can operate the transceiver. In the series' early episodes, a battery plays an important role as the castaways try to triangulate a signal. During "Numbers," Hurley uses the castaways' need for a battery as his reason for seeking Rousseau. The Frenchwoman gives him a battery, which Hurley later gives to Sayid (it will power the radar he salvages for use on the raft).

Beechcraft—Locke and Boone find a crashed Beechcraft airplane and its dead pilot in the jungle in "Deus Ex Machina." The plane carried drugs from Nigeria to an unknown destination. During "The 23rd Psalm," Mr. Eko burns the plane, its cargo, and the body of his brother, a priest killed on the plane's final drug run.

Bernard—Bernard is Rose's husband. When the plane depressurizes, Bernard is in the aft toilet and therefore in the section that breaks off first during the crash. However, Rose is certain that he is alive ("White Rabbit"). In subsequent episodes (e.g., "Homecoming," "Everybody Hates Hugo") Rose tells other characters that he is alive. In "Everybody Hates Hugo," Bernard makes his first appearance. He and Rose are reunited in "Collision."

Beth—Beth is Kate's friend who loves DriveShaft ("Pilot"). The name also belongs to the pregnant woman who dies during surgery, leading to an inquiry into Christian Shephard's performance as a surgeon ("White Rabbit").

"Beyond the Sea"—The words to this song are written throughout Rousseau's notes. Shannon eventually translates the notes and sings the song to Sayid during the ending scene of "Whatever the Case May Be."

Bible—In the Dharma Initiative facility found by the Tailies, a foot locker with an odd assortment of items is opened. Mr. Eko takes the Bible and treats it reverently ("The Other 48 Days"). In "What Kate Did," Mr. Eko shares the book's contents with Locke. Inside a hollowed space within the Bible is a segment of film edited out of the orientation film. *See also* Book of Law.

Black Rock—Rousseau notes the Black Rock on her maps and, in "Solitary," tells Sayid she created a new broadcast from there once her party died and she was alone. When Charlie reads Claire's diary ("All the Best Cowboys Have Daddy Issues"), he finds her reference to the black rock from her dreams. A black, rocky mountain also is shown in Walt's comic book ("Special"). In

"Exodus, Part 1" Rousseau leads Jack, Kate, Arzt, Hurley, and Locke to the *Black Rock*, which turns out to be a large, multimasted ship beached at least a mile inland.

blast doors—Michael discovers that the Hatch has blast doors, which are automatically lowered from the ceiling in the event of an explosion ("What Kate Did").

boar—Boars serve not only as a source of food for the survivors but as a catalyst to several actions. Boars first attack the fuselage soon after the crash ("Walkabout"), presumably attracted by the bodies in the wreckage. Locke becomes a boar hunter during "Walkabout." In "The Moth," Locke sets up traps for boars and is shown cleaning his kill after Charlie inadvertently "baits" Locke's trap so that it brings down a large animal. In "Outlaws," Sawyer believes a boar has targeted him, because the animal destroys only his belongings instead of attacking other castaways' living areas. In "...And Found," Jin is attacked by a boar in the jungle.

Book of Law—Mr. Eko uses this name for the Bible's Old Testament as he tells Locke the story of Josiah ("What Kate Did"). He then explains the parallel between the story of Josiah and the castaways' recent experiences.

Boone—*See* Carlyle, Boone.

bottle—Charlie gathers messages from the castaways to seal in a bottle, which then is taken on the raft in "Exodus, Part 1." When the message bottle washes ashore in "Everybody Hates Hugo," Claire finds it and gives it to Sun, who buries it. During "...And Found," Sun retrieves it and, in doing so, finds her missing wedding ring.

box company—Locke tells Boone that he was the regional sales manager for a box company ("All the Best Cowboys Have Daddy Issues"). Probably not-so-coincidentally, Hurley owns the company ("Numbers"). *See also* Randy.

Brennan, Tom—Kate's childhood love and adult friend Tom works at a hospital and helps fugitive Kate get a few minutes alone with her cancer-stricken mother ("Born to Run"). Tom ends up in Kate's getaway car and is accidentally shot by police as Kate attempts to crash through a barricade.

Brian—*See* Porter, Brian.

Bryan—Shannon's Australian boyfriend takes the money Boone offers him to leave Shannon ("Hearts and Minds").

C815 photocopier—Charlie tries to sell C815 photocopiers so that he can become a responsible employee and a regular guy. However, his first day on the job coincides with his first days of heroin withdrawal, and he fails miserably when he tries to demonstrate how the copier works ("Homecoming"). 815 is a combination of 8 and 15, two of the Numbers, as well as the doomed flight's number (Oceanic 815).

cable—In "Solitary," Sayid is intrigued by a cable (what he later calls a "wire") running from the jungle to the beach and apparently out to sea. (The purpose and origin of the cable have not yet been explained.) While following this cable, he is drawn closer to Rousseau's hideaway and is ensnared by one of her traps.

Candle, Dr. Marvin—The orientation film that Desmond suggests Locke and Jack view in the Hatch is narrated by Dr. Candle. Candle has an artificial left hand (or arm) and only makes the hand gesture for Namaste with his right hand. After Mr. Eko finds the film segment edited from the orientation film, he and Locke splice the missing segment into the rest of the film and view the longer version ("What Kate Did"). In this segment, Candle explains that the station's computer must not be used to communicate with the outside world, or another "incident" might take place.

Carlyle, Boone—Stepbrother to Shannon and the head of a division of his mother's wedding business, Boone is a rich man who often acts as guardian for his stepsister. After being fatally injured in a fall while transmitting a distress call from the drug runners' Beechcraft, he is the first of the fourteen main characters in the first season to die ("Do No Harm"). During the second season, he briefly appears in Shannon's backstory ("Abandoned").

Carlyle, Sabrina—Boone calls his mother the "Martha Stewart of weddings" ("Hearts and Minds") because she runs a business empire. Shannon's strained relationship with Sabrina is documented in the second season "Abandoned."

"Catch a Falling Star"—Claire's favorite lullaby is one her mother sang to her, and she wants to ensure that her child also will hear the song. She asks her baby's prospective adoptive mother if she knows that song ("Raised by Another").

Catholicism—The Reyes family (which includes Hurley) and Charlie are Catholic, and this religion is emphasized in both characters' backstories (e.g., "The Moth," "Numbers"). In addition, symbols from the Church make their way into other episodes. For example, the drug runner whose small plane also crashes on the island is dressed as a priest, and heroin is hidden inside statues of the Virgin Mary (e.g., "Deus Ex Machina," "Exodus"). In Season Two, Desmond crosses himself before rebooting the newly repaired computer ("Orientation"), implying that he is familiar with Catholicism. Mr. Eko is brought up Catholic until he is abducted by gun-wielding men and led into life as a drug lord. He becomes a priest on paper to fly drugs out of the country. However, on the island, he truly takes on the role of a priest ("The 23rd Psalm"), even baptizing Claire and Aaron ("Fire + Water").

caves—Jack discovers the caves in "White Rabbit," and they become the new home for several survivors, as well as a source of fresh water. The current survivors aren't the only ones to have lived here: the bones of "Adam and Eve," along with black and white stones, also are found in the caves. *See also* Adam and Eve.

Cedar Rapids, Iowa—Kate returns to Iowa to visit her terminally ill mother. Once there, she and her childhood friend Tom dig up a time capsule they buried years before ("Born to Run"). Her Iowa home, which she shares with mother Diane and stepfather Wayne, explodes, and she is charged with arson (and murder—Wayne is inside at the time), which starts her flight out of state ("What Kate Did").

census—In "Solitary," Hurley takes a census of the survivors to learn their names, place of origin, and age. He plans to use the information as a way to protect the survivors by learning more about each of them. The census reveals that Ethan Rom's name does not appear on the flight manifest, suggesting that he was never on the flight.

Charlie—*See* Pace, Charlie.

chief of surgery—Until a medical inquiry board finds him guilty of malpractice, Christian Shephard, Jack's father, is chief of surgery at St. Sebastian Hospital ("White Rabbit").

Christian—*See* Shephard, Christian.

Cindy—The Australian Cindy is a flight attendant on Oceanic 815 and a survivor of the crash. She tells the other Tailies she has a good memory for passengers' faces ("The Other 48 Days"). On the trek to the other side of the island, she disappears, and Ana Lucia believes she has been taken by the Others.

Claire—*See* Littleton, Claire.

Cline, Patsy—During Kate's backstory in "Tabula Rasa," Kate and Ray listen to a Patsy Cline song on the radio in Ray's truck. In "What Kate Did," Patsy Cline music again plays in the background. This time the song is "Walking After Midnight," which Kate plays on the Hatch's record player.

comic book—In the pilot episode, Walt finds a Spanish-language comic book in the wreckage and often is shown reading it. The title is translated as *Green Lantern and Flash: Faster Friends, Part One*. Pictures include a black mountain and a polar bear—images featured in real life on the island. Michael burns the comic book when his son prefers to read it instead of doing what he tells him to do ("Special"). In a flashback sequence during "Exodus, Part 2," we discover that the comic book belongs to Hurley, who is seen reading it on the plane.

communications officer—Sayid's role in the Iraqi Republican Guard is as a communications officer. Apparently his training includes the monitoring and repair of communication technology as well as interrogation techniques, as noted in "Solitary" and "The Greater Good."

compass—In "Hearts and Minds," Locke gives Sayid a compass, saying he no longer needs it. When Sayid works with the compass to help him in drawing a map, he discovers that "north" is in the wrong direction.

confidence man—Sawyer is the name of a confidence man who seduces a woman, swindles her and her husband, and leads to the couple's murder/suicide. The character known as "Sawyer" to the survivors became a confidence man as well, like the man he hates and tracks for vengeance. *See* Sawyer; Ford, James.

construction—Michael's trade before the crash is construction. On the island he tests the structural integrity of the caves before the survivors move into them ("The Moth"); constructs a raft, which sails during "Exodus"; and discovers that the Hatch has blast doors ("What Kate Did").

Cooper, Anthony—Locke's biological father (played by Kevin Tighe) is a rich man who manipulates his son into donating a kidney ("Deus Ex Machina"). He makes another appearance, to tell his son to get lost, in the Season Two Locke backstory episode "Orientation."

Cortez, Ana Lucia—She approaches Jack in an airport bar before Oceanic 815 leaves Sydney ("Exodus, Part 1"). The two briefly chat before she leaves to take a phone call. Played by Michelle Rodriguez, she becomes a series regular during the second season, beginning with "Adrift." Ana Lucia has a take-charge personality and harshly leads the Tailies prior to their encounter with the Season One survivors (e.g., "...And Found"). Her backstory is told in "Collision," in which her life as a police officer sheds light on her need for control, particularly of men.

CPR—Jack performs cardiopulmonary resuscitation techniques on Rose soon after the crash ("Pilot"). During "All the Best Cowboys Have Daddy Issues," he violently performs CPR on Charlie after his hanging and saves his life. In "Adrift," Sawyer pulls Michael onto a remnant of the raft and performs CPR, saving Michael from a near-drowning. In "The Other 48 Days," Ana Lucia knows CPR and saves Emma after the crash. Her role as a savior who jumps in to help others immediately after the crash parallels Jack's role in the pilot episode.

Curtis, Dr.—Dr. Curtis recognizes Hurley when he comes to the mental institution to visit Lenny in "Numbers." He may have treated Hurley at the institution—his history there is unclear. However, Dr. Curtis directs him to Lenny, who provides information about the mysterious numbers.

Danielle—*See* Rousseau, Danielle.

Danny—Apparently Ana Lucia's boyfriend or husband when she is an LAPD officer and most likely father to the unborn child Ana Lucia lost when she was shot ("Collision"). However, Danny leaves her.

Dark Territory—*See Territoire Fonce.*

Dawson, Michael—Michael and Susan Lloyd are parents to Walt, who is taken by his mother when she leaves Michael. An artist who fails to earn enough money from his art, he goes into the construction business. When Susan marries Brian Porter, he loses contact with his son. However, upon Susan's death, Michael regains custody of Walt. He begins active parenting on the island. Although their relationship is initially difficult, they finally bond, and then Walt is abducted by the Others.

DeGroot, Gerald—A doctoral student at the University of Michigan, Gerald, along with Karen DeGroot, founded the Dharma Initiative in 1970. Their work seems to have paved the way for the strange conditions often menacing the survivors of Oceanic 815 ("Orientation"). Gerald may be one of the Others on the island. *See also* DeGroot, Karen; Dharma Initiative.

DeGroot, Karen—With Gerald DeGroot, she gave birth to a "brainchild"—the Dharma Initiative. During her doctoral work at the University of Michigan in Ann Arbor, she helped develop the idea for a multidisciplinary research facility where scientists from around the world could conduct studies together. This work led to the Swan station where Desmond was held captive by the need to push a button every 108 minutes to keep the outside world "safe," although he is not sure from what ("Orientation"). Karen may be one of the Others. *See also* DeGroot, Gerald; Dharma Initiative.

Desmond—In the second season's "Man of Science, Man of Faith," Desmond appears twice. In Jack's backstory, he is a helpful runner who tends Jack's sprained ankle. On the island, Desmond later holds Locke hostage in the Hatch, where Desmond has been living. In a panic after he fails to fix the computer, Desmond leaves the Hatch and runs into the jungle ("Orientation"). Henry Ian Cusick plays Desmond.

destiny—Several characters ponder the concept of destiny in Season One. In "Exodus," Locke mentions that each person has been brought to the island by the island; it is part of their destiny. Conversely, Jack vehemently states his opposition to this belief. *See also* Fate.

dharma—*Dharma* is a spiritual concept, part of both Hindu and Buddhist thought, involving protection through living a balanced life in harmony with the rest of the universe. *Dharma* is a path of right living that brings peace and enlightenment. Dr. Candle's parting Namaste indicates the Hindu influence, fitting for the Dharma Initiative ("Orientation").

Dharma Initiative—In 1970, Gerald and Karen DeGroot, doctoral students at the University of Michigan, developed the Initiative as a research facility incorporating several different fields of study: psychology, parapsychology, zoology, utopian societies, meteorology, electromagnetism, behaviorism, remote viewing, and so on. The island hosted the Initiative, but an "incident" led to the need for a button to be pushed every 108 minutes—or something bad will happen. The orientation film for volunteers at the Swan station (the Hatch) are told only to push the button ("Orientation"). Another research facility, an abandoned storage area, is found by Ana Lucia's group of castaways ("The Other 48 Days"). This station bears an arrow in the Dharma logo.

Diane—*See* Jansen, Diane.

diary—Claire keeps a diary of her life on the island. After she is kidnapped ("All the Best Cowboys Have Daddy Issues"), Charlie loses his inner struggle not to read the diary ("Special"). In it he finds clues that he thinks may lead to her whereabouts. After her return ("Homecoming"), amnesiac Claire uses the diary as a way to regain her missing memories.

dictionary—Sun creates a Korean/phonetic English dictionary of basic words so Jin can learn English when he sails on the raft ("Exodus").

Diego—*See* Reyes, Diego.

Donald—Libby sets Donald's broken leg after the crash, but he later dies of an infection ("The Other 48 Days").

dream—Claire dreams that something bad happens to her baby and someone is trying to hurt her and her unborn child. Shortly thereafter, she and Charlie are kidnapped ("Whatever the Case May Be"). During "Fire + Water," Charlie's dreams of an endangered Aaron lead him to kidnap the baby. In response to the dreams and Charlie's strange behavior, Claire asks Mr. Eko to baptize Aaron to help protect him. *See also* vision.

DriveShaft—Charlie and his brother Liam form the rock band DriveShaft in England and end up with a hit, "You All Everybody," that takes them on a world tour. Liam is lead singer and spokesman for the group; Charlie writes several songs, sings backup, and plays bass. Life on the road is difficult, as the band loses jobs, such as television advertisements, because of Liam's drug-fueled behavior ("Fire + Water"). The band breaks up after their second tour of Finland, because Liam wants to become a drug-free family man. Charlie attempts to revive DriveShaft, but Liam refuses to come back ("Homecoming"). *DriveShaft* is also the title of the band's debut album, the one Locke tells Charlie he prefers to the second CD, *Oil Change* ("House of the Rising Sun"). Charlie's prize possession, in addition to his guitar, is his DS ring. During "Everybody Hates Hugo," Hurley and friend Johnny sing along to "You All Everybody" in a music store. Ironically, the CD is in the sale bin.

Duckett, Frank—The "Sawyer" who the castaway Sawyer wants to kill is also known as Frank Duckett, a retired confidence man operating a shrimp stand in Sydney, Australia. In "Outlaws," Sawyer shoots and kills Duckett but to his horror discovers he isn't the man he is searching for.

dynamite—As Arzt is quick to point out, dynamite is nitroglycerin surrounded by clay. Unfortunately, a stick blows Arzt up in front of a stunned group of castaways. Locke and Jack carefully carry six sticks of dynamite back to the Hatch to blow it open in "Exodus." In frustration over not knowing how to distribute the food from the Hatch's pantry, Hurley decides to blow up the pantry, an act designed to keep him from making decisions that will cause people to hate him. Rose, however, convinces him that this is not the best course of action ("Everybody Hates Hugo").

"Easy Money"—This song plays in the background as Hurley and pal Johnny drive around after they quit their jobs at Mr. Cluck's Chicken Shack. The title is especially appropriate for Hurley's situation: he carries a winning lottery ticket in his pocket but has yet to collect his winnings ("Everybody Hates Hugo").

electromagnetic fluctuations—In "Orientation," Jack and Locke view a film outlining the responsibilities of the volunteer button pushers at the Swan station. Their section of the island suffers from electromagnetic fluctuations. Problems with magnets and compasses also are noted in the first season episode "Hearts and Minds."

Emma—One of two children taken by the Others, Emma is sister to Zack. She is saved by Ana Lucia, who performs CPR on her shortly after the crash. Emma carries a teddy bear seen in other episodes being carried by one of the Others. Emma and Zack are headed to Los Angeles to meet their mother when Oceanic 815 crashes ("The Other 48 Days").

Ethan—*See* Rom, Ethan.

Execute—In the second season opener, "Man of Science, Man of Faith," the Execute button is highlighted on an old-style computer in the Hatch. Shannon sees Walt saying not to press the button, but she does not understand. When Jack belatedly follows Locke and Kate into the Hatch and discovers the computer, he seems ready to press the Execute button when he is stopped by Locke.

eye—The "eye" metaphor opens most first season episodes. A character's eye is shown in extreme closeup, indicating the person whose backstory is told in that episode or who will be prominently featured. In second and subsequent backstories (e.g., Jack has three in the first season), close-ups of a character's face, including both eyes, are a variation on the single-eye motif. A glass eye is found in the abandoned bunker that provides temporary shelter to the Tailies ("The Other 48 Days").

faith—During "In Translation," Locke tells Charlie that he has faith that the rocker will find his guitar; soon after, Charlie does. In "Exodus," Locke summarizes the differences between himself, a man of faith, and Jack, a man of science. Locke often uses the term *faith* to describe his conviction. Faith is an ongoing theme in the series. The second season opener is even entitled "Man of Science, Man of Faith."

FATE—Charlie likes to write on his taped fingers, especially in the first episodes ("Pilot"). FATE is the first word, although he later marks over the F to create LATE. Charlie's dream sequence ("Fire + Water") perhaps prophetically shows FATE once again on the tape, although in reality, Charlie hasn't decorated his fingers this way for several weeks.

fate—Throughout the first season, several characters ponder whether they have free will or are at the mercy of fate. In "Exodus," Sun believes that the castaways are being punished by fate, but Claire says she doesn't believe in fate. Mr. Eko seems to believe in fate, as he warns Locke not to confuse coincidence with fate ("What Kate Did").

Fiji—When Oceanic 815 first has equipment problems, the pilot heads for Fiji ("Pilot").

Fish 'n' Fry—Claire works at Fish 'n' Fry during the time she lives with Thomas and becomes pregnant ("Raised by Another").

fisherman—Jin's father is a poor fisherman who loves his son and suggests he leave his father-in-law's business in order to save his marriage to Sun ("House of the Rising Sun"). Jin has told his wife and father-in-law that his father is dead, but Jin is really just ashamed of his working class origins. On the island, Jin reveals himself to be an expert fisherman (e.g., "The Other 48 Days").

Ford, James—This name is listed by Sydney police as Sawyer's real name. Ford is wanted for a variety of crimes, including identity theft, and is deported from Australia in "Exodus, Part 1." *See* Sawyer.

French—The transceiver found in the cockpit and repaired by Sayid picks up a transmission originating from the island. The message, a distress signal in French, is reluctantly translated by Shannon ("Pilot"). In "Whatever the Case May Be," Shannon also translates a French document Sayid takes from Danielle Rousseau. The words form the French version of the song "Beyond the Sea."

geothermal generator—Sayid suspects that a geothermal generator is the power source behind the Hatch, but walls of concrete and titanium keep him from getting to the generator ("Everybody Hates Hugo").

golf—In "Collision," Kate practices long drives on the beach, much to Jack's amusement. However, when they challenge each other to playing a few holes of golf, Jack, who has been eager to give Kate advice, knocks his ball into the jungle after Kate makes a beautiful shot.

golf course—During "Solitary," Hurley develops a two-hole, par-three golf course to help the castaways relax.

Goodwin—In "…And Found," Mr. Eko identifies a body as that of Goodwin, apparently killed by the Others. The man was one of the twenty-three survivors from the tail section ("…And Found"). Until "The Other 48 Days," we assume that Goodwin is one of the Tailies from Oceanic 815. However, Ana Lucia discovers that he is one of the Others who has infiltrated their camp and killed Nathan, who Ana Lucia suspected of being one of the Others. Ana Lucia kills Goodwin with a spear during an altercation after she discovers his true identity.

Gulf War—Sayid is a veteran of the Gulf War, as is Hurley's buddy. During their first real conversation, Hurley is surprised to find that Sayid knows how to repair communication devices because he was in the war and seems surprised to learn that Sayid fought with the Republican Guard ("Pilot").

Halliburton case—The indestructible briefcase can only be opened with a key, as Sawyer discovers after trying every means he can imagine to open it ("Whatever the Case May Be"). The case, found at the bottom of a pool of water on the island, contains guns, ammunition, and a very special model airplane. Jack later wears the case's key around his neck to prevent anyone from getting the guns.

Hanso, Alvar—Danish philanthropist Hanso funded the Dharma Initiative. In "Orientation," he is shown on film as a somewhat shaded (or shady?) figure standing in a tall office building. *See also* Dharma Initiative.

Hart, Joan—In "Born to Run," Kate uses this alias when she picks up mail sent to her at a hotel.

Hatch—Boone accidentally discovers a bunker that seems impossible to open ("All the Best Cowboys Have Daddy Issues"); he and Locke keep the bunker a secret from the other survivors. The special numbers that pop up throughout the series also are engraved on the Hatch. In "Exodus," Locke and Jack set dynamite atop the excavated Hatch to blow it open. In "Man of

Science, Man of Faith," Kate, Locke, and Jack enter the Hatch and discover its inhabitant, Desmond. The underground research site they discover plays a prominent role in the second-season episodes, with many scenes taking place there or revolving around what happens there. *See also* Swan.

heart attack—Hurley's grandfather dies of a heart attack when the lottery check is presented in "Numbers." Jack's father dies of a heart attack, probably brought on by alcohol abuse and generally poor physical condition ("White Rabbit").

Heatherton, Francis Price—Frank is a successful business-man and one-time band member of Protestant Reformation. He assists Charlie in his new business venture, primarily because his daughter Lucy is dating Charlie ("Homecoming").

Heatherton, Lucy—Charlie's girlfriend in "Homecoming" is a rich girl from Knightsbridge, fresh from university graduation at Oxford. Her father helps Charlie get a job, but he steals from her to support his drug habit. Lucy rejects Charlie when he returns to make amends.

Helen—Locke invites Helen, his telephone "date," to accompany him to Australia in "Walkabout." He believes she really likes him after their month of long conversations, but she warns him that she is just doing her job by listening to him. Helen also is the name of Locke's former lover, who meets him in an anger-management group and tries to help him overcome his anger toward his biological father, Anthony Cooper. The couple is together at least six months, because Helen gives Locke a key to her apartment on their six-month anniversary. Katey Sagal plays Helen in "Orientation."

heroin—Charlie brings a bag of heroin onboard the flight and takes a quick hit immediately before the crash. He later locates the drug when he accompanies Jack and Kate to the cock-pit. During "The Moth," Charlie gives up the little heroin that remains and begins withdrawal. Locke and Boone discover a drug runner's plane full of heroin ("Deus Ex Machina"), which is being smuggled inside statues of the Virgin Mary. Charlie later comes across the heroin when he and Sayid track Rousseau ("Exodus") and smuggles one of the statues back to the caves. Mr. Eko discovers that Charlie has one of the statues and forces him to go to the Beechcraft; Eko burns the plane and its cargo ("The 23rd Psalm"). However, Charlie has a previously stored stash of statues, which Locke confiscates and stores in the Hatch's armory ("Fire + Water").

Hibbs—Sawyer's former partner in crime tells Sawyer about Duckett and sets up Sawyer to kill the man in "Outlaws."

hope—This concept also is mentioned conversationally in several Season One episodes—most tellingly when Hurley asks what Locke believes is in the Hatch. "Hope," Locke answers ("Exodus").

Hurley—"Hurley" is a nickname for Hugo Reyes. Although he confides to Jack that Hurley isn't his real name ("Raised by Another"), he won't divulge why he goes by that name.

hyperopia—Sawyer suffers from this vision problem, also known as far-sightedness, first diagnosed in "Deus Ex Machina."

"I Feel Good"—Hurley blasts into his rendition of this song to entertain Claire's baby and stop the child's crying, but his singing only makes the baby cry louder ("The Greater Good").

I Never—Sawyer teaches Kate to play this game similar to Truth or Dare in "Outlaws." Through the game, the two learn secrets about each other.

Islam—Sayid's backstories in "Solitary" and "The Greater Good" provide some insights into Islam, a religion alluded to in several episodes.

"Itsy Bitsy Spider"—Charlie sings the song to quiet Claire's baby, but the song fails to calm the child ("The Greater Good").

Jack—*See* Shephard, Jack.

James—In "Outlaws," Sawyer tells Frank Duckett his first name is James. *See also* Ford, James.

Jansen, Diane—Kate calls her mother by her first name when she visits her in a Cedar Rapids, Iowa, hospital, where she is dying of cancer. She seems distraught upon realizing that her daughter is with her and calls for the authorities. The meeting is shown as a flashback during "Born to Run."

Jarrah, Sayid—A former member of the Iraqi Republican Guard, Sayid uses his skills learned as a communications officer to attempt to send distress signals. He comes across Rousseau's traps and is for a time held captive by her. The notes he takes from her camp help him learn more about the island. Late in the first season, Sayid begins a romantic relationship with Shannon, which abruptly ends when Shannon is shot by Ana Lucia.

Jin—*See* Kwon, Jin-Soo.

Joanna—Crash survivor Joanna swims with Boone but is carried away by a rip current ("White Rabbit"). Although Jack swims out to save Boone, Joanna drowns before Jack can return to save her. In "Born to Run," Kate steals Joanna's passport so she can use the dead woman's identity.

John—*See* Locke, John.

Johnny—Hurley's buddy and partner in crime (e.g., stealing lawn gnomes to spell "Cluck You" in former boss Randy's front yard) is named Johnny. After Hugo abruptly quits his job at Mr. Cluck's, Johnny is inspired to do the same, and the two spend a memorable day and night just enjoying their freedom from the dead-end job ("Everybody Hates Hugo").

Kalgoorlie, Australia—Sam Toomey worked there when he learned about the mysterious numbers. Hurley travels to Kalgoorli, in the heart of Western Australia's gold fields, to track him down. Instead, Hurley finds Toomey's widow, who tells him about her family's misfortunes since her husband used the numbers to win a contest ("Numbers").

Karen—*See* Pace, Karen.

Kate—*See* Austen, Kate.

Katherine—Kate's mother refers to her as "Katherine" when she visits her in the hospital ("Born to Run"). *See also* Austen, Kate.

Kelvin—When Desmond's boat crashes upon the island's reef, Kelvin coerces Desmond to go into the Hatch, where Kelvin and Desmond share the responsibility for entering the code and pushing the button every 108 minutes. When Kelvin dies, Desmond is left alone with this responsibility ("Orientation").

Kevin—In "Man of Science, Man of Faith," Kevin is the fiancé of Sarah, who eventually becomes Mrs. Jack Shephard.

key—Keys figure prominently in *Lost*. In the pilot episode, Kate manages to use the marshal's key to her handcuffs after he is knocked out by falling luggage during the crash. This key frees Kate from being recognized as a captive or criminal. During "Whatever the Case May Be," Kate and Jack dig up the marshal's grave in order to retrieve the key to the metal case. In subsequent episodes, Jack wears the key around his neck. Only when he is drugged during "The Greater Good" is the key taken (by Shannon) to get a gun (to attempt to kill Locke in revenge for Boone's death). However, Jack soon gets the key back. In "Man of Science, Man of Faith," the key, again around Jack's neck, is magnetized by a strong field inside the Hatch. It pulls toward the magnet and leads him into Desmond's "home." In "Orientation," Helen gives Locke a key to her apartment on their six-month anniversary. Later, Helen removes Locke's car keys and throws them over the fence of Anthony Cooper's home.

kiss—Sawyer sets the price of information about Shannon's missing inhalers as one kiss from Kate ("Confidence Man"). Even torture fails to get him to reveal the inhalers' whereabouts, so Kate agrees to a lingering liplock. In "...And Found," Sun explains to Hurley that her dog's name means "kiss" in Korean.

knives—Locke's luggage includes a suitcase full of knives. He uses them to hunt boar, and he also teaches Walt how to throw a knife with deadly precision. Ana Lucia finds a U.S. Army knife in the pocket of a woman she kills when the Others attack the castaways' camp ("The Other 48 Days"). She later tells Goodwin that the knife is at least twenty years old.

Knoxville, Tennessee—Sawyer's letter to the man he hopes to kill is postmarked from Knoxville, TN, during the U.S. Bicentennial ("Confidence Man").

Korea—Sun and Jin are from Korea, where Jin worked for Sun's successful and powerful father. *See also* South Korea.

Kwon, Jin-Soo—The son of a fisherman and former waiter at the parties of the rich, Jin falls in love with rich girl Sun. He works hard and finally approaches Sun's father to ask for his daughter in marriage. Mr. Paik permits the marriage if Jin comes to work for him. He does, but discovers that his employer is ruthless. He plans to escape with Sun after one last business trip.

Kwon, Sun—Wife of Jin and daughter of a rich businessman, Sun seems to have an ideal life prior to the crash. However, she is estranged from her husband and eventually becomes an independent woman in the weeks following the crash. She and Jin eventually reconcile.

LATE—Another message Charlie writes in tape across his fingers ("House of the Rising Sun"). The letters later mark the trail after Charlie's and Claire's abduction.

LAX—Oceanic 815 is scheduled to arrive at LAX—the abbreviation for Los Angeles International Airport.

Lenny—*See* Sims, Leonard.

letter—Sawyer often reads a letter that he keeps folded in his pocket. When he later has Kate read the letter aloud ("Confidence Man"), she discovers that a boy wrote the letter to Sawyer, a confidence man who slept with the boy's mother and stole from his father. Only later does Kate realize that "Sawyer" is her fellow castaway.

Liam—*See* Pace, Liam.

Libby—A new character, introduced in the second season's "Everybody Hates Hugo," is played by Cynthia Watros. She has some medical knowledge and tells Ana Lucia she attended medical school for a year before dropping out ("The Other 48 Days"). She recognizes Hurley's crush on her and gives him tips on what women like to hear ("Fire + Water").

Lisa—*See* Reyes, Lisa.

Littleton, Claire—Single mother Claire is pregnant when she boards Oceanic 815 and gives birth to a son, Aaron, in "Do No Harm." Although she fears something bad will happen to her child, she tries to be a good parent to the baby she once wanted to give up for adoption. Claire's independence and determination gradually increase after Aaron is born, and she becomes a protective mother.

Lloyd, Susan—Susan takes baby son Walt with her when she travels to Amsterdam to take a lucrative job as an attorney ("Special"). She marries Brian Porter, who adopts Walt, and keeps biological dad Michael away from his son. Susan dies in Australia of a rare blood disease only a week after falling ill. Only after her death does Walt learn that his father loves him and wanted to keep in touch.

Lloyd, Walter—Walt is given Michael Dawson's father's first name and takes his mother's last name because Michael and Susan Lloyd are unmarried. The father/son relationship is often rocky, even as Walt comes to realize that his father loves him. Walt burns the first escape raft built by Michael but leaves with his father on the second raft. Walt is "special" and seems to have supernatural or psychic powers, which may be why the Others kidnap him. *See also* Porter, Walter Lloyd.

Locke, Emily Annabeth—Locke's biological mother (played by Swoosie Kurtz) eventually finds her son working in a toy store ("Deus Ex Machina"). As a private investigator reveals to Locke, Emily has been institutionalized for schizophrenia several times. She helps set up Locke's father's scheme to get a kidney from their son and receives money from Anthony Cooper. Emily also appears in Locke's vision before he finds the drug runners' plane.

Locke, John—Enigmatic Locke is confined to a wheelchair when the flight begins, but he is miraculously healed, he believes, by the island. Locke has the strongest connection to the island

and often acts as a spiritual advisor or counselor to the other survivors. He discovers the Hatch and later takes responsibility for making sure the button is pushed every 108 minutes. The Hatch also instigates more tension between Locke and Jack, who have widely differing ideas about how their little society should be run. As Claire turns away from Charlie, Locke also takes more interest in Claire and Aaron.

Los Angeles, California—The destination for Oceanic 815 is Los Angeles. DriveShaft's proposed comeback tour would begin there. The adoptive parents to whom the psychic encourages Claire to give her baby live in Los Angeles. Jin is scheduled to deliver watches to his father-in-law's business associates in LA. Jack is a surgeon at St. Sebastian's Hospital in the city and Ana Lucia a police officer.

Lottery—Hurley wins a lottery by playing supposedly cursed numbers ("Numbers," "Everybody Hates Hugo.") *See also* Mega Lotto Jackpot.

Lucy—*See* Heatherton, Lucy.

"Make Your Own Kind of Music"—Featured in "Man of Science, Man of Faith," the 1969 Cass Elliott hit provides a bouncy start to the second season as a mysterious man goes through his morning routine inside the Hatch

Malkin, Richard—In "Raised by Another," a psychic (played by Nick Jameson) hounds Claire to keep her baby, because danger surrounds the baby, and he will need his mother's positive influence.

Manchester, England—Charlie and brother Liam are from Manchester, where they establish DriveShaft as a popular local band prior to their global success ("The Moth").

manifest—Hurley matches the names gathered from survivors against the names listed in Oceanic 815's flight manifest. To his horror, he discovers that Ethan Rom is not listed as a passenger on the flight ("Solitary").

maps—Sayid takes maps from Rousseau's bunker in "Solitary" and then tries for days, unsuccessfully, to interpret her marks and notes. In "Whatever the Case May Be," Shannon finally breaks the "code" by translating the French notes; they are lyrics to "Beyond the Sea."

Margo—*See* Shephard, Margo.

Marley, Bob—The singer/songwriter is mentioned in "Exodus, Part 2," as Sawyer sings Marley's "Redemption." Michael asks Sawyer if he likes Marley, and he replies that everyone likes Marley.

Mars, Edward—The Oceanic-air.com website established by ABC-TV lists Edward Mars's name on the federal marshal's ID badge. Mars relentlessly pursued Kate until he could extradite her to the U.S. ("Tabula Rasa," "Born to Run," "What Kate Did"). *See also* marshal.

marshal—A federal marshal apprehends Kate in Australia and is bringing her back to the U.S. when Oceanic 815 crashes. The marshal survives the crash but is terribly injured. He regains consciousness long enough to warn Jack about Kate, but his injuries prove terminal ("Tabula Rasa"). *See also* Mars, Edward.

Mega Lotto Jackpot—Hurley plays the mysterious numbers in this lottery, which he wins. In "Numbers," the Jackpot drawing is shown on television, right before Hurley realizes he has the winning ticket and promptly faints. In "Everybody Hates Hugo," an episode which covers Hurley's day before he is identified as the lottery winner, his lottery ticket is shown up close. *See also* lottery.

Megan—*See* Pace, Megan.

Michael—*See* Dawson, Michael.

Mr. Cluck's Chicken Shack—In "Numbers," Hurley wears a shirt with a chicken logo, part of his uniform as a fast-food restaurant employee. During the second season, Hurley is shown working at Mr. Cluck's Chicken Shack. He tells Jack the chicken restaurant where he formerly worked was hit by a meteorite after his lottery win ("Man of Science, Man of Faith"). He works, unhappily, for manager Randy at Mr. Cluck's. When he wins the lottery, but has not yet revealed the winning ticket, he takes great pleasure in quitting his job ("Everybody Hates Hugo").

Mr. Eko—Sawyer learns the name of the man he calls "Shaft" in "...And Found." Mr. Eko (new regular Adewale Akinnuoye-Agbaje) is a skilled tracker, who helps Jin search for Michael. When he is attacked by two of the Others on the first night, Eko kills them with a rock and refuses to talk for forty days after the attack. He provides Locke with a missing section of the orientation film. After Mr. Eko finds the body of his brother, a priest mistakenly caught up in Eko's drug business, Eko becomes a priest in earnest ("The 23rd Psalm").

Monster—Locke sees the Monster, which he considers beautiful, and is later almost pulled underground by it ("Exodus"). Apparently huge, its path through the jungle is marked by swaying tree tops. It is large enough to uproot trees, and is certainly terrifying. It grabs the pilot from the cockpit and kills him. Its screech reminds Rose of something she has heard in New York City. Rousseau calls it a "security system" that protects the island. It may also be associated with a mysterious black cloud that seems to have a mind of its own. On a trek in the jungle with Charlie, Mr. Eko faces this black cloud, as well as his personal demons illustrated within the cloud. He survives, and he and Charlie have a new impression of the Monster ("The 23rd Psalm").

"Monster Ate the Pilot"—During "Born to Run," Charlie is convinced the raft will be found and help will arrive. He prepares for DriveShaft's big comeback after his miraculous return by writing songs for a new album. One song, for Track 2, is "Monster Ate the Pilot."

moth—A moth which helps show the way out of a cave-in ("The Moth") is symbolic of Charlie, who tries to shed his old life as an addict in favor of a sober life on the island.

Mullen, Ray—The one-armed sheep rancher turns in Annie (Kate) for a $23,000 reward ("Tabula Rasa"). When the marshal tries to apprehend Kate in a car chase, Ray's vehicle flips over, trapping him. Kate pulls him from the wreckage, but in saving Ray is captured.

mural—When Jack finally enters the Hatch ("Man of Science, Man of Faith"), he begins to explore the entryway to what becomes Desmond's living space. Jack sees a mural painted on one wall. Drawn like colorful graffiti, the mural features "108"—the total of Hurley's numbers. A dark-haired female figure on the right side of the mural could represent Rousseau. A house, like a child might draw, also is featured below the woman. 108 is somehow linked to the counter on Desmond's computer, which reads "108 00" when Hurley's numbers are keyed and the Execute button pressed. Some of the drawings bear a striking resemblance to Thomas's paintings in Claire's apartment in "Raised by Another" ("Adrift").

music box—Sayid is able to fix a broken music box and somewhat win Danielle's Rousseau's trust in "Solitary." It had been an anniversary gift from her husband; on its top a bridal couple dance. She treasures it, especially in her lonely life on the island.

Nadia—*See* Abed-Jazeem, Noor.

Nathan—The Tailies think Nathan is one of the survivors of the crash, but Ana Lucia fears he is one of the Others. Throughout "The Other 48 Days," the parallels between Nathan and Ethan are numerous: both are "from Canada," neither were on the plane (at least according to a flight attendant and the other survivors), both are creepy, both teach survivors how to hunt small animals (Ethan, rats; Nathan, rabbits). Nathan is killed by Goodwin after he is set free from the pit where Ana Lucia has been interrogating him.

Nelson, Willie—Surprisingly, a Willie Nelson song completes Sun's backstory, "In Translation." The lyrics—"Are you sure this is where you want to be?"—fit each castaway as the song closes this episode. *See also* "Are You Sure."

Nigeria—The drug runners who crashed on the island apparently came from Nigeria ("Deus Ex Machina"). Season Two's Mr. Eko is a Nigerian.

nitroglycerin—Arzt explains that nitroglycerin—the key ingredient in dynamite—is the most unstable explosive and must be handled carefully ("Exodus").

Numbers—The numbers, 4, 8, 15, 16, 23, and 42, can be found, individually or in combination, throughout the series' episodes, beginning in the episode "Numbers." In the second season they take on special meaning in relation to the Hatch. Not only are they imprinted on the outside ("Exodus"), but they are entered into a computer inside. Desmond demands that Locke type the Numbers and press Execute ("Adrift"). In "Orientation," the Numbers are revealed as the required code to save the world, at least according to Desmond and the Dharma Initiative orientation film. "Everybody Hates Hugo," Hurley's second-season backstory, emphasizes the Numbers on the day before Hurley is identified as the lottery winner.

Oceanic 815—The flight originates in Sydney, Australia, and is bound for Los Angeles. Approximately an hour into the flight, mechanical and communication problems force the pilot to turn toward Fiji. However, the flight is approximately one thousand miles off course when the plane breaks into three parts and crashes, the aft section plummeting into the ocean, the center section landing on the beach, and the front section ending up in the jungle.

Oil Change—The title of DriveShaft's second album, according to Locke ("House of the Rising Sun") a pale follow-up to the band's first, self-titled album. *See also* DriveShaft.

Others—Rousseau calls the mysterious whisperers on the island the Others. She claims they killed her team and took her child and are a group to be feared, an assessment with which the Tailies would certainly concur, after the Others abduct and murder several of their group of survivors. The castaways suspect Ethan Rom is one of them, and possibly more assist in Charlie's and Claire's abduction and Scott's murder. "Exodus" provides a first view of the Others, when a motley group of sailors take Walt from the raft, shoot Sawyer, and burn the raft. Jin and Mr. Eko hide from a band of silently walking Others as they trek through the jungle. The trouser legs, bare legs, and teddy bear imply that the band includes men, women, and a child/young adult ("...And Found). Jack and a "rescue" party searching for Michael are surrounded by the Others and talk with their spokesman, the man who shot Sawyer on the night the raft is attacked. The Others warn Jack and company to stay on their side of the island, because the island is really the home and property of the Others ("The Hunting Party").

Pace, Charlie—Charlie becomes bassist for the rock band DriveShaft. He loves music but is caught up in the band's temporary fame and becomes a heroin addict. When the band breaks up, he has difficulty in dealing with the aftermath of his limited fame. He "adopts" Claire and Aaron as his family and tries to protect them on the island. However, when Claire learns that Charlie lied to her about heroin hidden in a Virgin Mary statue, she kicks him out of their shared tent. Charlie becomes an outcast after he kidnaps Aaron in an attempt to "protect" him.

Pace, Karen—Wife of Liam and mother to Megan, she lives in Sydney ("The Moth"). Karen angrily tosses her husband out of her life when he not only fails to show up at the hospital to greet new daughter Megan but drops the baby when he does visit ("Fire + Water").

Pace, Liam—Older brother to Charlie, Liam proves to be a bad influence on his sibling ("The Moth"). Liam destroys Charlie's dreams of fame for DriveShaft and even sells his brother's prized piano for travel money so that he can try to patch up his failing marriage ("Fire + Water"). After he's gone straight, he refuses Charlie's insistent invitation to front the band again.

Pace, Megan—The daughter of Charlie's brother Liam, she lives with her parents in Sydney, Australia, and is approximately five years old at the time of Oceanic 815's crash ("The Moth"). Liam's daughter is named for his mother, Megan Pace ("Fire + Water").

Paik—Sun's father's name (Mr. Paik) is all that he is called during "House of the Rising Sun." Paik is a ruthless, rich businessman. He thinks nothing of bringing his son-in-law into the family automobile business and turning him into an enforcer. He sends Jin on a business trip to deliver watches to clients in Sydney and Los Angeles.

peanut butter—When Claire admits she craves peanut butter, Charlie tries to find some—or a suitable substitute—on the island ("Confidence Man"). If he finds peanut butter for her, she promises to move to the caves. When his search fails, Charlie brings "imaginary peanut butter," and his creative approach motivates her to relocate. In "Homecoming," amnesiac Claire tells Charlie she remembers "peanut butter" and associates it with him. Charlie finally is able to present real peanut butter to Claire in "Everybody Hates Hugo," when Hurley distributes the wealth of the Hatch's pantry, giving everyone one item special to them.

photocopier—*See* C815 photocopier.

pilot—The pilot of Oceanic 815 survives to tell Jack and Kate the flight was off course before the crash, but he is soon lifted from the wreckage by the Monster. His mangled body is later found in a tree. Although Jack is not a pilot, he tells Kate that he once took flying lessons but decided that flying was not for him. However, he knows enough about aeronautics to search for the transceiver.

polar bear—In the pilot episode, Sawyer shoots a polar bear that charges a group of the survivors. Also in the pilot episode, a comic book (later revealed to belong to Hurley) Walt finds includes a picture of an attacking polar bear. The polar bear makes another appearance, as the bear menaces Walt as he hides in a stand of bamboo in "Special." With Locke's help, Michael saves his son from the bear, and the bear is chased off by Vincent. Danielle Rousseau mentions polar bears as fairly tame beings compared to the other dangers of the island. She seems unconcerned when Sayid warns her against them ("Solitary"). In "Adrift," Michael's backstory reveals his sad parting with toddler

Walt before the boy's mother takes him to live in Rome. Michael is coerced into giving up parental rights to his son, but he tells Walt how much he loves him and his parting gift for Walt is a plush polar bear. During the orientation film to the Dharma Initiative, polar bears are shown as Dr. Candle explains that biological and zoological research is part of the Initiative ("Orientation").

police officer—Ana Lucia is a Los Angeles police officer relieved of duty after she is shot during a burglary. Once back on duty, she has difficulty refraining from pulling her weapon on threatening men ("Collision"). She murders the man who shot her.

Porter, Brian—Brian is the husband of Susan, Walt's mother. Overcome with grief and hesitant to be a true father to Walt, the Australian tells Michael to take Walt ("Special").

Porter, Walter Lloyd—Brian Porter adopts Walt Lloyd, and his legal name most likely then is changed to Walter Lloyd Porter. *See* Lloyd, Walter.

pregnancy—Claire is eight months pregnant at the time of the crash. In "Raised by Another," Claire's early stages of the pregnancy are shown, as she learns about the unplanned baby and, once her relationship with the baby's father, Thomas, ends, decides to give up the child for adoption. Claire gives birth to a healthy son ("Do No Harm"). In "Exodus," Danielle Rousseau tells the castaways that she was seven months pregnant when she was shipwrecked; she delivered the baby herself. Ana Lucia reveals to Sayid she was pregnant at the time she was shot while on police patrol ("Collision").

psychic—In Australia, Claire visits a psychic on a lark with a friend, but the psychic turns her away a few moments into the reading. A shaken Claire does not know what the psychic saw, but he correctly tells her that she is pregnant, which only a few people know. The psychic, Malkin, later hounds Claire to keep her child, but eventually gives her a ticket for Oceanic 815, supposedly so she can give up the baby for adoption in Los Angeles ("Raised by Another").

quarantine—In "Man of Science, Man of Faith," Kate points out to Locke, Jack, and Hurley that the door blown off the Hatch is marked "quarantine"—a word only seen from the inside of the locked hatch. It seems to indicate that whatever the world outside the Hatch holds has been labeled as quarantined, whereas the Hatch itself ironically might be perceived as "safe." In "The Other 48 Days," the inside of the bunker's door is marked Quarantine. The Dharma Initiative's abandoned storage facility, which the Tailies find, is marked the same way as the interior side of the Hatch.

radar—Sayid takes the radar unit from the wrecked Beechcraft and modifies it so Michael can use it on the raft to detect any passing ships. In "Exodus, Part 2," Sawyer spots a blip on the screen and urges Michael to set off their lone flare to alert whoever is passing by. Unfortunately, the blip turns out to be a small pirate vessel belonging to the Others.

radio—The Tailies find a radio in an abandoned Dharma Initiative storage facility. Bernard makes contact with Boone when he hears his mayday, but Ana Lucia ends the transmission because she thinks the Others are trying to draw out the castaways ("The Other 48 Days").

raft—Michael begins to build a raft that will take four castaways off the island. The first raft is destroyed by arson, but Michael, Jin, Sawyer, and Walt build a second raft. Sawyer buys his way onto the raft by donating supplies from his "home." After a difficult launch, the raft finally sails in "Exodus." However, the voyage is short lived, as the Others attack the crew and set the raft ablaze. In "Adrift," Sawyer and Michael survive by floating on sections of the destroyed raft.

Randy—Locke's despised boss in "Walkabout," he ridicules Locke about his plans for a walkabout. Locke gets satisfaction in telling him off. Randy is also, mysteriously, Hugo's manager in

"Everybody Hates Hugo," in which he has the same overbearing personality and creates in Hurley the same resentment that Locke feels toward his manager.

Ray—*See* Mullen, Ray.

Republican Guard—Sayid tells Hurley he served in the Gulf War ("Pilot"), a veteran of this elite branch of the Iraqi military. During his five years in the Republican Guard, Sayid was a communications expert who learned not only how to operate and create communication devices but how to interrogate prisoners ("Confidence Man").

Reyes, Carmen—Hurley's mother seems like a no-nonsense woman ("Numbers"). Just before he wins the lottery, Hurley lives at home with her. When he buys her a new house, she breaks her ankle getting out of the car. His relationship with his mother is briefly shown in "Everybody Hates Hugo," in which she is domineering in trying to get her son to improve his life.

Reyes, Diego—Hurley's brother is married to Lisa until Hurley wins the lottery. Then Diego's wife leaves him for a woman, to Hurley's surprise and Carmen's disgust ("Numbers").

Reyes, Hugo—Known to most castaways only as Hurley, the young man is worth $156 million as the result of playing the mysterious numbers and winning the lottery. However, he believes the numbers are cursed and he is the cause of accidents that befall everyone around him.

Reyes, Lisa—Hurley's brother's wife leaves her husband for a waitress. He believes this turn of events is the result of a curse brought on by using the numbers ("Numbers").

Rom, Ethan—Ethan Rom is an anagram for "other man." In "Solitary," Hurley discovers that his name is not on Oceanic 815's manifest. He seems strangely familiar with the island. He kidnaps Charlie and Claire ("All the Best Cowboys Have Daddy Issues") and, after she escapes, insists upon her return. To protect Claire from any future attack, Charlie kills Ethan ("Homecoming"). Ethan is played by William Mapother.

Rose—An important secondary character, Rose comforts Charlie after his near death and Claire's abduction. She is a religious woman who firmly believes (correctly) her missing husband is still alive; she and Bernard are reunited in "Collision." Rose rejoins the cast in Season Two's "Everybody Hates Hugo," in which she provides advice and comfort to Hurley.

Rousseau, Alex—In "Solitary," Danielle Rousseau tells Sayid that she killed her husband, as well as her colleagues, after they are stranded on the island. She repeatedly asks Sayid what he knows about Alex, her missing child. Viewers may assume that Alex is Danielle's son, but in "Exodus," Danielle says that the baby was a week old when "she" was taken by the Others.

Rousseau, Danielle—The Frenchwoman (played by Mira Furlan) is the sole survivor of a scientific expedition marooned on the island. For sixteen years she evades the Others and the beasts of the island. Rousseau provides the new group of survivors with warnings about the island's dangers. Seven months pregnant when she came to the island, her child was taken when it was only a week old.

Rousseau, Robert—Danielle Rousseau's true love, Robert (whose last name is presumed to be Rousseau), gave her a music box for their anniversary. To her delight, Sayid fixes the music box ("Solitary").

runner—Both Jack and Desmond run the stairs at a nearby stadium when they want to work off excess energy ("Man of Science, Man of Faith"). However, Jack runs for health reasons only, while Desmond proclaims himself as a professional in training for an around-the-world run. He tells Jack ("Orientation") that this trek brought him close to the island, where his boat crashed on a reef.

Rutherford, Adam—When accident-victim Sarah is brought into the hospital after her car collided with an SUV, Jack immediately begins working on her. The driver of the SUV, who is also in a life-threatening situation, dies, but Jack saves Sarah ("Man of Science, Man of Faith"). Rutherford is Shannon's father, and his death drastically changes his daughter's fortunes.

Rutherford, Shannon—Shannon is a spoiled rich girl, more interested in tanning than in helping other survivors. However, as the first season progresses, she becomes more self-sufficient. She builds a shelter and also translates Rousseau's notes from French. As she works more closely with Sayid, the two begin to develop a romantic relationship. However, after Boone's death, Shannon seems more bent on revenge than romance. She and Sayid fall in love, but Shannon's life is cut short by Ana Lucia.

Ryan, Kate—The name listed by entertainment sources, such as *E!Online*, for Kate's character. Possibly she keeps an earlier alias, Ryan, or her last name may be a married name (she tells Sawyer that she was briefly married).

Ryan, Maggie—Another alias used by Kate ("Whatever the Case May Be") during a bank robbery in Taos, New Mexico. Not even Kate's "gang" knows her name isn't Maggie Ryan.

safe deposit box—The marshal keeps the model airplane in box 815 in a Taos, New Mexico, bank. Kate holds up the bank just to retrieve the plane, which belonged to her former love Tom ("Whatever the Case May Be").

Sarah—Jack's fiancé and later wife, this young woman owes her health to Jack. He performs surgery so that she might walk again after a car accident leaves her with spinal injuries. In "Man of Science, Man of Faith," the extent of her spinal injuries is revealed; however, she makes a miraculous recovery. In "Exodus," Jack tells Ana Lucia that he is no longer married. Sarah finds someone new after workaholic Jack spends more time with his patients than his wife; she leaves him ("The Hunting Party").

Sawyer—"Sawyer" is an alias the man has used for many years. A former confidence man who looks out for himself, he also has eyes for Kate and can't resist needling Jack. *See also* Ford, James.

Sawyer, Frank—The con man first seduces (the character) Sawyer's mother and steals from his father. The boy's hatred is so strong he takes Frank Sawyer's name when he vows to kill the original for what he did ("Confidence Man"). *See also* Ford, James.

Sayid—*See* Jarrah, Sayid.

Scott—Scott seems to be close with Steve, another survivor, so much so the castaways have trouble distinguishing them. In "Homecoming," Scott falls victim to Ethan, who wants Claire back.

scratches—Both Rousseau and Ethan sport similar scratches. Claire likely scratches Ethan during her escape, and in "Exodus," she also remembers scratching Rousseau. Claire's returning memory causes her to recoil from Rousseau, who wants to hold the baby.

sea urchin—In the pilot episode, Jin forages food from the ocean. He prepares sea urchin and presents the food first to Hurley, who laughingly refuses it, and then Claire, who, after taking a bite, feels the baby kick for the first time in days ("Pilot"). Hurley steps on a sea urchin ("...In Translation"). During "Do No Harm," Sun removes the long, thin spines from a sea urchin to make a needle fine enough for Jack to transfuse blood into Boone.

security system—Rousseau tells the group accompanying her to the Black Rock that the Monster is a security system to protect the island ("Exodus").

Shannon—*See* Rutherford, Shannon.

shark—The fin of a great white shark flashes across the screen as the shark looks ready to attack Sawyer ("Adrift"). The shark appears to bear the logo of the Dharma Initiative.

Shephard, Jack—Jack is a talented spinal surgeon who nonetheless feels inadequate around his father, who is also a surgeon. Jack becomes the survivors' leader, as well as their physician. As leader, Jack often adamantly tells the other castaways what to do in his efforts to protect them (and control what happens to the group). He and Locke argue more frequently once the Hatch has been opened.

Shephard, Christian—Jack's father is chief of surgery at a Los Angeles hospital. After a patient dies during an operation, Christian (played by John Terry) is relieved of his title and right to practice medicine. Ostracized by his friends and former colleagues, he escapes to Sydney, Australia, where he drinks to excess and eventually dies in an alley from a heart attack ("White Rabbit").

Shephard, Margo—Jack's mother begs him to go to Australia to retrieve his father's body ("White Rabbit"). When Jack is reluctant, Margo accuses him of causing his father's current predicament; she tells him he owes his parents. Margo is played by Veronica Hamel.

showers—During "Solitary," Michael draws plans for showers within the caves. He devises a scheme to collect water in two basins and then let it flow in a controlled shower. During "Everybody Hates Hugo," Kate enjoys a shower in the facilities provided in the Hatch. To cool Sawyer, burning with a fever, Jack places him in the Hatch's shower ("Collision").

Silverman, Mark—Jack's friend Mark is best man at his wedding to Sarah ("Do No Harm"). He is also Jack's childhood friend, the one Jack tries to save from a beating by schoolyard bullies ("White Rabbit").

Sims, Leonard—Currently a patient in a California mental institution, Lenny once was a sailor who, with friend Sam Toomey, heard a repeated broadcast of mysterious numbers in the South Pacific. Lenny constantly repeats the numbers, which Hurley plays in the lottery. After Hurley discovers that the numbers are "cursed," he visits Lenny, who warns Hurley to get as far away from the numbers as possible ("Numbers").

smoke—According to Rousseau in "Exodus," black smoke indicates the Others are planning an attack. Black smoke presaged the attack in which Rousseau's baby was taken. It appears on the horizon in "Exodus," prompting the castaways to prepare quickly. The raft is launched, the Hatch is blown open with dynamite, and a group of castaways head to the caves.

South Korea—In "..And Found," Hurley asks Sun if she is from the "good Korea," and she assures him that she is from South Korea. Scenes in Jin's second-season backstory also show Seoul as the place where Jin and Sun first met. *See also* Korea.

spinal surgeon—Jack specializes in spinal surgery. In the pilot episode, he tells Kate about some of his harrowing experiences in surgery and how they helped him overcome fear.

St. Sebastian Hospital—Jack's name tag on his blue surgical scrubs lists St. Sebastian Hospital in Los Angeles, where future wife Sarah becomes his patient after her horrific car accident. Jack's father, Christian, chief of surgery at St. Sebastian, gives his son advice about his bedside manner in a flashback in "Man of Science, Man of Faith."

Steve—A friend to Scott and fellow survivor, the two peripheral characters are, to the other survivors, interchangeable. In "Exodus," Sawyer reads messages castaways placed in a bottle to be taken on the raft and learns that Steve has paired up on the island with Tracy, a married woman.

Sullivan—This peripheral character suffers from hives and is treated by Jack. He later joins the other survivors on Hurley's new golf course ("Solitary").

Sun—*See* Kwon, Sun.

Swan—Not only is a swan part of the Dharma logo on everything from food to clothing in the Hatch, but in "Orientation" it is revealed to be the third of six research stations. The area around the Swan is noted for strange electromagnetic fluctuations and one infamous "incident" that prompted the need for a two-person team to take turns entering code and pressing the Execute button on the station's lone computer. *See also* Dharma Initiative. In a strange verb choice, Charlie complains to Locke that he is just as important as everyone who went "swanning" off to the Black Rock and then to the Hatch ("Everybody Hates Hugo").

Sydney, Australia—The originating point for Oceanic 815, the city also is home to characters related to the survivors, such as Charlie's brother Liam. The survivors also have many personal links to the city.

Tahiti—Rousseau's scientific expedition sails from the South Pacific island of Tahiti.

Taos, New Mexico—Kate robs a bank in Taos in order to retrieve a model airplane from a safe deposit box. She ends up shooting her accomplices during the robbery ("Whatever the Case May Be"). *See also* safe deposit box.

tattoos—Jack sports several tattoos, which fascinate Kate. She cannot imagine a surgeon with tattoos and suggests that he may be wilder than he seems ("House of the Rising Sun"). Charlie also has a few tattoos.

teddy bear—In "…And Found," one of the Others dangles a teddy bear by a leash/tether as the band walks silently through the jungle.

Tennessee—Sawyer tells Frank Duckett that he is from Tennessee ("Outlaws").

Territoire Fonce—Danielle Rousseau names a section of the island the "Dark Territory" on a map that Sayid takes from her camp. Rousseau's party became infected when they entered the area, and one man lost his arm. The Black Rock is located within this territory.

Thomas—Thomas fathers Claire's baby but later ends the relationship before the child is born. He is a struggling artist in Australia with whom Claire lives before the unplanned pregnancy ("Raised by Another").

Tikrit, Iraq—Sayid is stationed with the Republican Guard in Tikrit.

titanium—Sayid tells Jack it is lucky that titanium has almost no magnetic attraction; the Hatch's walls are made from titanium over concrete ("Everybody Hates Hugo").

Tito—Hurley's beloved grandfather dies just as the lottery check is presented and he is ready to provide his grandfather with a secure retirement. The old man had worked three jobs for fifty-two years and was seventy years old ("Numbers").

Tommy—In "Homecoming," Charlie talks with "friend," fellow addict, and drug supplier, Tommy. Tommy sets up meetings between Charlie and the women from whom he steals. He cuts off

Charlie's heroin supply when he fails to steal from Lucy, a woman who manages to win his heart and motivate him to get a job.

Toomey, Martha—Sam Toomey's wife loses her leg in a car accident on the evening that he wins a contest by using the magical numbers ("Numbers").

Toomey, Sam—A former navy buddy of Leonard Sims, Toomey also knows about the mysterious numbers and plays them in a bean-counting game. When he wins, he discovers the numbers' curse. Toomey moves his wife to an isolated part of the Australian outback to protect them, but he still dies at a fairly young age ("Numbers").

torture—With Jack's guidance, Sayid tortures Sawyer to find Shannon's inhaler. Rousseau tortures Sayid to learn information about the castaways ("Solitary").

transceiver—Jack, Kate, and Charlie trek to the cockpit to find the plane's transceiver. Jack brings it to Sayid, who tries to use it to send a distress call.

trebuchet—Locke, with Boone's assistance, builds the device to smash through the Hatch. Instead, the trebuchet breaks, causing Locke to become further frustrated by his inability to open the Hatch ("Deus Ex Machina").

Turnip Head—When Claire fails to name her son, Charlie dubs the baby Turnip Head ("The Greater Good").

Vincent—Originally belonging to Walt's stepfather, Brian, Michael tells Walt that he can take the dog on the trip to Los Angeles ("Special"). Vincent is the first survivor Jack encounters after the crash. When Walt sails on the raft, he leaves the dog with Shannon ("Exodus").

vision—Locke sees a vision of his mother and hears a plane overhead right before he finds the Beechcraft. He convinces Boone of the correctness of this vision by revealing his role in the vision, which, eerily enough, is part of Boone's past ("Deus Ex Machina"). Boone has an hallucination, possibly because of his injury and then treatment by Locke, or a true vision. In it, he sees Shannon killed by the Monster ("Hearts and Minds"). *See also* dream.

Walt—*See* Lloyd, Walter; Porter, Walter Lloyd.

watch—Mr. Paik asks Jin to deliver a watch to an associate in the U.S. After the crash, when he sees Michael wearing the watch, he attacks him in order to protect his employer's property. After Sun explains to Michael why Jin reacted so violently, Michael angrily returns the watch to Jin. In "Exodus," Jin presents the watch to now-friend Michael.

wedding planner—Boone tells Locke he runs a highly lucrative wedding planning business for his mother, the "Martha Stewart of weddings" ("All the Best Cowboys Have Daddy Issues").

wedding ring—Rose wears husband Bernard's wedding ring when the couple flies, because his fingers swell ("Pilot"). She shows Jack the ring, which she wears on a chain around her neck ("Walkabout"). In "...And Found," Sun loses her wedding ring, which she later finds close to the bottle of messages she buries and a day later digs up. On the other side of the island, Jin is identified by Mr. Eko as a married man because he wears a wedding ring. Jack tells Sun he once lost his wedding ring but secured a duplicate before his wife found out. Now unmarried Jack's wedding ring is relegated to the sock drawer back home ("...And Found").

whispers—According to Rousseau, the Others whisper in the jungle, and she has heard them. Sayid also hears the whispers after he escapes Rousseau's hideaway in "Solitary." In "Outlaws," Sawyer hears whispers as well, prompting him to ask Sayid what he heard. In "Exodus," Rousseau tells Sayid and Charlie that she heard the Others say that they would be coming for the boy. In "Man of Science, Man of Faith," Shannon also hears whispers.

"You All Everybody"—DriveShaft's big hit is written by Charlie, who uses the song's popularity as a way to get women interested in him ("Pilot"). The song plays in the background in "Homecoming," as Charlie chats up a group of women. In "Everybody Hates Hugo," Hurley and buddy Johnny sing along in a music store, although Johnny refers to DriveShaft as "Suckshaft." The CD is in the sale bin.

Zack—Brother to Emma, Zack and his sister survive the crash only to be kidnapped by the Others ("The Other 48 Days").

CHARACTER SKETCHES

KATE AUSTEN

Interests—Steering clear of the authorities. Getting and keeping Tom's model airplane. **Home base (approximately)**—Originally Iowa, most recently Australia. **Family**—mother Diane Jensen (possibly deceased); legal stepfather but also biological father Wayne Jensen (deceased) legally recognized "biological" father Sam Austen. **Former job(s)/career**—Ranch worker, bank robber. **Closest friend(s) on the island**—Jack, sometimes Sawyer—but Kate is friendly to just about everyone and never completely trusts anyone. **Key moments on the island**—Helping Sayid transmit a distress signal. Volunteering for every dangerous mission into the jungle. Kissing Sawyer. Trying to take a dead castaway's identity and escape on the raft. Being the first to enter the Hatch. Fighting the Others. **Greatest personal challenge on the island**—Trusting others. **Greatest personal achievement on the island**—Retrieving the model airplane from the marshal's briefcase. **Backstory episodes**—"Whatever the Case May Be" (Season 1); "Born to Run" (Season 1); "What Kate Did" (Season 2)

BOONE CARLYLE

Interests—Shannon, mother's business. **Home base (approximately)**—California, formerly lived in New York. **Family**—Mother Sabrina, father (deceased), stepsister Shannon, stepfather Adam Rutherford (deceased). **Former job(s)/career**—Manager of a division of his mother's wedding business. **Closest friend(s) on the island**—Shannon, Locke. **Key moments on the island**—Joining forces with Locke. Uncovering the Hatch.

Sending a distress signal from the Beechcraft. Dying as a result of injuries from a second plane crash. **Greatest personal challenge on the island**—Living his own life, separate from Shannon. **Greatest personal achievement on the island**—Working with Locke. **Backstory episodes**—"Hearts and Minds" (Season 1); "Abandoned" (Season 2).

ANA LUCIA CORTEZ

Interests—Unknown. **Home base (approximately)**—Los Angeles, CA. **Family**—mother, Theresa. **Former job(s)/career**—Police officer; airport screener. **Closest friend(s) on the island**—Mr. Eko, at first; Jack. **Key moments on the island**—Leading the Tailies. Killing Shannon. Finding Henry Gale's balloon. Dying. **Greatest personal challenge on the island**—Keeping her group of survivors safe from the Others. Joining the other castaways after killing Shannon. **Greatest personal achievement on the island**—Maintaining control of the Tailies, as well as keeping them safe. Refusing to kill Henry Gale. **Backstory episodes**—"The Other 48 Days" (Season 2); "Two for the Road" (Season 2).

MICHAEL DAWSON

Interests—Art, son Walt. **Home base (approximately)**—New York, NY. **Family**—Son Walt; unnamed mother (to whom he speaks on the phone in the Sydney airport; "Exodus"). **Former job(s)/career**—Construction worker, artist. **Closest friend(s) on the island**—Early attraction to Sun; surprising friendship with Jin. **Key moments on the island**—Engineering a way to rescue Jack from a cave-in. Rescuing Walt from a polar bear. Building and sailing the raft. Killing two castaways. Retrieving Walt from the Others. **Greatest personal challenge on the island**—Building a positive relationship with Walt. Finding Walt after his abduction. **Greatest personal achievement on the island**—Gaining Walt's love. Being reunited with Walt. **Backstory episodes**—"Special" (Season 1); "Adrift" (Season 2); "Three Minutes" (Season 2).

MR. EKO

Interests—Religion. **Home base (approximately)**—Nigeria. **Family**—Brother, Yemi. **Former job(s)/career**—Drug lord/self-appointed priest. **Closest friend(s) on the island**—Ana Lucia Cortez, although he shares interest in the Hatch with Locke and begins to build a church with Charlie. **Key moments on the island**—Killing the Others who attack him; serving as tracker and guide as the Tailies travel to the other side of the island; facing the Monster; finding the Pearl station. **Greatest personal challenge on the island**—Overcoming remorse from killing others, even in self-defense; returning to his religious roots. **Greatest personal achievement on the island**—Finding his brother's body in the Beechcraft and gaining closure about this death; bringing a missing segment of the orientation film to the Hatch and helping Locke splice the film; finding spiritual purpose in pushing the button. **Backstory episodes**—"The 23rd Psalm" (Season 2); "?" (Season 2).

SAYID JARRAH

Interests—Electronics and occasionally romance (with Shannon). **Home base (approximately)**—Tikrit, Iraq (although he left home several years ago and had been searching for his friend Nadia). **Family**—Unknown now; an overprotective mother was mentioned in "Solitary." **Former job(s)/career**—Communications officer in the Republican Guard. **Closest friend(s) on the island**—Shannon, as a love interest; Jack, as an ally. **Key moments on the island**—Triangulating source of the Frenchwoman's distress call. Torturing Sawyer. Being tortured by Rousseau. Fixing Desmond's computer. Falling in love with Shannon. Torturing Henry Gale. **Greatest personal challenge on the island**—Overcoming his shame for his role during Sawyer's interrogation. Overcoming his grief and rage after Shannon's death. **Greatest personal achievement on the island**—Getting Shannon to believe in herself. **Backstory episodes**—"Solitary" (Season 1); "The Greater Good" (Season 1); "One of Them" (Season 2).

JIN-SOO KWON

Interests—Being a successful businessman; taking care of his wife. **Home base (approximately)**—Seoul, South Korea. **Family**—Fisherman father; father-in-law Mr. Paik; mother-in-law; wife Sun. **Former job(s)/career**—Employee of Mr. Paik (generally his "enforcer"); formerly a waiter and doorman. **Closest friend(s) on the island**—Michael, although he is sometimes solicitous of Sawyer; Sun, once they are reunited in Season 2. **Key moments on the island**—Attacking Michael for "stealing" his watch. Ending, for the time being, his relationship with Sun. Building and sailing the raft with Michael. Being reunited with Sun (Season 2). **Greatest personal challenge on the island**—Becoming a better husband. **Greatest personal achievement on the island**—Becoming a part of the group, instead of staying apart from the castaways. Becoming a prospective father. **Backstory episodes**—". . . In Translation" (Season 1); "House of the Rising Sun," in Sun's backstory (Season 1); ". . . And Found" (Season 2); "The Whole Truth," in Sun's backstory (Season 2).

SUN KWON

Interests—Art; her dog Popo; gardening; healing methods; her marriage. **Home base (approximately)**—Seoul, South Korea. **Family**—Wealthy but overbearing parents in Seoul; husband Jin. **Former job(s)/career**—Graduate with an art history degree; wife. **Closest friend(s) on the island**—Kate and, for a time Michael; Jin, once they are reunited. **Key moments on the island**—Revealing that she speaks English. Rebuilding a relationship with Jin. Finding herbal remedies to ease Shannon's asthma and to assist in Boone's surgery. Planting a garden and an orchard. Discovering that she is pregnant. **Greatest personal challenge on the island**—Rebuilding her marriage with Jin. **Greatest personal achievement on the island**—Becoming a more independent woman. **Backstory episodes**—"House of the Rising Sun" (Season 1); ". . . In Translation," in Jin's backstory

(Season 1); ". . . And Found," in Jin's backstory (Season 2); "The Whole Truth" (Season 2).

CLAIRE LITTLETON

Interests—Baby; astrology. **Home base (approximately)**—Sydney, Australia. **Family**—Estranged mother; Thomas, former lover and father to her son Aaron; (speculation) father, Christian Shephard; half brother, Jack Shephard. **Former job(s)/career**—Fast-food employee at Fish 'n' Fry. **Closest friend(s) on the island**—Charlie (until he lies to her and kidnaps Aaron); Locke (after he steps in as a protector). **Key moments on the island**—Being kidnapped by Ethan. Giving birth to Aaron. Having Aaron kidnapped by Rousseau and later by Charlie. Recovering memories about her abduction. **Greatest personal challenge on the island**—Being a good mother. **Greatest personal achievement on the island**—Being a good mother. **Backstory episodes**—"Raised by Another" (Season 1); "Maternity Leave," (Season 2).

JOHN LOCKE

Interests—Games of all types. **Home base (approximately)**—Tustin, CA. **Family**—Biological father. **Former job(s)/career**—Regional collections manager for a box company; once a toy store employee and a home inspector. **Closest friend(s) on the island**—The Island. **Key moments on the island**—Hunting boar. Finding, helping to open, and exploring the Hatch. Accidentally luring Boone to his death. Serving as a counselor/advisor to characters who are having an emotional crisis. Organizing a system for inputting the code into the Hatch's computer. Having a crisis of faith about pushing the button. **Greatest personal challenge on the island**—Determining what The Island wants him to do. **Greatest personal achievement on the island**—Becoming "found." Regaining the ability to walk. **Backstory episodes**—"Walkabout" (Season 1); "Deus Ex Machina" (Season 1); "Orientation" (Season 2); "Lockdown," (Season 2).

CHARLIE PACE

Interests—Music (playing professionally, composing). **Home base (approximately)**—Manchester, later London, England. **Family**—brother Liam, sister-in-law Karen, niece Megan, mother Megan (possibly deceased). **Former job(s)/career**—Bassist for DriveShaft, sometime grifter. **Closest friend(s) on the island**—Claire (until he loses her trust), Hurley. **Key moments on the island**—Saving Jack during the cave-in. Shooting Ethan. Bringing back Claire's baby. Giving up heroin, later finding a stash on the island, and finally destroying it. Having horrific dreams that lead him to kidnap Aaron and set a fire. **Greatest personal challenge on the island**—Staying away from heroin. Regaining Claire's trust. **Greatest personal achievement on the island**—Looking after Claire and Aaron. **Backstory episodes**—"The Moth" (Season 1); "Homecoming" (Season 1); "Fire + Water" (Season 2).

WALTER LLOYD PORTER

Interests—Comic books, dog Vincent, backgammon. **Home base (approximately)**—Sydney, Australia, most recently; although he has lived in New York, Amsterdam, and Rome. **Family**—Mother Susan Lloyd (deceased); stepfather Brian Porter, who adopted Walt; father Michael Dawson. **Former job(s)/career**—Student. **Closest friend(s) on the island**—Vincent. **Key moments on the island**—Learning to throw a knife. Burning the raft. Giving Vincent to Shannon. Being kidnapped by the Others. Sending messages while abducted. **Greatest personal challenge on the island**—Getting to know his father; possibly surviving the Others. **Greatest personal achievement on the island**—Rebuilding the raft with his father and learning more about him in the process. Being reunited with his father. **Backstory episodes**—"Special" (Season 1); "Adrift" (Season 2—featured as a baby and toddler).

HUGO (HURLEY) REYES

Interests—Popular culture (at least he knows about a lot of movies). Music, including CDs and concerts. Backgammon. **Home base (approximately)**—California, possibly Santa Clara. **Family**—mother Carmen, brother Diego, former sister-in-law Lisa, grandfather Tito (deceased). **Former job(s)/career**—Counter man at Mr. Cluck's Chicken Shack, lottery winner, wealthy investor. **Closest friend(s) on the island**—Charlie, sometimes Jack (but he is more of an authority figure), Libby. **Key moments on the island**—Building a golf course. Getting a battery (and information) from Rousseau. Distributing food (twice—most recently from the Hatch) to the castaways. Dating "Libby." **Greatest personal challenge on the island**—Stepping on a sea urchin. **Greatest personal achievement on the island**—Keeping in everyone's favor, even when he is in charge of something. Dating "Libby." **Backstory episodes**—"Numbers" (Season 1); "Everybody Hates Hugo" (Season 2).

SHANNON RUTHERFORD

Interests—Tanning, ballet. **Home base (approximately)**—California originally, most recently Sydney, Australia. **Family**—Father Adam Rutherford (deceased), mother deceased, stepbrother Boone (deceased), stepmother Sabrina Carlyle. **Former job(s)/career**—Student, dance teacher. **Closest friend(s) on the island**—Sayid. **Key moments on the island**—Wearing an orange bikini while others established a camp. Translating the Frenchwoman's notes. Attempting to kill Locke for his role in Boone's death. Searching for Walt. Making love with Sayid. Being shot and killed by Ana Lucia. **Greatest personal challenge(s) on the island**—Overcoming grief at Boone's death. Believing in her self-worth. **Greatest personal achievement on the island**—Finding someone who loves her unconditionally. **Backstory episodes**—"Hearts and Minds" (Season 1). "Abandoned" (Season 2).

Sawyer (James Ford)

Interests—Women, reading. **Home base (approximately)**— Not known: he travels throughout the U.S. South as he runs cons; as a child, lived in Tennessee. **Family**—Parents deceased. **Former job(s)/career**—Confidence man. **Closest friend(s) on the island**—surprisingly, late in Season 2, Jack; Kate; a fragile friendship with Michael and Jin. **Key moments on the island**— Kissing Kate. Hoarding luxuries gathered from the plane and survivors' belongings. Sailing on the raft. Surviving a bullet wound inflicted by the Others. Having sex with Ana Lucia. **Greatest personal challenge on the island**—Dealing with his grudge toward everyone. **Greatest personal achievement on the island**—Telling Jack about Christian's feelings toward his son. **Backstory episodes**—"Confidence Man" (Season 1); "Outlaws" (Season 1); "The Long Con" (Season 2).

Jack Shephard

Interests—Mostly work related, but perhaps wilder in the past—he sports several tattoos and took flying lessons; possibly running. **Home base (approximately)**—Los Angeles, CA. **Family**—mother Margo, father Christian (deceased), former wife Sarah; (speculation) half sister, Claire Littleton. **Former job(s)/career**—Spinal surgeon at St. Sebastian's Hospital. **Closest friend(s) on the island**—Kate; Ana Lucia. **Key moments on the island**— Accepting leadership of the castaways. Treating injuries (e.g., giving CPR to Rose and Charlie, treating Sawyer's stab wound, transfusing his own blood into Boone). Confronting Desmond—and part of his past. Planning revenge on the Others. **Greatest personal challenge on the island**—Being able to let go of situations he cannot control. **Greatest personal achievement on the island**—Keeping as many people alive as possible. **Backstory episodes**—"White Rabbit" (Season 1); "All the Best Cowboys Have Daddy Issues" (Season 1); "Do No Harm" (Season 1); "Man of Science, Man of Faith" (Season 2); "The Hunting Party" (Season 2).

CHARACTER CONNECTIONS

During the complete first season and first half of the second, the characters share not only space on the island, but facts from their histories or actions on the island that mirror each other's. The connections do not include every task that characters have done together, only events and traits mirrored between characters are included. The following list provides an indication of the links between and among characters that help us make meaning from *Lost* and help the characters begin to understand themselves and each other.

CHARACTER	AND	CONNECTION
Ana Lucia	Charlie	Shoot and kill their attackers, who once left them for dead
	Claire	Become pregnant and are later abandoned by the baby's father
	Danielle (Rousseau)	Capture and tie up Sayid for interrogation
	Hurley	Live and work in Los Angeles
	Jack	Share a drink in a bar at the Sydney airport; live and work in Los Angeles; follow a parent into the "family business"; know Christian Shephard
	Kate	Flirt with Jack; are called Ann or a variation of that name during part of their lives
	Locke	Live in California
	Michael	Accidentally shoot and kill a female castaway from Oceanic 815

CHARACTER	AND	CONNECTION
Ana Lucia (cont)	Sawyer	Are influenced by Christian Shephard after drinking with him in a bar; Sawyer runs into the door of the car Ana Lucia is driving
	Sayid	Feel dead inside because they have lost loved ones; know how to interrogate prisoners
	Shannon	Are shot and killed by another castaway from Oceanic 815; die soon after having a first sexual experience with a new partner; find "redemption" just before death
Bernard	Jin	Are separated from their wives for a time on the island
Boone	Hurley	Have lots of money; live in California
	Jack	Jack fails to save Boone's stepfather after an accident brings Adam Rutherford into the emergency room where Jack is working; live in California
	Locke	Live in California
	Michael	Live in New York City for a time
	Rose	Live in New York City for a time
	Shannon	Share past history as stepsiblings and lovers; die on the island
Charlie	Ana Lucia	Shoot and kill their attackers, who once left them for dead
	Claire	Are kidnapped and traumatized by Ethan
	Desmond	Come from the U.K.; are Catholic
	Hurley	Have listened to DriveShaft and like music; stay in the same hotel the night before they take Oceanic 815; are Catholic; are comforted by Rose during an emotional crisis; keep a stash in the jungle to feed their addictions; destroy what they are addicted to
	Jack	Have tattoos; save each other's life on the island

CHARACTER	AND	CONNECTION
Charlie (cont)	Jin	Believe that a real man takes care of his wife/girlfriend, sometimes to the point of being obsessive or jealous toward others
	Locke	Enjoy DriveShaft's music; are called "special" by their mothers
	Mr. Eko	Are Catholic; believe they turned away from religion and toward drugs because of their brothers; return to religion on the island; have prophetic dreams
	Walt	Are called "special" by a parent; set a fire on the island
Cindy	Claire	Are Australian
	Walt	Are kidnapped by the Others
Claire	Ana Lucia	Become pregnant and later are abandoned by the baby's father
	Charlie	Are kidnapped and traumatized by Ethan
	Cindy	Are Australian
	Danielle (Rousseau)	Give birth on the island; have a child kidnapped
	Hurley	Work at a fast-food restaurant
	Jack	Possibly share a father (speculation only)
	Kate	Have taken a pregnancy test
	Michael	Go through the process of giving up a child for adoption; are the single parent of a child on the island; have a child kidnapped
	Mr. Eko	Talk with Richard Malkin; receive messages from the Malkin family
	Sun	Have taken a pregnancy test; are distressed after discovering they are pregnant
Danielle (Rousseau)	Ana Lucia	Capture and tie up Sayid for interrogation

CHARACTER	AND	CONNECTION
Danielle **(Rousseau)** (cont)	Claire	Give birth on the island; have a child kidnapped
	Hurley	Understand the significance of the "cursed" Numbers
	Michael	Have a child kidnapped by the Others
	Sayid	Know how to interrogate and torture others
	Shannon	Speak French
Desmond	Charlie	Come from the U.K.; are Catholic
	Hurley	Are Catholic
	Jack	Like running; talk briefly in Los Angeles
	Locke	Spend much of their time pushing the button and believe the job must be done
Hurley	Ana Lucia	Live and work in Los Angeles
	Boone	Have lots of money; live in California
	Charlie	Have listened to DriveShaft and like music; stay in the same hotel the night before they take Oceanic 815; are Catholic; are comforted by Rose during an emotional crisis; keep a stash in the jungle to feed their addictions; destroy what they are addicted to
	Claire	Work at a fast-food restaurant
	Desmond	Are Catholic
	Danielle (Rousseau)	Understand the significance of the "cursed" Numbers
	Jack	Live in California
	Jin	Quit a job after being reprimanded by the boss; as boys, fish with their fathers; Hurley may have been seen by Jin on Korean television after Hurley wins the lottery
	Libby	Stay in the same mental institution

CHARACTER	AND	CONNECTION
Hurley (cont)	Locke	Have Randy as a boss; are connected to the box company (Locke works there; Hurley owns the company)
	Mr. Eko	Are Catholic
	Sayid	Lose the women they love, who have been shot by an Oceanic 815 survivor
	Sun	Have fond memories of owning a special dog
	Walt	Read the same comic book; are known in their youth as playing backgammon well
Jack	Ana Lucia	Share a drink in a bar at the Sydney airport; live and work in Los Angeles; follow a parent into the "family business"; know Christian Shephard
	Boone	Jack fails to save Boone's stepfather after an accident brings Adam Rutherford into the emergency room where Jack is working; live in California
	Charlie	Have tattoos; save each other's life on the island
	Claire	Possibly share a father (speculation only)
	Desmond	Like running; talk briefly in Los Angeles
	Hurley	Live in California
	Libby	Treat a man's leg injury immediately after the crash
	Locke	Live in California
	Sawyer	Have talked with Christian Shephard; perform CPR on a castaway to save a life; flirt with Kate; kiss Kate
	Shannon	Jack walks past Shannon when she learns of her father's death; Jack fails to save Shannon's father after an accident brings Adam Rutherford into the emergency room where Jack is working; grow up in California

CHARACTER	AND	CONNECTION
Hurley (cont)	Sun	Share an interest in healing; lose a wedding ring
	Walt	Have difficulties understanding their respective fathers
Jin	Bernard	Are separated from their wives for a time on the island
	Charlie	Believe that a real man takes care of his wife/girlfriend, sometimes to the point of being obsessive or jealous toward others
	Hurley	Quit a job after being reprimanded by the boss; as boys, fish with their fathers; Jin may have seen Hurley on Korean television after he wins the lottery
	Rose	Are separated for a time from a spouse on the island
	Sun	Share a history as spouses; speak Korean
Kate	Ana Lucia	Flirt with Jack; are called Ann or a variation of that name during part of their lives
	Libby	Say they have "trust issues"
	Locke	Are good trackers
	Mr. Eko	Are good trackers
	Sawyer	Are forced to leave Australia because of a criminal past; use different names to conceal their true identities
	Sun	Have taken a pregnancy test
Libby	Ana Lucia	Are shot and killed by Michael
	Hurley	Stay in the same mental institution
	Jack	Treat a man's leg injury immediately after the crash
	Kate	Say they have "trust issues"

CHARACTER	AND	CONNECTION
Libby (cont)	Shannon	Are shot and killed by another castaway from Oceanic 815
Locke	Ana Lucia	Live in California
	Boone	Live in California
	Charlie	Enjoy DriveShaft's music; are called "special" by their mothers
	Desmond	Spend much of their time pushing the button and believe the job must be done
	Hurley	Have Randy as a boss; are connected to the box company (Locke works there; Hurley owns the company); live in California
	Jack	Live in California
	Kate	Are good trackers
	Mr. Eko	Are good trackers; face the monster and survive; have prophetic dreams; at one time believe that pushing the button is important and part of their destiny
	Michael	Locke rolls past Michael in the Sydney airport
	Rose	Have been healed by the island
	Sayid	Have talked with Nadia
	Walt	Are called "special" by a parent
Mr. Eko	Charlie	Are Catholic; believe they turned away from religion and toward drugs because of their brothers; return to religion on the island; have prophetic dreams
	Claire	Talk with Richard Malkin; receive messages from the Malkin family
	Desmond	Are Catholic
	Hurley	Are Catholic

Character	And	Connection
Mr. Eko (cont)	Kate	Are good trackers
	Locke	Are good trackers; face the monster and survive; have prophetic dreams; at one time believe that pushing the button is important and part of their destiny
	Rose	Actively profess their religion and pray for survivors
Michael	Ana Lucia	Accidentally kill a female castaway from Oceanic 815
	Boone	Live in New York City for a time
	Claire	Go through the process of giving up a child for adoption; are the single parent of a child on the island; have a child kidnapped
	Danielle (Rousseau)	Have a child kidnapped by the Others
	Locke	Locke rolls past Michael in the Sydney airport
	Rose	Live in New York City
	Sun	Share a love of art, she with an art history major, he as an artist
Rose	Boone	Live in New York City for a time
	Jin	Are separated for a time from a spouse on the island
	Locke	Have been healed by the island
	Mr. Eko	Actively profess their religion and pray for survivors
	Michael	Live in New York City
	Sun	Separated from their husbands on the island, for a while

Character	And	Connection
Sawyer	Ana Lucia	Are influenced by Christian Shephard after drinking with him in a bar; Sawyer runs into the door of the car Ana Lucia is driving
	Jack	Have talked with Christian Shephard; perform CPR on a castaway to save a life; flirt with Kate; kiss Kate
	Kate	Are forced to leave Australia because of a criminal past; use different names to conceal their true identities
	Sayid	Lose a lover (killed by another Oceanic 815 survivor) soon after a first sexual encounter with her
Sayid	Ana Lucia	Feel dead inside because they have lost loved ones; know how to interrogate prisoners
	Danielle (Rousseau)	Know how to interrogate and torture others
	Hurley	Lose the women they love, who have been shot by an Oceanic 815 survivor
	Locke	Have talked with Nadia
	Sawyer	Lose a lover (killed by another Oceanic 815 survivor) soon after a first sexual encounter with her
	Shannon	Talk to each other in the Sydney airport; are lovers on the island
Shannon	Ana Lucia	Are shot and killed by another castaway from Oceanic 815; die soon after having a first sexual experience with a new partner; find "redemption" just before death
	Boone	Share past history as stepsiblings and lovers; die on the island
	Jack	Jack walks past Shannon when she learns of her father's death; Jack fails to save Shannon's father after an accident brings Adam Rutherford into the emergency room where Jack is working; grow up in California

CHARACTER	AND	CONNECTION
Shannon (cont)	Danielle (Rousseau)	Speak French
	Libby	Are shot and killed by another castaway from Oceanic 815
	Sayid	Talk to each other in the Sydney airport; are lovers on the island
	Walt	Lose a close family member and grieve on the island; take care of Vincent
Sun	Claire	Have taken a pregnancy test; are distressed after discovering they are pregnant
	Hurley	Have fond memories of owning a special dog
	Jack	Share an interest in healing; lose a wedding ring
	Jin	Share a history as spouses; speak Korean
	Kate	Have taken a pregnancy test
	Michael	Share a love of art, she with an art history major, he as an artist
	Rose	Separated from their respective husbands on the island, for a while
Walt	Charlie	Are called "special" by a parent; set a fire on the island
	Cindy	Are kidnapped by the Others
	Hurley	Read the same comic book; are known in their youth as playing backgammon well
	Jack	Have difficulty understanding their respective fathers
	Locke	Are called "special" by a parent
	Shannon	Lose a close family member and grieve on the island; take care of Vincent

Similar Names

Names are another way to make meaning in *Lost*. Several characters have similar names, either by name origin, root, translation, or similar sounds (e.g., close-sounding names in English, rhyming names). The following table indicates some connections among characters or perhaps some interesting coincidences among character names.

Name	Description of Character	Episode(s) or Recurring Character
Adam	Dubbed Adam and Eve as the "first people" on the island; bones found in the caves.	"House of the Rising Sun"
Adam Rutherford	Accident victim who dies in the emergency room before Jack can treat him; Shannon's father	"Man of Science, Man of Faith"
Annie	Kate uses this name during her stay on a farm in Australia	Recurring character (Kate); Annie only in "Tabula Rasa"

Emily Annabeth Locke	John Locke's biological mother, who helps Locke's biological father, Anthony Cooper, trick John into donating a kidney to his father	"Deus Ex Machina"
Ana Lucia Cortez	Survivor from Oceanic 815's tail section; brutal leader of the "Tailies"	Introduced in "Exodus"; recurring character in the second season
Ann	Ana Lucia is called Ann by her police partner.	"Collision"
Beth	Kate's friend who loves DriveShaft	"Pilot"
Beth	Pregnant woman who dies during surgery begun by Jack's father, Christian, which was taken over by Jack when he learns that his father is incapacitated	"White Rabbit"
Emily Annabeth Locke	John Locke's biological mother	"Deus Ex Machina"
Elizabeth	Libby's real first name; the name of her boat	"Live Together, Die Alone"

Brian Porter	Walt's stepfather, Walt's mother's husband who adopted the boy but later gave him up to Michael	"Special"
Bryan	Shannon's boyfriend in Sydney, Australia, who takes money from Boone and abandons Shannon	"Hearts and Minds"
Christian Shepherd	Jack's father; former chief of surgery at St. Sebastian's Hospital in Los Angeles	"White Rabbit"; "All the Best Cowboys Have Daddy Issues"; "Do No Harm"; "Man of Science, Man of Faith"
Crissy	Oceanic representative who tells Jack that his father's body cannot travel on flight 815	"Exodus"
Kristen	Newlywed who, with husband Steve, dies in the crash of Oceanic 815.	"Walkabout"
Dave	Hurley's imaginary friend	"Dave"
David	Libby's husband	"Live Together, Die Alone"
David	Jessica's husband, who Sawyer is trying to con	"Confidence Man"

Desmond David Hume	Inhabitant of the Hatch who explains to Locke the need to push the button	"Live Together, Die Alone" (when Desmond's full name is revealed)
Emily Annabeth Locke	John Locke's biological mother	"Deus Ex Machina"
Emma	Child kidnapped by the Others shortly after the crash	"The Other 48 Days"
Ethan Rom (similar in structure to Nathan, also the characters seem to mirror each other's behavior in much of their individual story arcs)	Reportedly one of the Others	Recurring character, "Whatever the Case May Be"; "All the Best Cowboys Have Daddy Issues"; "Homecoming"
Nathan (similar in structure to Ethan, also the characters seem to mirror each other's behavior in much of their individual story arcs)	Mistakenly believed to be one of the Others	"The Other 48 Days"
Frank Duckett	Reported alias of Frank Sawyer, the man who conned James Ford's/ Sawyer's mother; man Sawyer seeks to kill; not the right man that Sawyer seeks, although Sawyer finds that out too late	"Confidence Man"

Frank Sawyer	Confidence man who Sawyer wants to kill for destroying his family	"Confidence Man"
Francine	Young woman in Locke's anger-management group	"Orientation"
Frances (Frank) Heatherton	Father of Lucy Heatherton, Charlie's one-time girlfriend	"Homecoming"
Helen	Locke's phone-a-date	"Walkabout"
Helen	Locke's lover; a member of Locke's anger-management group	"Orientation"
James Ford	Sawyer's real name	"Exodus"
Diego Reyes (Diego is a Spanish nickname for James)	Hurley's brother's name	"Numbers"
John Locke	Regional collections manager for a box company; the castaways' primary hunter; a believer in destiny; a challenger for leadership of the castaways	Recurring character
Jack Shephard (Jack is a nickname for John)	Spinal surgeon; the castaways' physician and leader	Recurring character
Zack (although not a "John" name, rhymes with Jack)	Child kidnapped by the Others shortly after the crash	"The Other 48 Days"

Johnny	Hurley's good friend and former co-worker at Mr. Cluck's Chicken Shack	"The Moth"; "Everybody Hates Hugo"
Karen DeGroot	University of Michigan doctoral student; creator of the Dharma Initiative	"Orientation"
Karen Pace	Liam Pace's wife and Charlie's sister-in-law	"Man of Science, Man of Faith"; "The Moth"
Kevin	Sarah's fiancé, who abandons her during her surgery	"Pilot"
Kelvin Inman	Man who, according to Desmond, ran from the jungle to drag Desmond into the Hatch; a "volunteer" who pushed the button	"Orientation"; "Live Together, Die Alone"
Marc Silverman	Jack's childhood friend and best man	"White Rabbit"
Mark Wickland	Another name for Dr. Marvin Candle on a second orientation film	"?"
Megan Pace	Liam's daughter and Charlie's niece	"The Moth"; "Fire + Water"
Megan Pace	Liam's and Charlie's mother	"Fire + Water"
Randy	Locke's boss at the box company	"Walkabout"

Randy	Hurley's boss at Mr. Cluck's Chicken Shack	"Everybody Hates Hugo"
Ray Mullen	Farmer who hires Annie (Kate) as a temporary worker; man who turns her in for the reward money	"Tabula Rasa"
Reyes (e.g., Hugo, Carmen, Diego)	Hurley's family name	First mentioned in "Numbers"; family members in "Numbers" and "Everybody Hates Hugo"
Sam Austen	The man Kate believed to be her biological father	"What Kate Did"
Sam Toomey	Navy buddy of Leonard Sims, who also heard the numbers; Australian who played the numbers and believed them cursed	"Numbers"
Sarah Shephard	Jack's (now ex-) wife	"White Rabbit"; "The Hunting Party"
Sarah	Alias given to Ana Lucia by Christian Shephard when they work together in Australia	"Two for the Road"
Steve	Survivor of Oceanic 815; background person who occasionally assists	Recurring minor character

Steve	Newlywed who, with wife Kristen, dies in the crash of Oceanic 815	"Walkabout"
Tom Brennan	Kate's best friend and love, who dies during a shootout when Kate escapes the law	"Born to Run"
Thomas	Biological father of Claire's baby, Aaron	"Raised by Another"
Tommy	Charlie's supplier and "friend"	"Homecoming"
Tom	Real name of Mr. Friendly (one of the Others)	"Live Together, Die Alone"
Tom	Alias used by Christian Shephard when he works with Ana Lucia in Australia	"Two for the Road"

EPILOGUE

LOST IN THE FUTURE

After the previous chapters were written, *Lost*'s second season continued to provide more resolution to fan favorites' backstories. The enigmatic Mr. Eko's pre-island life was tantalizingly revealed in "The 23rd Psalm," itself not only a Biblical reference to walking through the valley of the shadow of death (certainly an accurate description of *Lost*'s island) and fearing no evil, but also a numerical reference to one of the cursed Numbers. Like Locke, Mr. Eko faces the Monster and survives. In "The Hunting Party," the mystery of Jack's lost love, Sarah, is finally put to rest when we learn how his marriage ended. Charlie's childhood and DriveShaft life are shown in "Fire + Water," an apt description of his relationship with older brother Liam and his parents, as well as the means by which he tries to "save" baby Aaron. These episodes, with a smattering of information about Sawyer's backstory episode, "The Long Con," ended the original edition of this book.

As expected, the remaining episodes, shown in the U.S. through May 2006, provided the conclusion to some castaways' stories, but led other characters in exciting and sometimes frightening new directions. Michael's and Walt's story seems to end with their reunion and apparent exodus from the island. However, in true *Lost* style, we don't see what happens to the little boat once the father and son motor off screen. Perhaps they return home but never tell their tale, but more likely, also in true *Lost* fashion, they remain spiritually if not geographically lost for some time to come.

Michael, at least, someday must deal with the ramifications of murdering two people, even if he currently feels that the sacrifice of his friends is necessary for Walt to be freed from the Others' camp.

And what of the Others? Late-season addition Henry Gale, whose real name and identity we are no closer to knowing at the end of the season than when he is first captured by Rousseau and delivered to Sayid for questioning, gives us a new perspective about island life. Gale can be charming as well as infuriating, and his mind games, even on such a savvy character as Locke, make us question what's really happening on the island. Also as anticipated, other Others are playing a more dominant role in the castaways' lives and thus receiving more screen time. Mr. Friendly, Miss Klugh, Pickett, and Alex, along with Henry Gale, are only a few new faces that promise further intrigue in the coming season. As the plot quite literally thickens, with new characters and even more layers of meaning, the question of who is "good" and who is not continues to bedevil the castaways and the audience. "We *are* the good guys," Gale tells Michael, but the events manipulated by the Others, as shown during Season 2, indicate that their definition of "good" may not be ours—but then, the beloved castaways, even good Doctor Jack, also are looking a lot shadier by the second-season finale.

Faith, a continuing theme, is highlighted in the finale, as Locke and Eko each define what faith requires them to do. Redemption will likely be a prominent theme again in the third season, as the castaways not only must face themselves and the implications of recent cataclysmic events, but also new alliances with or attacks against the Others.

A common question about this book after the second-season finale aired is: How much information is now outdated? Our answer is none. Even the many conspiracy theories outlined in the last chapter have been embellished with information gained through the most recent episodes. In fact, several elements of these theories—electromagnetism, experimentation, even aliens—are mentioned or shown in the finale. Granted, some are tongue-in-cheek allusions, such as Sawyer mentioning aliens, but *Lost* fans can add to, rather than completely dismiss, many theories being discussed online or referenced in this book. With the introduction of Charles and Penelope Widmore and more of Desmond's backstory, conspiracy theorists undoubtedly will be busy for awhile as they try to unravel the true story behind the island's mystery and its ever-growing cast of characters.

In May, ABC announced its fall schedule, and, as expected, *Lost* has been renewed for a third season. During a *Lost* convention in June 2005, Lindelof told fans that story arcs had been projected for three seasons and five seasons; the series wouldn't go longer than five years to tell the complete story, which could be told basically within three years. (However, in late January 2006, original cast members received a hefty per-episode raise, with the caveat that they also sign a contract for an additional year. Obviously, the producers and ABC are banking on *Lost*'s continued success, which could prolong the original estimated storyline.) Although Lindelof admitted that some aspects of the story (such as the Numbers) take on a life of their own, which then requires reworking the primary arcs to accommodate new details and sidestories, the series' basic concept had been outlined. He promised that there would be no "reunion" shows or spinoffs. It seems doubtful that we'll someday follow Charlie's new band on a third tour of Finland, see a sitcom featuring those wacky next door neighbors Sun and Jin, or watch Kate evade the law as *The New (and Incredibly Hot) Fugitive*. Even a movie seems farfetched. *Lost* is and should remain a mini-movie each week, shown on small screens, whether television, mobile phone, or computer.

Since the renewal, Lindelof and Cuse have indicated that, in the third season, the Others will play a more prominent role, but relationships, always a series' strength, also will be emphasized. Romance, or at least perhaps something longer lasting than a promised picnic or one night of passion, may become reality for at least some characters. Charlie and Claire (relation)shippers can hope that the pair's tentative reunion in the finale bodes well, and the Jack/Kate/Sawyer quandary still may offer some interesting twists.

Typical of ratings trends with a sophomore series, *Lost* didn't please all of the viewers all of the time. Nevertheless, it succeeded in winning over more critics, maintaining a high number of regular viewers for all first-run episodes, and keeping the hardcore faithful guessing online. To appease viewers, and to help maintain the ever-necessary ratings, ABC's 2006-2007 *Lost* schedule allows more rerun-free broadcasts. A block of episodes premiering later in 2006 will be followed by an even longer block of first-run episodes beginning in the U.S. in January or February 2007 and continuing through the May "sweeps" rating period. The executives behind ABC's schedule realize the new realities of programming; popular series like *24* begin later than the formerly "typical" start to the new television season, offer episodes without repeats, and capture the audience's continued interest through momentum in the storytelling. The serialized *Lost* needs to maintain this momentum so that viewers stay with the many plot twists and character developments. The promised scheduling of *Lost*'s third-season episodes should help keep viewers riveted on Wednesday nights and allow the series' writers to develop at least two clearly defined story arcs for the season.

Lost's marketing machine continues to roll out new products and, better yet, interactive experiences. During episodes broadcast in May, commercials with information for the Lost Experience helped fans begin what ABC bills as a hiatus-long role-playing "game" to learn more about the Hanso Foundation and its potential role in the island's mystery. In addition, pictures of upcoming action figures adorned the Web late in the season. Even the departed Shannon is immortalized in plastic, wearing the famous orange bikini. Hurley's action figure arrives with a lottery ticket; Kate's, a tiny airplane. Games and toys are only a small part of a vast marketing campaign that continues even when the show is on hiatus.

Now in mid-2006, it seems safe to say that many of us will find ourselves watching *Lost* for the foreseeable future, and hardcore fans likely will spend a great deal of time analyzing details, reading background materials featured in episodes, and participating in activities like the Lost Experience. The show continues to provoke discussion, pique our curiosity, and promote itself in innovative ways. So far, the series hasn't *Lost* its way, and we hope that Abrams, Lindelof, Cuse, and company keep us heading in a plausible direction for seasons to come.

Appendix A

LOST EPISODE GUIDE

Seq. #	EP #	Air Date	Title	Writer	Director
1	1.1	9/22/2004	"Pilot (1)"	J. J. Abrams & Damon Lindelof	Abrams
2	1.2	9/29/2004	"Pilot (2)"	Abrams & Lindelof	Abrams
3	1.3	10/6/2004	"Tabula Rasa"	Lindelof	Jack Bender
4	1.4	10/13/2004	"Walkabout"	David Fury	Bender
5	1.5	10/20/2004	"White Rabbit"	Christian Taylor	Kevin Hooks
6	1.6	10/27/2004	"House of the Rising Sun"	Javier Grillo-Marxuach	Michael Zinberg
7	1.7	11/3/2004	"The Moth"	Jennifer Johnson & Paul Dini	Bender

8	1.8	11/10/2004	"Confidence Man"	Lindelof	Tucker Gates
9	1.9	11/17/2004	"Solitary"	Fury	Greg Yaitanes
10	1.10	12/1/2004	"Raised by Another"	Lynne E. Litt	Marita Grabiak
11	1.11	12/8/2004	"All the Best Cowboys Have Daddy Issues"	Grillo-Marxuach	Stephen Williams
12	1.12	1/5/2005	"Whatever the Case May Be"	Lindelof & Johnson	Bender
13	1.13	1/12/2005	"Hearts & Minds"	Carlton Cuse & Grillo-Marxuach	Rod Holcomb
14	1.14	1/19/2005	"Special"	Fury	Yaitanes
15	1.15	2/9/2005	"Homecoming"	Lindelof	Hooks
16	1.16	2/16/2005	"Outlaws"	Drew Goddard	Bender
17	1.17	2/23/2005	"...In Translation"	Grillo-Marxuach & Leonard Dick	Gates

18	1.18	3/2/2005	"Numbers"	Fury & Brent Fletcher	Tucker Gates
19	1.19	3/30/2005	"Deus Ex Machina"	Lindelof & Cuse	Robert Mandel
20	1.20	4/6/2005	"Do No Harm"	Janet Tamaro	Williams
21	1.21	5/4/2005	"The Greater Good" (a.k.a. "Sides")	Dick	David Grossman
22	1.22	5/11/2005	"Born to Run"	Edward Kitsis, Adam Horowitz, & Grillo-Marxuach	Gates
23	1.23	5/18/2005	"Exodus (I)"	Lindelof & Cuse	Bender
24	1.24	5/25/2005	"Exodus (II)"	Lindelof & Cuse	Bender
25	2.1	9/21/2005	"Man of Science, Man of Faith"	Lindelof	Bender
26	2.2	9/28/2005	"Adrift"	Dick & Steven Maeda	Williams

27	2.3	10/5/2005	"Orientation"	Grillo-Marxuach & Craig Wright	Bender
28	2.4	10/12/2005	"Everybody Hates Hugo"	Horowitz & Kitsis	Alan Taylor
29	2.5	10/19/2005	"...And Found"	Lindelof & Cuse	Williams
30	2.6	11/9/2005	"Abandoned"	Elizabeth Sarnoff	Adam Davidson
31	2.7	11/16/2005	"The Other 48 Days"	Lindelof & Cuse	Eric Laneuville
32	2.8	11/23/2005	"Collision"	Dick & Grillo-Marxuach	Williams
33	2.9	11/30/2005	"What Kate Did"	Maeda & Wright	Paul Edwards
34	2.10	1/11/2006	"The 23rd Psalm"	Lindelof & Cuse	Matt Earl Beesley
35	2.11	1/18/2006	"The Hunting Party"	Sarnoff & Christine M. Kim	Williams
36	2.12	1/25/2006	"Fire + Water"	Horowitz & Kitsis	Bender
37	2.13	2/8/2006	"The Long Con"	Maeda & Dick	Roxann Dawson

38	2.14	2/15/2006	"One of Them"	Lindelof & Cuse	Williams
39	2.15	3/1/2006	"Maternity Leave"	Dawn Robertson Kelly & Matt Ragghianti	Bender
40	2.16	3/22/2006	"The Whole Truth"	Kim & Sarnoff	Karen Gaviola
41	2.17	3/29/2006	"Lockdown"	Lindelof & Cuse	Williams
42	2.18	4/5/2006	"Dave"	Kitsis & Horowitz	Bender
43	2.19	4/12/2006	"S.O.S."	Maeda & Dick	Laneuville
44	2.20	5/3/2006	"Two for the Road"	Kim & Sarnoff	Edwards
45	2.21	5/10/2006	"?"	Cuse & Lindelof	Dean Sarafian
46	2.22	5/17/2006	"Three Minutes"	Kitsis & Horowitz	Williams
47	2.23	5/24/2006	"Live Together, Die Alone, Part 1"	Lindelof & Cuse	Bender

| 48 | 2.24 | 5/24/2006 | Live Together, Die Alone, Part 2 | Lindelof & Cuse | Bender |

LOST'S AWARDS AND NOMINATIONS 2004–2006

AWARD TITLE	ORGANIZATION/ AWARD NAME	NOMINEE(S)	DATE PRESENTED	NOMINEE/ WINNER
Best Network Television Series	Academy of Science Fiction, Fantasy, and Horror Films, Saturn Award	*Lost*	2005	**Winner**
Best Supporting Actor in a Television Series	Academy of Science Fiction, Fantasy, and Horror Films, Saturn Award	**Terry O'Quinn**	2005	**Winner Best Actress in a Television Series**
Best Actress in a Television Series	Academy of Science Fiction, Fantasy, and Horror Films, Saturn Award	**Evangeline Lilly**	2005	Nominee

Category	Award	Recipient	Year	Result
Best Actor in a Television Series	Academy of Science Fiction, Fantasy, and Horror Films, Saturn Award	**Matthew Fox**	2005	Nominee
Best Supporting Actor in a Television Series	Academy of Science Fiction, Fantasy, and Horror Films, Saturn Award	**Dominic Monaghan**	2005	Nominee
Best Network Television Series	Academy of Science Fiction, Fantasy, and Horror Films, Saturn Award	*Lost*	2006	**Winner**
Best Actor in a Television Series	Academy of Science Fiction, Fantasy, and Horror Films, Saturn Award	**Matthew Fox**	2006	**Winner**
Best DVD Television Release	Academy of Science Fiction, Fantasy, and Horror Films, Saturn Award	Lost (Season 1)	2006	**Winner**
Best Actress in a Television Series	Academy of Science Fiction, Fantasy, and Horror Films, Saturn Award	**Evangeline Lilly**	2006	Nominee
Best Supporting Actor in a Television Series	Academy of Science Fiction, Fantasy, and Horror Films, Saturn Award	**Adewale Akinnuoye-Agbaje**	2006	Nominee

Best Supporting Actor in a Television Series	Academy of Science Fiction, Fantasy, and Horror Films, Saturn Award	**Terry O'Quinn**	2006	Nominee
Best Supporting Actress in a Television Series	Academy of Science Fiction, Fantasy, and Horror Films, Saturn Award	**Michelle Rodriguez**	2006	Nominee
Outstanding Female TV Performance	Asian Excellence Award	**Yunjin Kim**	2006	**Winner**
Outstanding Male TV Performance	Asian Excellence Award	**Daniel Dae Kim**	2006	**Winner**
Outstanding Achievement in Television, Dramatic Series, Night (Pilot episode, Part 2)	Director's Guild of America	**J. J. Abrams**	2005	Nominee
Television Drama Multi-Episode Storyline (*Lost*— Charlie's Addiction)	Entertainment Industries Council, Prism Award	*Lost*—**"Pilot," "House of the Rising Sun," "The Moth"**	2005	**Winner**
Performance in a Drama Storyline	Entertainment Industries Council, Prism Award	**Dominic Monaghan**	2005	Nominee
Best New Series	Family Friendly Programming Forum, Family Television Award	*Lost*	2004	**Winner**

Best Drama	Family Friendly Programming Forum, Family Television Award	*Lost*	2005	**Winner**
Best Drama	Hollywood Foreign Press Association, Golden Globe	*Lost*	2005	Nominee
Best Drama Series	Hollywood Foreign Press Association, Golden Globe Award	*Lost*	2006	**Winner**
Actor in a Drama, TV Series	Hollywood Foreign Press Association, Golden Globe Award	**Matthew Fox**	2006	Nominee
Supporting Actor, series or miniseries	Hollywood Foreign Press Association, Golden Globe Award	**Naveen Andrews**	2006	Nominee
Actor in a Series, Drama	International Press Academy, Satellite Award	**Matthew Fox**	2005	**Winner**
Actress in a Series, Drama	International Press Academy, Satellite Award	**Evangeline Lilly**	2005	Nominee
Television Series, Drama	International Press Academy, Satellite Award	*Lost*	2005	Nominee
Television Series, Drama	International Press Academy, Satellite Award	*Lost*	2006	Nominee

Best DVD Release of a Television Show	International Press Academy	*Lost*	2006	Nominee
Outstanding Drama Series	NAACP, NAACP Image Award	*Lost*	2006	Nominee
Outstanding Supporting Actor in a Television Series	National Council of La Raza, Alma Award	**Jorge Garcia**	2006	**Winner**
Outstanding Supporting Actress in a Television Series	National Council of La Raza, Alma Award	**Michelle Rodriguez**	2006	**Winner**
Favorite New Series	People's Choice	*Lost*	2004	Nominee
Television Series: Drama	Producers Guild of America, PGA Award	**J.J. Abrams, Damon Lindelof, Bryan Burk, Jack Bender, Jean Higgins, Carlton Cuse**	2006	**Winner**
Outstanding Performance by an Ensemble in a Drama Series	Screen Actors Guild, SAG Award	*Lost*	2006	**Winner**
Outstanding Drama Series*	Television Academy of Arts and Sciences, Emmy Award	*Lost*	2005	**Winner**

* Emmy Trivia: *Lost* is the first series since *The West Wing* to win an Emmy for best drama series in its first season.

Outstanding Casting for a Drama Series	Television Academy of Arts and Sciences, Emmy Award	*Lost*	2005	Winner
Outstanding Directing for a Drama Series	Television Academy of Arts and Sciences, Emmy Award	J. J. Abrams (pilot episode)	2005	Winner
Outstanding Single-Camera Editing for a Drama Series	Television Academy of Arts and Sciences, Emmy Award	*Lost*	2005	Winner
Outstanding Music Composition for a Series (Dramatic Underscore)	Television Academy of Arts and Sciences, Emmy Award	Michael Giacchino	2005	Winner
Outstanding Supporting Actor in a Drama Series	Television Academy of Arts and Sciences, Emmy Award	Naveen Andrews	2005	Nominee
Outstanding Supporting Actor in a Drama Series	Television Academy of Arts and Sciences, Emmy Award	Terry O'Quinn	2005	Nominee
Outstanding Writing for a Drama Series	Television Academy of Arts and Sciences, Emmy Award	J. J. Abrams, Damon Lindelof, Jeffrey Lieber (*Lost*— Pilot episode, Parts 1 and 2)	2005	Nominee

Outstanding Writing for a Drama Series	Television Academy of Arts and Sciences, Emmy Award	David Fury (*Lost—* Walkabout)	2005	Nominee
Outstanding Sound Editing for a Series	Television Academy of Arts and Sciences, Emmy Award	*Lost* (Pilot episode, Parts 1 and 2)	2005	Nominee
Outstanding Special Visual Effects for a Series	Television Academy of Arts and Sciences, Emmy Award	*Lost* (Pilot episode, Parts 1 and 2)	2005	**Winner**
Outstanding Single-Camera Sound Mixing for a Series	Television Academy of Arts and Sciences, Emmy Award	*Lost* (Outlaws)	2005	Nominee
Outstanding New Program of the Year	Television Critics Association	Lost	2005	**Winner**
Outstanding Achievement in Drama	Television Critics Association	*Lost*	2005	**Winner**
Program of the Year	Television Critics Association	*Lost*	2005	Nominee
Outstanding Achievement in Drama	Television Critics Association	Matthew Fox	2005	Nominee
Outstanding Achievement in Drama	Television Critics Association	*Lost*	2006	Nominee
Program of the Year	Television Critics Association	*Lost*	2006	Nominee

Award	Organization	Recipient	Year	Result
Outstanding Supporting Visual Effects in a Broadcast Program (for the pilot episode's plane-crash sequence)	Visual Effects Society	Digital Dimension	2005	Winner
Outstanding Supporting Visual Effects in a Broadcast Program (Pilot episode, Part 2)	Visual Effects Society	Kevin Blank, Mitch Suskin, Benoit Girard, Jerome Morin	2005	Winner
Outstanding Supporting Visual Effects in a Broadcast Program (Exodus, Part 2)	Visual Effects Society	Kevin Blank, Mitchell ferm, Eric Chauvin, John Teska	2006	Winner
Best Dramatic Presentation in Short Form	World Science Fiction Society, Hugo Award	*Lost*	2005	Nominee
Writing in a Dramatic Series	Writer's Guild of America	*Lost*	2006	Winner

* Emmy Trivia: *Lost* is the first series since *The West Wing* to win an Emmy for best drama series in its first season.

NOTES

Page 1. *At the pit of exhaustion from directing*—Jensen, "Treasured Islanders," 44.

Page 1–2. *"Its Season Two ratings"*—Jensen, "Treasured Islanders," 43.

Page 2. *"By late 2005, Lost had become the most frequently downloaded series for iPod"*—Hinman, "Lost Podcast #1."

Page 3. *"During August 2005, the pilot episode was popular among passengers on Virgin Airline's Britain-to-U.S. flights"*—Virgin Airlines 13; also personal conversations with other passengers in flight on August 29, 2005.

Page 7. *In December 2005, Entertainment Weekly named the cast of Lost its "Entertainer of the Year"*—Jensen, "Treasured Islanders."

Page 7. *"If [Lost] works at all, it's because"*—Hiberd, 19.

Page 7. *"not spectacular, but good"*—Grover.

Page 7. *A network "that recently seems to have set the world record for airing stinkers"*—Grover.

Page 7–8. *It was his fired predecessors Susan Lyne—who discovered and supported Housewives—and Lloyd Braun*—Sellers, 40.

Page 8. *"Braun brought the basic concept"*—Snierson, 31.

Page 9. *"I lucked into this incredible medium…exist in features"*—Stafford and Burnett, 2.

Page 9–10. *"[A]s someone who was…really want to publicize?"*—Stafford and Burnett, 2.

Page 10. *"Memory circuits wired to the mythic mainframe of pop culture"*—Vaz, Alias Declassified, 17.

Page 10. *"Spy drama, comedy, romance…Mission Impossible, and Avengers"*—Stafford and Burnett, 5.

Page 10. *"I loved all sorts of movies…the films of David Cronenberg*—Dillmore, 20–21.

Page 10. *"He always enjoyed about writing…compelling to watch"*—Dilmore, 21.

Page 10. *"When you write a pilot…you're not bored"*—Stafford and Burnett, 5.

Page 11. *"It wouldn't work for me"*—Gross, "Man on a Mission," 36.

Page 12. *"I'm not sure how the process works in me"*—Dilmore 21.

Page 13. *"The deal on Lost"*—Gross, "Man on a Mission," 34.

Page 13. *"You'll have to ask J. J. why he needs me*—"Herc Chats Up the Co-Creator."

Page 13. *Lindelof would offer Ain't It Cool News…the greatest show ever The Simpsons"*—"Herc Chats Up the Co-Creator."

Page 13. *Alias addict for almost three years"*—AIC News.

Page 14. *"Damon showed up and…shot for shot what's there"*— Ryan.

Page 15. *"We're on a first name basis with all our viewers"*— Carlton Cuse on *The Adventures of Brisco County, Jr.* ("Save Our Show," *TV Guide,* quoted on www.the11thhour.com).

Page 16. *In Entertainment Weekly's "Best of 2005" issue…"man of science" Jack and "man of faith" Locke*—Jensen, "Treasured Islanders," 44.

Page 17. *"Lost Boys"*—Cover of *Entertainment Weekly,* 15 April 2005.

Page 17. *[C]ontinuous serials"*—Dolan, 35.

Page 17. *"There's never been anything like it on TV…Carter for letting it happen"*—King, "Lost's Soul," 150.

Page 18. *"A Daily Variety story reported in July 2004"*— McClintock, 5.

Page 18. *Joss Whedon-alum David Fury…that network interference had intensified*—DiLullo, 41.

Page 19. *"A frustration for me…we had to draw the line."*— DiLullo, 41.

Page 20. *"We were holding back, but…mystical, or not, by perception"*—DiLullo, "Deepening," 41.

Page 20. *"We are respecting the network's desire…keep things more subtle and grounded and that's a good thing"*—DiLullo, "Deepening," 41.

Page 20. *"Are content with the mysteries…not content with the answers"*—DiLullo, "Deepening," 41.

Page 21. *"There is the challenge of how long…enough concrete answers"*—DiLullo, "Deepening," 41.

Page 21. *"We answer some of these questions…the core audience of the series"*—DiLullo, "Deepening," 42.

Page 22. *As both creative consultant Jeff Pinkner…and Lindelof have acknowledged*—Jensen, "Treasured Islanders," 44.

Page 23. *In an interview for The Lost Chronicles, Lindelof…"stock this world with all the elements and hints and clues"*—Vaz, 78.

Page 23. *"With most shows, the 'watercooler' moments…engage, interact, and imagine"*—Jensen, "Treasured Islanders," 44.

Page 23. *"The mantra at [ABC] these days…'a marathon, not a sprint'"*—Jefferson.

Page 23. *From the outset…complex enough to take years to tell*— Nelson, 12.

Page 47. *The irony of Lost is that…shackled to their pasts*— Vargas, "*Lost* Special."

Page 53. *Yunjin Kim, the actress portraying…were criticized as being stereotypical.*—Susan King, "Stereotype not 'Lost,'" E3.

Page 57. *In November 2005, People magazine included Kim as one of the sexiest men alive*—"2005's Sexiest Men Alive."

Page 58. *Michelle Rodriguez expressed concern*—Keck, "She Shot Shannon."

Page 61. *Dharma sounds like DARPA*—Jayepmills. "DHARMA…DARPA and ARPA?"* Discussion board post.

Page 70. *A Time article in January 2005 suggested that like "a* *religious text, Lost is open to endless interpretation"*—Poniewozik, "Welcome to His Unreality," 61.

Page 71. *"Hindu concept of* dharma*"*—Several online sites provide an introduction to the concept of *dharma*: For example, "In Hinduism, the consciousness of forming part of an ordered universe, and hence the moral duty of accepting one's station in life" resonates with life on the island, not only the survivors' attempt to make sense out of the island, but their acceptance of life there; "station" is also an interesting word, given that the Dharma Initiative requires the castaways to push the button in Station 3: The Swan. Retrieved October 1, 2005, from www.tiscali.co.uk. Essential elements and doctrines. Retrieved October 1, 2005, from www.hindunet.org/quickintro/hindudharma. Living dharma. Retrieved October 1, 2005, from www.livingdharma.org.

Page 71. *Do not want to be considered guinea pigs in an ongoing experiment*—*Lost's* site for the Dharma Initiative provides the film shown in "Orientation."Retrieved November 1, 2005, from thedharmainitiative.org. The Hanso Foundation also has a separate site with further information pertinent to *Lost*. Interestingly, the site retains a 2005 copyright date most likely suitable only for the series' copyrighted information, not as a commentary on the active status of the Dharma Initiative on *Lost's* mysterious island. On the site, the Dharma Initiative is listed as an "active project" dealing with human development to advance the human race. With the violence and paranoia typical of Season Two, we might question the project's success if the castaways are indeed subjects in this experiment. Retrieved November 1, 2005, from thehansofoundation.org/dharma.html.

Page 77. *Oceanic 815's flight date...near a pagan equinox holiday).*—Oceanic Air. Retrieved November 25, 2005, from www.oceanic-air.com.

Page 77. *In which pregnant Claire nervously waits for Ethan to come for her*—*Lost*, The Complete First Season DVD.

Page 81. *Damon Lindelof conceded that "[e]very single name...one* *who tends the flock"*—Matthew Gilbert, "TV Characters' Names."

Page 81. *According to Fox, Jack "is not...into very deep-gray areas"*—Hatty, "Matthew's Moral Center," 9.

Page 89. *Series creator Damon Lindelof calls the episodes "redemptive stories... redeem themselves"*—Dinah Eng, "Ten Writers Examine Life's Diverse Journey on *Lost*."

Page 93. *Even the series' cast and crew question...only Ian Somerhalder (Boone) raised his hand*—Ain't It Cool News, "Moonshine Has Seen the Museum of Radio & Television *Lost* Event."

Page 95. *"Lost is like...in the face of their flaws and struggles"*— Jensen, "Beach Boys," 22.

Page 95. *"A U.S. television commercial for the second season...He asks if there can be redemption*—ABC Television. "Charlie. Redemption." *Lost* Season 2 television commercial, September 2005.

Page 95. *"Dominic Monaghan explained that he plays Charlie as a bad good guy at this point, but he could very easily become a good bad guy"*—Kristin Veitch. *Watch with Kristin.* "Lost in Hawaii: Dominic Monaghan."

Page 102. *"The survivors' lives are 'intertwined before they all got on that plane,' Damon Lindelof told TV Guide in October 2004.*— Malcolm, "Secrets of *Lost*," 28.

Page 103. *Because of the network's reticence in having mystical or supernatural explanations...even if such answers have not yet been provided*—DoLullo, 41; Bond, 38–41.

Page 107. *The witty formulation of film scholar Robert Stam*— Stam, 202.

Page 107. *According to the literary critic and bestselling author Harold Bloom*—Bloom, *Anxiety of Influence.*

Page 108. *"The result of wanting to do 'something with dramatic stakes a few notches higher than the romantic turmoil of a college coed'"*—Dilmore, 22.

Page 110. *"If eight or nine million people are watching*

276 UNLOCKING THE MEANING OF LOST

Alias...creation or the reception of the show"—Gross, "Man on a Mission," 35.

Page 110–111. *"The job is exactly the same...I think the audience we have is terrific"*—Gross, "Man on a Mission," 35.

Page 124. *John Keats once told us to distrust..."a palpable design upon us"*—311.

Page 130. *"We took The Stand," Cuse insists, for example, "and put it on an island"*—Cuse and Lindelof Podcast.

Page 154. *"Whatever 'out there' truth Mulder and Scully discovered"*—Lavery, 243.

Page 157. *"[Lost fans are] like Talmudic scholars. They have created a body of scholarship about every episode."*—Rivenburg, "An Island of Losties."

Page 161. *In July 2004, DavidFury.net interviewed Fury...jokingly responded that he hoped to create a "Lost fan fight club"*—"Q&A with David Fury," davidfury.net/qanda2004.html.

Page 162. *"The Internet has really changed the way we watch TV...and you'd be moronic not to listen to the fans"*—Kristin Veitch, "Secrets to TV's Hottest New Show."

Page 180. *The authenticity of the video was eventually disproven...on The Fuselage message boards*—Grillo-Marxuach, Javier, "Classification Video a Fake?"

Page 180. *When asked about the websites on The Fuselage website, Marxuach offered...but overall, I'd rather neither confirm nor deny!"*—Grillo-Marxuach, Javier, "Check Out."

Page 182. *A Boston Globe article in October...those that attract a "lively, game audience"*—Gilbert, "Getting Lost."

Bibliography

This bibliography directs you to some interesting interviews and tidbits about one of your favorite television series. It includes information about the series in general, actors, the creators and crew, and critical reviews. Of course, with a series as hugely popular with critics and fans worldwide, *Lost* generates many thousands of words in the press each year. The following bibliography is by no means an attempt to catalog all these articles. Online articles are not listed, simply because they are too numerous. Excellent websites like www.lost-tv.com and www.lost-media.com can guide you to recent online articles regarding *Lost* and its cast and crew.

Armstrong, Jennifer. "Love, Labor, Lost." *Entertainment Weekly*, September 9, 2005, 838/839: 28–32, 41 (poster 33–40).

Armstrong, Jennifer, Jeff Jensen, and Dan Snierson. "Lost Glossary." *Entertainment Weekly*, November 11, 2005, 849: 28–30, 33.

Blackmoor, Eric, and Judy Ewens. "The Patient Englishman." *TV & Satellite Week*, August 20–26, 2005: 15. [UK publication]

Bond, Jeff. "Finding *Lost*." *Cinefantastique*, September/October 2005, 37(6–7): 38–41.

Brady, James. "In Step with Evangeline Lilly." *Parade*, October 23, 2005: 15.

Byrne, Ciar. "Record Numbers Tune in to Channel 4 to See *Lost*, *Big Brother*, and cricket." *The Independent*, August 16, 2005: 3. [UK newspaper]

Cairns, Bryan. "Bear Everything." *Lost*, January/February 2006, 1(2): 25–27.

—"Destination Boone." *Dreamwatch*, July 2005, 9: 42–43.

—"Leading the Flock." *Cult Times*, August 2005: 14–17.

—"Sail Away." *Lost*, January/February 2006, 1(2): 48–49.

—"Sins and the Father." *Lost*, January/February 2006, 1(2): 14–21.

Calhoun, John. "Treachery in the Tropics." *American Cinematographer*, February 2005, 86(2): 44–48, 50–55.

Carrillo, Jenny Cooney. "Little Lilly Lost." *Dreamwatch*, May 2005, 7: 52–56.

—"Lost Boy." *Dreamwatch*, February 2005, 4: 52–55.

"Catch-Up Guide: *Lost*." *Inside TV*, June 13–19, 2005, 1(8): 34–37.

Cimbalo, Guy. "Q&A: Dominic Monaghan." *Stuff*, October 2005: 78.

David, Greg. "Paradise Lost." *(Canadian) TV Guide*, November 6–12, 2004, 28(45): 22–25.

DiLullo, Tara. "Agent Exposition." *Alias*, March/April 2005, File 9: 40–43.

—"Falling from Grace." *Lost*, January/February 2006, 1(2): 14–21.

—"The Island and the Agents." *Lost*, January/February 2006, 1(2): 25–27.

—"Leaders of the Pack." *Lost*, November/December 2005, 1(1): 20–27.

—"Lost in Translation." *Dreamwatch*, June 2005, 8: 48–50.

—"Lost Souls." *SFX*, September 2005, 134: 40–42, 44.

—"*SFX* Profile: Josh Holloway." *SFX*, November 2005, 136: 32–33.

DiLullo, Tara, and Jenny Carillo Cooney. "The Lost World." *Dreamwatch*, September 2005, 132: 38–41.

Earp, Stephanie. "Lost Souls." *(Canadian) TV Guide*, March 26, 2005: 18–21.

Eden, Jenny. "Desert Island Disco." *TV Zone*, November 2005, 195: 20–22, 24, 26.

—"From Hobbit to Rock Star." *TV Times*, August 13–20, 2005: 16–17. [UK magazine]

—"The Good Doctor." *TV Zone*, October 2005, 194: 20–23.

—"It's a Battle to Keep My Clothes On." *Grazia*, August 15,

2005: 18–19. [UK publication]

—"The Mighty O'Quinn." *Xposé*, December 2005, 96: 38–41.

—"Most Wanted." *TV Zone*, October 2005, 194: 24–26.

Edwards, Gavin. "Little Girl Lost." *Rolling Stone*, October 6, 2005, 984: 50–52.

—"Lost Boy." *Rolling Stone*, February 10, 2005, 967: 45–46.

Elgar, Nick, Bryan Cairns, and Richard Matthews. "Full of Maggie Grace." *Dreamwatch*, November 2005, 13: 54–56.

Elgar, Nick, and Richard Matthews. "Medicine Man." *Dreamwatch*, November 2005, 13: 57.

Eramo, Steven. "Make Room for Daddy." *Starburst*, September 2005, 327: 38–44.

Golder, Dave. "*Lost*: Review (The Journey)." *SFX*, June 2005, 132: 87.

Graves, Stephen. "Reviews: *Lost* (Homecoming, Outlaws, …In Translation)." *Xposé*, May 2005, 94: 62.

—"Reviews: *Lost* ("The Moth," "Confidence Man," "Solitary," "Raised by Another")." *Xposé*, February 2005, 92, 62–63.

Gross, Ed. "Mysterious Island." *SFX*, January 2005, 126: 60–61.

Gross, Edward. "Overview: *Lost*." *SFX*, January 2005, 126: 58–61.

Hatty, Michele. "Matthew's Moral Center." *USA Weekend*, May 6–8, 2005: 9.

Hayes, K. Stoddard. "Lost and Found." *Dreamwatch*, February 2005, 4: 22–23.

Hockley, Ian. "Preview: *Lost*." *Cult Times*, Fall 2004, Special 32: 68–69.

Huddleston, Kathie. "By the Numbers." *SciFi*, October 2005, 11(5): 44.

—"Down the Hatch." *SciFi*, October 2005, 11(5): 40–42, 44.

—"TV in Focus: *Lost*." *SciFi*, June 2005, 11(3): 16.

Jensen, Jeff. "The Beach Boys." *Entertainment Weekly*, April 15, 2005, 815: 20–24.

Knoll, Corina. "*Lost* in Paradise." *KoreAm Journal*, October 2004, 15(16): 74–81.

"*Lost* Season One Episode Guide." *Cinefantastique*, September/October 2005, 37(6–7): 42–50.

Loudon, Christopher. "Lost and Found." *(Canadian) TV Guide*, November 19–25, 2005, 29(47): 17–19.

Lynch, Jason, and Monica Rizzo. "Fantasy Island." *People*, January 30, 2006: 73–74.

Malcom, Shawna. "Foxy!" *TV Guide*, January 16–22, 2006, 53(3): 22–27.

—"*Lost*: Burning Questions." *TV Guide*, October 17–23, 2005, 53(42): 18–21.

—"*Lost*: The Episode Guide." *TV Guide*, August 28, 2005, 53(35): 34–40. (with CD)

—"*Lost*: The Ultimate Guide." *TV Guide*, January 30, 2005, 53(4): 22–28, 30–32.

—"Lost Boy." *TV Guide*, April 3–9, 2005: 24–26, 28–29.

—"RIP Boone!" *TV Guide*, April 17–23, 2005, 53(16): 8–9.

—"Secrets of *Lost*." *TV Guide*, October 24–30, 2004, #52(43): 22–24, 26–28.

Mallory, Michael. "Steve LaPorte Gets Lost in his Work." *MakeUp*, February/March 2005, 53: 42–47.

Miller, Kirk. "Evangeline Lilly." *Co-Ed*, Fall 2005, 1(3): 106–109.

Potts, Kimberly. "*Lost* Mysteries Revealed!" *Inside TV*, June 6, 2005, 1(7): 26–27.

Power, Rob. "Reviews. *Lost* ("Pilot, Part One"; "Pilot, Part Two")." *SFX*, December 2004, 124: 111.

"Returning Favorites." *TV Guide*, September 18, 2005, 53(38): 42–43.

Roush, Matt. "Great Expectations: Can Last Year's Faves Live Up to Hype?" *TV Guide*, September 18, 2005, 53(58): 16.

—"Matt Roush's Top 10 List for 2004." *TV Guide*, December 19–25, 2004, 52(51): 40.

—"Matt Roush's Top 10 List for 2005." *TV Guide*, December 19–25, 2005, 53(51): 40.

Rudolph, Ileane. "Evangeline Lilly." *TV Guide*, December 19–25, 2004, 52(51): 41.

—Insider. "*Lost* Clues Revealed!" *TV Guide*, December 19–25, 2005, 53(51): 16.

—"Matthew Fox." *TV Guide*, December 19–25, 2004, 52(51): 42.

Sloane, Judy. "Jorge Garcia: Man of Action!" *Starburst*, February 2005, 319: 18–19.

—"Land of the Lost." *TV Zone*, 2005, Special 59: 120–124.

—"The Lost World." *Xposé*, April 2005, 93: 50–54.

—"Nothing Lost." *Starburst*, November 2005, 329: 38–39.

—"Terry O'Quinn: Locke Unlocked." *Starburst*, February 2005, 319: 20–21.

—"Two Against Nature." *Starburst*, February 2005, 319: 16–21.

Sloane, Judy, and Paul Spragg. "Sun Shines." *Cult Times*, October 2005: 18–21.

Spelling, Ian. "The Adventures of Lost Sawyer." *Starlog*, June 2005, 335: 19–22.

—"Calling Mr. Eko." *Starlog*, March 2006, 343: 73–75.

—"Cuse Control." *Dreamwatch*, August 2005, 10: 50–52.

—"Hurley Burley." *Starlog*, May 2005, 334: 73–75.

—"Lost Soul." *Starlog*, March 2005, 232: 28–34.

—"Ravin,' I'm Ravin." *Cult Times*, Fall 2004, Special 32: 70–74.

Spragg, Paul. "*Lost*: Reviews ("Whatever the Case May Be," "Hearts and Minds," "Special," "Homecoming")." *TV Zone*, 2005, 187: 64, 65, 66, 68.

—"*Lost*: Reviews ("White Rabbit," "House of the Rising Sun")." *TV Zone*, 2005, 184: 80, 82.

—"Review of Tabula Rasa." *TV Zone*, Fall 2004, 184: 80.

Stein, Joel. "Matthew Fox." *Details*, September 2005, 23(10): 276–279.

Terry, Paul. "Between a Rocker and a Dark Place…." *Lost*, November/December 2005, 1(1): 42–49.

—"Meet…Carlton Cuse." *Lost*, January/February 2006, 1(2): 50–54.

Weightman, Stewart. "Reviews: *Lost* ("Deus Ex Machina," "Do No Harm")." *Starburst*, June 2005, 324: 96.

—"Reviews: *Lost* ("The Moth," "Confidence Man," "Solitary,"

"Raised by Another," "All the Best Cowboys Have Daddy Issues," "Whatever the Case May Be," "Hearts and Minds," "Special")." *Starburst*, March 2005, 321: 108–109.

White, Cinday. "Road Map for the Fall TV Season. Fall TV '05. What You Are Watching: *Lost*." *Now Playing*, Fall 2005, 1(3): 44–45.

Withers, Simon. "Reviews: *Lost* ("Deus Ex Machina," "Do No Harm")." *SFX*, June 2005, 131: 103.

—"Reviews: *Lost* ("Homecoming," "Outlaws," "...In Translation," "Numbers")." *SFX*, May 2005, 130: 100.

—"Reviews: *Lost* ("Man of Science, Man of Faith")." *SFX*, December 2005, 137: 76.

—"Reviews: *Lost* ("Raised by Another," "All the Best Cowboys Have Daddy Issues")." *SFX*, February 2005, 127: 102.

—"Review: *Lost* ("Special")." *SFX*, April 2005, 129: 103.

—"Reviews: *Lost* ("Tabula Rasa," "Walkabout," "White Rabbit," "House of the Rising Sun")." *SFX*, December 2004, 125: 111.

WORKS CITED

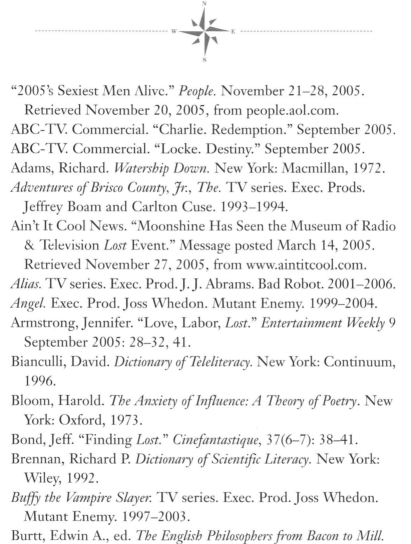

"2005's Sexiest Men Alive." *People*. November 21–28, 2005.
Retrieved November 20, 2005, from people.aol.com.

ABC-TV. Commercial. "Charlie. Redemption." September 2005.

ABC-TV. Commercial. "Locke. Destiny." September 2005.

Adams, Richard. *Watership Down*. New York: Macmillan, 1972.

Adventures of Brisco County, Jr., The. TV series. Exec. Prods.
Jeffrey Boam and Carlton Cuse. 1993–1994.

Ain't It Cool News. "Moonshine Has Seen the Museum of Radio
& Television *Lost* Event." Message posted March 14, 2005.
Retrieved November 27, 2005, from www.aintitcool.com.

Alias. TV series. Exec. Prod. J. J. Abrams. Bad Robot. 2001–2006.

Angel. Exec. Prod. Joss Whedon. Mutant Enemy. 1999–2004.

Armstrong, Jennifer. "Love, Labor, *Lost*." *Entertainment Weekly* 9
September 2005: 28–32, 41.

Bianculli, David. *Dictionary of Teleliteracy*. New York: Continuum,
1996.

Bloom, Harold. *The Anxiety of Influence: A Theory of Poetry*. New
York: Oxford, 1973.

Bond, Jeff. "Finding *Lost*." *Cinefantastique*, 37(6–7): 38–41.

Brennan, Richard P. *Dictionary of Scientific Literacy*. New York:
Wiley, 1992.

Buffy the Vampire Slayer. TV series. Exec. Prod. Joss Whedon.
Mutant Enemy. 1997–2003.

Burtt, Edwin A., ed. *The English Philosophers from Bacon to Mill*.
New York: The Modern Library/Random House, 1939.

Carroll, Lewis. *Alice in Wonderland*. Norton Critical Edition. Ed.
Donald J. Gray. New York: W.W. Norton, 1971.

Cast Away. Dir. Robert Zemeckis. 20th Century Fox. 2000.

Crichton, Michael. *Jurassic Park*. New York: Knopf, 1990.

Cuse, Carlton. "Save Our Show" *TV Guide*. Quoted on www.the11thhour.com.

Cuse, Carlton, and Damon Lindelof. "Podcast 1." November 8, 2005. Retrieved December 28, 2005, from abc.go.com/prime time/lost/podcasts/html.

Defoe, Daniel. *Robinson Crusoe*. Ed. Michael Shinagel. Norton Critical Edition. New York: W.W. Norton, 1975.

DeGroot, Samuel. Forum post. The Fuselage. Retrieved December 29, 2005 from thefuselage.com.

"Dharma." Retrieved October 1, 2005, from www.tiscali.co.uk.

"Dharma Initiative." Retrieved November 1, 2005, from thedharmainitiative.org.

DiLullo, Tara. "Deepening the *Lost* Mystery." *Dreamwatch*, March 2005, 5: 41.

Dilmore, Kevin. "Of Spies and Survivors." *Amazing Stories*, February 2005, 74(2): 20–24.

Dolan, Marc. "The Peaks and Valleys of Serial Creativity: What Happened to/on *Twin Peaks*." *Full of Secrets: Critical Approaches to* Twin Peaks. Ed. David Lavery. Detroit: Wayne State University Press: 30–50.

Ebert, Roger. "Cast Away." Chicago Sun-Times, December 22, 2000, Retrieved from rogerebert.suntimes.com.

Edelstein, David. "Stand and Deliver: Cast Away Maroons a Bunch of Half-Baked Ideas on a Desert Island." Slate, December 22, 2000. Retrieved from www.slate.com.

Eng, Dinah. "Ten Writers Examine Life's Diverse Journey on *Lost*." *Denver Post*, November 23, 2005. Retrieved November 26, 2005, from www.denverpost.com.

"Essential Elements and Doctrines." Retrieved October 1, 2005, from www.hindunet.org/quickintro/hindudharma.

Firefly. TV series. Exec. Prod. Joss Whedon. Mutant Enemy. 2002.

Fox, Matthew. (Interview.) *The View*. ABC Television. May 17, 2005.

Fury, David. "Q&A with David Fury" DavidFury.net. Retrieved December 28, 2005 from davidfury.net/qanda2004.html.

Gilbert, Matthew. "Getting Lost: Show Pursues TV's Most Elusive Genre—Mythology. Or Maybe That's Not It at All." *The Boston Globe*, October 27, 2004.

—"TV Characters' Names Often Say Something about Who They Are." *The Boston Globe*, February 22, 2005. Retrieved November 26, 2005, from www.northjersey.com.

Gilligan's Island. TV series. Exec. Prod. Sherwood Schwartz. Gladysya Productions. 1964–1967.

Golding, William. *Lord of the Flies*. Casebook Edition. Ed. James R. Baker and Arthur P. Ziegler, Jr. New York: Putnam's, 1954.

Grillo-Marxuach, Javier. Forum post. The Fuselage "Check Out." Retrieved December 29, 2005 from www.thefuselage.com.

—Forum post. The Fuselage. "Classification Video a Fake?" Retrieved December 29, 2005 from www.thefuselage.com.

Gross, Edward. "Man on a Mission." *Cinefantastique*, February/March 2005, 36(1): 34–36.

Grover, Ronald. "Has ABC Found Its Way with Lost? The New Drama May Have Broken the Ailing Network's Hit Drought. A Smart New Programming Exec and a Buzz-worthy Fall Lineup Also Helps." *Business Week Online*, September 29, 2004.

Hanso Foundation. Walt Disney Corporation. Retrieved November 1, 2005, from thehansofoundation.org/dharma.html.

Hatty, Michele. "Matthew's Moral Center." *USA Weekend*, May 6–8, 2005: 9.

Hibberd, James. "*Lost* Finds Top Spot." *Television Week*, 3 Jan. 2005: 19.

Hilton, James. *Lost Horizon*. New York: Pocket Books, 1939.

Hinman, Michael. "Lost Podcast #1." SyFy Portal. November 28, 2005. Retrieved December 29, 2005, from www.craveon line.com.

Hintz, Martin, and Kate Hintz. *Halloween: Why We Celebrate It the Way We Do*. Mankato, MN: Capstone Press, 1996.

"History of Halloween." Retrieved November 25, 2005, from www.redmoonhorror.com/halloween/the-history-of-halloween.htm.

James, Henry. *The Turn of the Screw.* Unabridged edition. New York: Tor Books, 1993.

Jayepmills. "DHARMA...DARPA and ARPA?" Discussion board post. September 29, 2005. The Fuselage. Retrieved November 20, 2005, from www.thefuselage.com.

Jefferson, David J. "Desperate? Not ABC. The network hasn't been able to buy a big hit in years. But with Desperate Housewives, Lost and Wife Swap, ABC has Found a Groove." *Newsweek,* October 25, 2004: 96.

Jenkins, Henry. "Do You Enjoy Making the Rest of Us Feel Stupid?" alt.tv.twinpeaks, the Trickster Author, and Viewer Mastery." *Full of Secrets: Critical Approaches to* Twin Peaks. Ed. David Lavery. Detroit: Wayne State U P: 51–69.

Jensen, Jeff. "The Beach Boys." *Entertainment Weekly,* April 15, 2005, 815: 20–24.

—"Treasured Islanders: The Cast of *Lost.*" *Entertainment Weekly,* 30 December 2005–January 2006: 43–44.

Kang, Sugwon. *The Philosophy of Locke and Hobbes.* New York: Monarch Press, 1965.

Keats, John. *Selected Poetry and Letters.* Ed. Richard Harter Fogle. New York: Holt, Rinehart, and Winston, 1969.

Keck, William. "She Shot Shannon; What's Ana Lucia's Next Target?" *USA Today.* November 15, 2005. Retrieved November 20, 2005, from www.usatoday.com.

King, Stephen. "*Lost*'s Soul." *Entertainment Weekly,* 9 September 2005: 150.

—*The Langoliers.* New York: Signet, 1995.

—*The Stand.* New York: Gramercy Books, 1978.

King, Susan. "Stereotype not 'Lost' on Korean Actress." *Los Angeles Times.* May 1, 2005. E3.

Klein, Joshua. "X-Files Set Cherry-Picks Myth-Making Episodes." Chicago Tribune, June 10, 2005. Retrieved from metromix. chicagotribune.com.

L'Engle, Madeleine. *A Wrinkle in Time.* New York: Dell, 1963.

"Living Dharma." Retrieved October 1, 2005, from www. livingdharma.org.

Locke, John. *Two Tracts on Government.* Ed. Philip Abrams. London: Cambridge UP, 1967.

Lost: The Complete First Season. DVD. Buena Vista Home Entertainment, 2005.

"*Lost* Finds Another ABC Win Wednesday." Retrieved November 20, 2005, from tv.zap2it.com.

Malcom, Shawna. "Secrets of *Lost.*" *TV Guide,* October 24, 2004, 52(43): 28.

Millenium. Dir. Michael Anderson. Live/Artisan, 1989.

Nelson, Resa. "Television: *Lost* Breaks Out as the Cult Hit with Mass Appeal." *Realms of Fantasy,* April 2005, 11(3): 8, 10–12.

O'Brien, Flann. *The Third Polceman.* Normal, IL: Dalkey Archive Press, 1999.

"Oceanic Air." Retrieved November 25, 2005, from www. oceanic-air.com.

Poniewozik, James. "Welcome to His Unreality." *Time,* January 17, 2005, 165(3), 61.

Ryan, Leslie. "Damon Lindelof." Television Week, 2 August 2004: www.tvweek.com.

Santino, Jack. *The Hallowed Eve: Dimensions of a Culture in a Calendar Festival in Northern Ireland.* Lexington: University Press of Kentucky, 1998.

Sellers, Patricia. "ABC's Desperate Measures Pay Off." *Fortune,* 15 November 2004: 40.

Smith, Andrew. Forum post. "Numbers." Retrieved December 29, 2005 from www.4815162342.com.

Snierson, Dan. "Almost Paradise." *Entertainment Weekly,* December 3, 2004, 795: 28–31, 34, 36.

Stafford, Nikki and Robyn Burnett. *Uncovering Alias: An Unofficial Guide.* Toronto: ECW Press, 2004.

Stam, Robert. *Film Theory: An Introduction.* Malden, MA: Blackwell, 2000.

Survivor. TV series. Exec. Prod. Mark Burnett. Castaway Television Productions. 2000–continuing.

Twilight Zone, The. TV series. Desilu Productions. 1959.

Twin Peaks. TV series. Exec. Prod. David Lynch. Lynch/Frost Productions. 1990.

Vargas, Elizabeth. Episode 1240. "*Lost* Special." *20/20.* ABC Television. May 6, 2005.

Varley, John. "Air Raid." *The John Varley Reader.* New York: Ace Trade, 2004.

Vaz, Mark Cotta. *Alias Declassified: The Official Companion.* New York: Bantam Books, 2002.

—*The Lost Chronicles.* New York: Hyperion, 2005.

Veitch, Kristin. "Secrets to TV's Hottest New Show: 'Lost' in the moment: E!s TV Expert Goes Beyond Plotlines to Find the Secrets to This Small Screen Megahit. Plus, the Show's Creators Reveal What's Next." *USA Weekend,* May 6–8, 2005: 8–9.

—Watch with Kristin. "*Lost* in Hawaii. Dominic Monaghan." *E!Online.* May 18, 2005. Retrieved November 26, 2005, from www.eonline.com.

Vowell, Sarah. "Please Sir May I Have a Mother?" *Salon,* 2 Feb 2000. www.salon.com.

"Wyrdology: The Halloween Pumpkin Head." Retrieved November 25, 2005, from www.wyrdology.com/festivals/halloween/pumpkin-head.html.

X-Files, The. TV series. Exec. Prod. Chris Carter. 1013 Productions. 1993–2002.

Zacharek, Stephanie. "Cast Away: Melancholy! Eternal Solitude! Tom Hanks and Robert 'Forrest Gump' Zemeckis Reunite for the Year's Most Unlikely Blockbuster." *Salon,* 22 December 2000. Retrieved from www.salon.com.

INDEX

ABOUT THE AUTHORS

Lynnette Porter has authored or coauthored six books, including *Unsung Heroes of* The Lord of the Rings: *From the Page to the Screen*, a literary and film criticism of J. R. R. Tolkien's characters. She has presented more than 150 conference papers before the Popular Culture Association, Popular Culture Association in the South, Tolkien Society, Society for Technical Communication, and other professional associations in the U.S., U.K., Canada, Australia, and New Zealand. She also speaks at fan-related conferences such as the One Ring Celebration and Fellowship Festival. She teaches at Embry-Riddle Aeronautical University in Daytona Beach, Florida.

David Lavery teaches at Middle Tennessee State University. In the Fall of 2006 he will become chair in Film and Television at Brunel University, London. He is the author of over one hundred published essays and reviews and author/editor/coeditor of eleven books, including *Reading Deadwood: A Western to Swear By* and *Reading* The Sopranos: *Hit TV from HBO* in the Reading Contemporary Television Series. He co-edits the e-journal *Slayage: The Online International Journal of* Buffy *Studies* and is one of the founding editors of the new journal *Critical Studies in Television: Scholarly Studies of Small Screen Fictions*.